POLITICAL SCIENCE
AND
SAINT THOMAS AQUINAS

Donald G Boland

En Route Books and Media, LLC

Saint Louis, MO

⚙ *ENROUTE*
Make the time

En Route Books and Media, LLC

5705 Rhodes Avenue

St. Louis, MO 63109

contact@enroutebooksandmedia.com

Cover Credit: Sebastian Mahfood inspired by an image of St. Louis IX from the Private Collection / The Stapleton Collection / The Bridgeman Art Library, Abraham Lincoln, a portrait by Mathew Brady taken February 27, 1860, the day of Lincoln's Cooper Union speech, and Pericles' Funeral Oration (Perikles hält die Leichenrede) by Philipp Foltz (1852). Foreground: Parthenon; Background: Saint Chapelle de Paris

ISBN-13: 978-1-956715-77-4

LCCN: 2022943369

To Ambrogio Damiano Achille Ratti

Pope Pius XI

who in the encyclical *Quas primas (1925)*
proclaimed the feast of Christ the King.

" ... and of his Kingdom there shall be no end." (Luke 1: 33)

Table of Contents

Preface i

Introduction 1

PART I
Commentary on Aristotle's *Politics*

BOOK I: SECTION I, Chapter One 31

BOOK I: SECTION 2, Chapters Two, Three, Four and Five 53

BOOK I: SECTION 3, Chapters Six, Seven, Eight and Nine 67

BOOK I: SECTION 4, Chapter Ten 99

BOOK II: SECTION 1, Chapters One, Two, Three, Four and Five
.... 107

BOOK II: SECTION 2, Chapters Six, Seven, Eight, Nine, Ten,
Eleven and Twelve 117

BOOK II: SECTION 3, Chapters Thirteen, Fourteen, Fifteen,
Sixteen and Seventeen 125

BOOK III: SECTION 1, Introduction 137

BOOK III: SECTION 2, Chapters One, Two, Three and Four 149

BOOK III: SECTION 3, Chapters Five and Six 157

PART 2
ST. THOMAS ON KINGSHIP

BOOK I 167

BOOK II: Chapters One and Two 185

BOOK II: Chapters Three and Four 197

CONCLUSION 213

Appendices

Appendix A: The Merchant and the Middleman 223

Appendix B: The Business of Business 253

Appendix C: Chesterton and Capitalism 269

Appendix D: Marx's Small Mistake 307

Justice being taken away, then, what are kingdoms but great robberies? For what are robberies themselves, but little kingdoms? The band itself is made up of men; it is ruled by the authority of a prince, it is knit together by the pact of the confederacy; the booty is divided by the law agreed on. If, by the admittance of abandoned men, this evil increases to such a degree that it holds places, fixes abodes, takes possession of cities, and subdues peoples, it assumes the more plainly the name of a kingdom, because the reality is now manifestly conferred on it, not by the removal of covetousness, but by the addition of impunity. Indeed, that was an apt and true reply which was given to Alexander the Great by a pirate who had been seized. For when that king had asked the man what he meant by keeping hostile possession of the sea, he answered with bold pride, "What thou meanest by seizing the whole earth; but because I do it with a petty ship, I am called a robber, whilst thou who dost it with a great fleet art styled emperor." **St. Augustine (354-430), in Book IV of *The City of God*, trans. by Marcus Dods (1834-1909)**

"Let the king understand, therefore, that he has received the duty of being to his kingdom what the soul is to the body and what God is to the world. **If he reflect seriously upon this, a zeal for justice will be enkindled in him** when he contemplates that he has been appointed to this position in place of God, to exercise judgment in the kingdom; further he will acquire the gentleness of clemency and mildness when he considers as his own members those individuals who are subject to his rule." –**St. Thomas Aquinas, "On Kingship," Book I, ch. 13 (n. 95)**

†

"I see in the near future a crisis approaching that unnerves me and causes me to tremble for the safety of my country ... Corporations have been enthroned and an era of corruption in high places will follow, and the money power will endeavour to prolong its reign by working on the prejudices of the people until wealth is aggregated in a few hands and the Republic is destroyed." –**attributed by some to Abraham Lincoln**

Preface

This is the fourth book in a series of five on our consideration of the relation between the modern study of human affairs, called the human and social sciences, and the practical/moral philosophy of Aristotle as interpreted by Saint Thomas Aquinas. The first published was "Economic Science and Saint Thomas Aquinas", the second published was "Natural Law: Australian Style", the third published was "Ethics Today and Saint Thomas Aquinas" and the last will be "The Social Encyclicals and Saint Thomas Aquinas". This last though also able to be considered within Moral Theology is actually able to be regarded from a moral philosophical point of view, which is our main focus in the series.

In the first we had to explain how Economic Science belonged not to theoretical philosophy or science but to what Aristotle and Aquinas called practical philosophy or science, and indeed to ethics or moral philosophy taken most generally.

This was necessary to counter the modern reduction (and effective distortion) of such a study to a quasi-theoretical science modeled on the physico-mathematical sciences and the univocally conceived "scientific method".

We can apply what is said about where Economic Science should be placed in the whole spectrum of Moral Philosophy in that book to Political Science as presented here but ending up not in the ancient marketplace but in the forum, the meeting place where matters of policy and legislation were "exchanged" among the citizens of the ancient city/state. This political assembly today equates with our word "Parliament", which literally means "talk-fest", amusingly allegorized in mediaeval times by Geoffrey Chaucer in his poem "Parlement of Foules" (a coop of cackling chooks).

The last book will bring in the contribution of the popes of the Catholic Church from Leo XIII to the consideration mainly of the modern situation of politico-economic affairs. For the revolution in social organization wrought by the revolutions that ushered in the modern era, centering on the religious (Protestant Reformation) but involving all aspects of society from the economic (especially commercial and financial) to cultural (the sciences and the arts) had profound effects particularly on the economic and political organization of European or Western civilization.

This resulted in a huge deterioration in the condition of the majority in economic and political terms as the aristocratic or baronic element of the political constitution of medieval Christendom took the opportunity to oust from power the monarchical element (either totally as it turned out in France, or by enfeebling it as was early achieved in England) and at the same time to enrich themselves at the expense of the Church's charitable patrimony and of the lands of the emerging small proprietors (yeomanry). This brought about an effective oligarchical rule hiding at first behind an enfeebled monarchy and then masquerading as the champion of the poor ("democracy") against the "old regime".

In reality despite an industrial revolution that released all the power of the new science and technology the condition of the poor majority (the newly "freed" army of "workers") only got worse and worse under the new regime, come to be called liberal Capitalism as we explain. So desperate had things become by the end of the nineteenth century that the Catholic popes felt constrained to "intervene" in the secular sphere and condemn both the evils of the liberalist and capitalist system that was its cause and the false socialistic and communistic ideologies that were being put forward to overthrow that system.

The clash of these ideologies dominated the twentieth century in the "cold war" between the USSR and the USA. The popes clearly saw that the "cure" of Communism was infinitely worse than the evident "disease" of Capitalism (as death is not preferable to life no matter how diseased), and so their strictures were mainly aimed at the former. But with the USSR's political collapse under its own weight at the end of the 20th century the evils of the politico-economic system of Capitalism have come to the fore again. Indeed, both ideologies have a common root, in an individualist liberalism that fundamentally rejects all authority, religious and political, involving an extreme individualism that is an irrational reaction against the faith and morals of Catholicism, and that seeks to undermine all traditional moral and social institutions.

Thus it is that the Communist ideology has joined forces, as it were, with "enlightenment" liberalism in the attack on even natural religion and natural morality, with a concerted opposition by the communist only against "the Establishment", i.e. against Capitalism seen as representing that political order that has been used to protect (and hide) the oligarchical element in modern politics in the name of free market economics. This has caused a kind of schizophrenia in the political parties, for they are now composed of those who want to conserve the status quo economically (who generally belong to the privileged few wealthy and their "hangers-on") and those relatively few (claiming to be a vanguard fighting social injustice in the name of the working poor) who wish to carry through the cultural destruction of laws and institutions built on traditional religion and morality. These two relatively few belonging to opposing groups within modern society, both radically liberalist, are generally described as "conservative" and "progressive".

The "Conservatives", however, are confused as to what they wish to conserve. For, their belief in "Enlightenment values" would commit them to many of the anti-religious and anti-moral "reforms" proposed (as may be seen in the recent "same-sex marriage" debate). The only thing they seem to be fully "sold on" is the need to preserve the existing "free market" economic system – against Socialism. For this reason, the "Progressives" are meeting with little resistance to the more socially immoral of their proposals.

The popes were early alive (as in Pope Pius IX) to the dangers of such liberalist thinking in the West. But, as noted, the more threatening danger was in the revolutionary extreme of Communism. This danger has changed but (outside of China) this is only in its modality. It has now become absorbed into the radical liberalism in the West itself, which has been of an evolutionary kind. It will be interesting to see how this will be dealt with in subsequent social encyclicals. For not only do we have this imminent cultural collapse but also the old capitalist oppression of the working poor has returned in a systemization of financial indebtedness, of which the GFC is but a symptom.

That is the practical moral/political side of the picture, with which religion is more immediately concerned. What we have wished to bring out, however, is the change in the understanding of theoretical science and philosophy, which is a most fundamental characteristic of modern life and education. This we have developed at some length in our first, second and third books, but now wish to develop even further as it impacts perhaps most dramatically and seriously upon our understanding of modern politics in theory and practice. This we plan to do mainly by expounding on Aristotle's *Politics* as interpreted by Saint Thomas but supplemented by the latter's "On Kingship".

There is here however a serious complication in this effort. That is in having to deal with the problem of slavery, which it seems comes into Aristotle's political philosophy. We believe the socio-political and legal institution of slavery, which was so fundamentally a part of ancient society, and whose legal status in its mode of serfdom did not fully disappear in Western civilization until late mediaeval times, has to be judged as inherently inconsistent with the dignity of every human person, man woman or child. Therefore, insofar as Aristotle, even as interpreted by

Aquinas, can be judged to have approved of it, no matter how qualifiedly, his moral position in this regard is to be considered flawed. (We say something about the modern mode of servitude in many places)

However, it is not an easy matter of interpretation and one that we must examine closely. For one thing, as dealt with by Aristotle it overlaps with what he regarded as Domestic Science. Aristotle made it as something coming within relationships belonging to the household (a broader concept than the modern one of the family). Moreover, it only applied to some men of a certain lack of intelligence, not to women or children, whose family relationships were separate. His philosophical position therefore is not to be blandly equated with how slavery was actually legally regarded in ancient times, let alone in modern times.

He would certainly have condemned, as all do today, the ancient legal right of paterfamilias, by which the father had power of life and death over his own children. But we ought not be congratulating ourselves, for today we have adopted an equally horrific "right" to own-child murder, which might be given the Latin name of materfamilias, of a mother over her child in the womb. Being people of clear moral conviction, we now condemn the ancient practice of child murder and assert the modern equivalent as a "right" to kill one who is now recognized scientifically as human. The ignorant can salve their consciences because they close their eyes and choose not to think about what they are really doing, leaving the execution, as Pope Francis says, to the hitman (or woman) who gets paid to do the ugly deed. In this most grievous species of modern murder there is no one so blind who chooses not to see.

We could therefore deal with the problem in domestic ethics, which is one way some seek to avoid it as a political issue. It is there an offence against the obligation to care for one's child. But an issue such as murder within the family calls for action at the civil (criminal) level, just as any matter of serious child or spouse abuse, and even more so. So too with an individual's right of free use of his or her will in dealing with others, Hence, we need to make some attempt to understand how the problem of man's (and woman's) inhumanity to others of their own "race" in respect of enslavement might be resolvable.

This will involve considering the problem to some extent within Revelation, particularly the Old Testament. For in the USA, particularly by Protestant slave owners, appeal was early made to Scripture to justify the institution of slavery. This necessarily involved a consideration of the black people shipped from Africa as objectively inferior (in intelligence and hence the ability to rule themselves). The early science of anthropology and the scientific theory of evolution were also used to make such eugenic-type arguments. Even as late as the early twentieth century we may find enthusiasts of the scientific theory of evolution, including Catholics (check out Teilhard de Chardin), who leaned in this direction.

Here too, however, it was something viewed in a quasi-domestic (in a broad sense) relationship, a sort of beneficent business dictatorship, not necessarily justifying cruelty, and so able to be regarded as compatible with Christian charity.

This despotic power over others is now universally condemned; and even by those who still argue for the theories of Eugenics and Evolution, both materialistically based. But one can see how complex the discussion of the problem can be made.

For instance, as for the interpretation of Old Testament Scripture we need to take into account what Christ said about divorce in Jewish practice, being permitted to the chosen people "because of the hardness of their hearts". Such a possible explanation may be available for other practices prohibited to Christians, thinking for instance of the practice of usury, which was prohibited in regard to Jewish borrowers but not in regard to gentiles.

So one has to be careful in arguing from what was in Jewish law or practice with regard to the social institution of slavery. A similar consideration has to be kept in mind in reading early Christianity, where the acceptance of the institution of slavery in pagan law is concerned. (Refer to St. Paul's letter to Philemon). We do not plan to enter into the moral theological aspects of the problem but will try to reach some kind of resolution from the viewpoint of moral philosophy. But this particular problem arising within the consideration of Political Science should not distract us from attempting to discover "the truth of thing" about it as a whole, which was obviously St. Thomas's principal aim in commenting on Aristotle. And there is much of practical wisdom to be gleaned therefrom.

We should therefore first try to put the subject matter in its proper terms and context. This is not easy, not just because of the difference between the use of language about Politics in Aristotle and modern political philosophy and science, but also because there is so much variation in terminology even within the one field of discourse.

Take the use of terms for what in Greek is *polis*, and in Latin is *civitas*, which both are strictly translated simply as "city". In ancient Greek and Roman times this association of human beings was contrasted with *oikos* and *domus,* the words for "household," from which we get our word for domestic, and from which we get economy, *oikos nomos*, the rule or law of the household. But the modern word "family" is not quite an accurate translation for what was intended by household.

Aristotle distinguished two natural associations or societies, that of the household and that of the city, or of domestic and civil societies. But in modern times we generally identify the word "social" with the latter. So, too there is a difference in the modern use of the word "nation". This rather referred to an intermediate state between that of the household and the city, which Aristotle called the equivalent of a tribal or village association of people initially derived from a common ancestor from which the people derived their name.

Thus, there would develop in time a city made up of several nations. The notion of city was understood in terms of political control or rule. It was not necessarily identified with a geographical centre as in modern times, where we tend to think in quantitative terms in everything including moral/political. This order "of perfection" has been reversed in modern language. Aristotle regarded the *polis* as the highest form of human association, and the nation a transitory or intermediate form that naturally would end up in the institution of a city.

Then we see developed the use of the word "State". This comes from the most general sense of an established position in anything. But when used in a social or political context came to signify what Aristotle meant by *polis*, the association of human beings into an ordered condition under a ruler (one, few or many) who/which was a principle of unity of the society, now able to be understood as a community.

He will distinguish this ruling principle into three basic forms, or six if the more fundamental moral quality of good or bad, as acting or not acting for the common or community good, is taken into account. Aristotle will point out that qualitative differences are more important than quantitative in political, moral, analysis.

The modern mind, immersed in thinking in terms of quantity (and Mathematics) will be easily duped into ignoring the notion of common good, and indeed that of good or value at all, though nearly all discussion of "politics" will be insistently and nonsensically talked of (spruiked) in terms of "values". Democracy as the rule of the many, good or bad, then becomes a form of political organization, and indeed the only kind now acceptable. Since the French and American Revolutions, the old "bad" regimes are those of the *Ancien Regime*, of the one and the few.

This is all very convenient for those tyrannies and oligarchies which can claim we still have a democracy for every rule is a rule of many, and our dictatorships, contrary to their definitions are benevolent. It helps to have set up a system of compulsory education (secular and "free" of course) and the population is well indoctrinated in the new political science according to modern scientific method.

However, the notion of law becomes connected with that of *polis*, or city, or State. It is the function of ruling or making and carrying out laws that marks the idea of what is instituted. The basic law, not necessarily written but handed down, then comes to be referred to as the constitution.

In the course of history various other words become used to signify such an organisation of people united under a ruler or rulers somehow united and the notion of a political organization will be applied to an ever wider and wider group of people of which the city is but a part, as developed in the Roman Empire.

In modern times the words State and Nation get intertwined, and the process of aggregation grows ever greater so we have one rule extended to a population that Aristotle would have not conceived of, and if he did would no doubt have regarded as not natural, growing without limit, even in what are still called cities, like a cancerous thing. As early as the 1800s people living there were speaking of London as a growing wen (ugly cancer) on the face of England (William Cobbett).

Indeed, in modern times the notion of limit, let alone natural limit has been lost altogether –for reasons that we have tried to explain. So, in modern times we speak of the Spanish Empire, the Holy Roman Empire, the French Empire and the latest so named the British Empire. For reasons that pertain more to propaganda than reality we do not refer to the Russian Empire or the American Empire – for both claim the political name of Democracy. The language of federation or union has taken over, and even of "blocs" – for the rulers are generally blockheads (refer to quote of St. Augustine in the title pages). The modern kind of political rule seems to involve a growth without limit, and this is seen as a good thing, bringing us all together into one world sized cancerous whole. At a more profound philosophical level, such is the power of being bewitched by thinking in terms of quantity rather than being or reality.

So we could go on but we must return to Aristotle's definitions and try to fit in afterwards these other kinds of political unity and rule. It will help at the start to clarify the notion of political since it should not be simply equated with a society or organization of people that we might refer to as a community. That can be taken in the most general sense, as we might refer to human life simply as life. To do this we need to refer to our discussion of the comparison between individual human life and associated human life as it refers to civil society or political life intended by Aristotle, which meaning St. Thomas takes on. We are already familiar with the practice of applying the organization of a human body to a society so understood, referring for instance to the body as a whole, then the head and its members. But what we need to use are the distinctions between the various levels of life of an individual human person. We will shortly refer to it here, but we take it up in more detail in the Introduction.

Remember that human life exists on three levels incorporating those of plants and animals below. The form of life that is proper to it is spiritual, to which the names intellectual and rational belong. But, as we have seen, we need to divide the proper level into two according to the possession of two spiritual powers, one of knowledge, intellect, and one of inclination or appetite, will. By reason of this, sciences are divided into theoretical and practical, as we have discussed.

Without going too far again into details we can then relate the aspects of associated human life to the individual, the two lowest, vegetative and sensitive, to the socio-economic and socio-recreative orders, which have the refinements previously discussed. Then we can relate the highest level of individual human life, understanding and willing, to the theoretical and practical sides of intellectual and rational life, which as concerns us here as wisdoms are occupied with the metaphysical and moral objects of human knowledge and desire.

The distinctions get rather subtle at this point. It is the whole life of a community that we are concerned with but only from the aspect of one, just as morality is concerned with the whole of human individual life, unconscious, sense conscious and intellectually conscious but only through the operation of our free will as directed by reason. Not all of the operations of human life are totally under our control, though they still are to some extent, as for example nutrition as to its initiation. Once freely begun the digestive processes proceed automatically or naturally in a physical sense.

So, the political order as understood by Aristotle and Aquinas is concerned with the social order or the human community directly as it is a moral order, though it can be considered theoretically in various other ways. Our study can limit to the lowest socio-economic level, like that of biology in the individual in medicine, but it has to bring in humans operating according to natural moral law, somewhat as now done in bioethics. Then rising to the sense level in an analogous way, according to reason and even to the cultural level according to reason, both from a physical point of view and a moral one. The voluntary and moral life of human beings in society is concerned with "the city" conceived as a common unity, or community, that is a life in common from a natural/rational point of view. But there is only one aspect of this whole social life with which we are focused on. The *polis* for Aristotle is the city as it is self-ruling, for every human person is both free and rational, truly free only if he or she acts in accord with reason.

That is the precise object of Political Science. That is where we live and operate according to our free will, in the governance of the community, principally according to political prudence and justice. There are other sciences, the knowledge of which is presupposed, and arts (technical at a high animal level) that have to be used, but the principal "art" is prudence, which as we have noted in "Ethics Today" is all but forgotten in modern thought, sadly even among Catholic moralists. However, let us leave this comparison as a preliminary clarification of the precise object of Political Science. We should say something now about the relation between this understanding of the subject matter and that of the modern "politician", both in theory and practice.

As explained in our earlier books, and repeated here, we have put the difference between pre-modern and modern science in terms of the dethronement of Metaphysics in favor of Physics or Natural Science. But, there is more to it than that. Recall that the old Physics had a rational/formal character and the new Physics saw itself as replacing this with a purely empirical/material character. This was an inadequate basis for an ordered science. If it were the only part of the scientific method, we could not organize our thinking in natural science. We would be confined to simply accumulating unrelated "facts" (information), as Hume concluded.

Aristotle's insistence on Natural Science having not only an empirical/material part but also a rational/formal part would not be denied. For reasons already adverted to, what replaced it, however, was not a better integration of natural forms but mathematical forms or formulas in imitation of the mixed or medial kinds of science. The empirical "data" came to be organized mathematically. That slotted well into the identification of science with the mixed science of physico-mathematics, as explained in earlier books.

For, relatively speaking, mathematics is meta-physics. It does not depend except remotely upon empirical evidence. It prefers deduction to induction. Having lost the true notion of Metaphysics, the modern mathematically minded thought they found an adequate substitute for the rational part of physical science in the mathematical part of modern science. But there was here no true transcendence of the material and physical order of things.

Because of the loss of metaphysical grounding the mathematical/rational component of the new physics passed from being categorical or apodictic to being hypothetical or probable in its principles and conclusions. The meaning of "theory", which was from the Greek for what is known (seen), changed to what is assumed; similarly "speculation", which was from the Latin for seeing (as in a mirror), became changed to mean almost baseless postulating. The advance of Science came to be seen, as proposed by Popper, by disproof rather than proof, by falsification rather than verification.

That is not to say that physical and mathematico-physical sciences do not need to use hypotheses, but this only applies where convincing experiential evidence is lacking, at the edge of science, as it were. Who doubts that water is able to come from hydrogen and oxygen, and vice versa? Now the philosophy of doubt has reached to the root. For it is possible, is it not, to speculate that when next attempted that scientific "fact" may be disproved? Indeed, if we do not admit this skepticism, are we not offending against the principle of falsification which is the basis of all modern (Popperian) science?

What we wanted to point to in our earlier books, and what we want to bring out more clearly here, is that this modern theoretical scientific method, so to be taken as forever provisional, has been applied universally to all subject matters, and in particular to those of the practical/moral/political sciences, called today the human and social sciences. But there is a further consideration, which we had to bring out in our treatment of Natural Law. There is a division now between political prudence and the art(s) of politics, much the same as there developed even earlier in regard to law the division described in our book. We could apply it also to modern Economics, between economic science and policy.

In the pre-modern (Aristotelian) treatment of these practical subject matters there was no sharp division between theory and practice, as occurs in the difference imagined in modern notions between theory and practice in regard to practical matters or affairs. For ethical or moral sciences are practical right from the start, even in their most universal principles, and they are complemented seamlessly not by an art but by the virtue of prudence. How theory and art were related in this case has been indicated throughout.

In the modern treatment of the same practical/moral/political subject matters the (purely theoretical) "scientific method" is applied to the human and social sciences as if they were Psychology and Social Psychology, based upon empirical observations and measurements of individual and social "phenomena" (i.e. human behavior, warts and all), therefrom drawing (inductively at first and then deductively) "scientific" conclusions/theories (generalizations) that go to make up the ever-needing-to-be-radically-revised science (called "paradigm shifts" by Kuhn). This science is then made to be the basis for technical "policy", decisions of an artificial kind that are invariably mistaken (because of the false "science") and, at the legal and political level, requiring constant legislative "reforms". This process of "reformation" fuels the cyclical rotation of political parties that "in theory" at least subscribe to one or other of the two political ideologies of our times. Such is the merry-go-round of modern politics, surely a social situation that cannot last, and indeed seems to be rapidly falling apart at the present time.

Therefore, what we propose to do in our present work is to return to the examination of political science as it is meant to be, that is as a practical science completed in political prudence. The main lines of this study are to be found in the ancient and medieval masters of these sciences. However, it is not to be denied that we should not rely exclusively upon them. For, they could not provide for what comes to light in the concrete history of human and social affairs. Though first principles are immune from change, secondary principles and conclusions may need to be amended in the light of the long experience of mankind. This we shall address for instance in the discussion of human freedom and the ancient institution of slavery.

Nor should we deny the additional need for a collection of arts and skills in cooperation with prudence. For, the political governor must be well versed in the concrete conditions of the community concerned, within which there are as St. Thomas puts it citizens not of perfect virtue. But, even if they were all perfectly just citizens, there is still a whole host of decisions that have to be taken that depend more on experience of the facts than knowledge of the principles and laws of the practical science. In that respect as well, the leaders need the assistance of many advisors in matters not so much moral as technical.

That is to say there is a place for the modern focus on what is empirically and mathematically discoverable about the concrete conditions of human and social behavior. It is not these aspects of science and technique as such that are a problem but the philosophical prejudice behind their employment that eschews direction and motivation from the moral and prudential levels of human thought and practice. Divorced from these higher levels of human understanding, judgment and reasoning these lower levels must go awry, as they have done and do now all the time.

The transition from the pre-modern practical moral philosophy/science of Politics (from Aristotle) to the modern amoral science was effected at a fundamental theoretical level by the double shift we have discussed in relation to philosophy and science generally. There was the contempt for any method of science that was not solidly experimentally based. This meant that the physical sciences of the ancients and the scholastics were disdained, because it was seen, quite justifiably, that, as they had developed over a long period of time, they were weak empirically, and overly rationalist.

Francis Bacon was a key thinker who pioneered the modern promotion of the experimental method. Along with this however there came the powerful combination of Mathematics with Physics. Descartes was a pioneer in this regard, but he also contribut-

ed, by introducing his method of doubt, to the philosophical desire "to wipe the slate clean" so far all previous science was concerned. These influences culminated as we have seen in the work
of Isaac Newton.

The triumph of the new vision of science over the old, and
the sidelining of "philosophy" as "metaphysics", took some time
therefore to be complete. Eventually, the new "scientific method"
spread to all human knowledge including as we have noted the
practical moral and political sciences. However, the penchant for
substituting a more empirical approach was particularly evident
in the study of political affairs quite early.

The rejection of the older Aristotelian ethical method of
study of such matters appeared for instance in Machiavelli, 1468-
1527, (for whose approach Francis Bacon, basically a lawyer, had
some sympathy precisely because of its empirical/"realist" character). Such thinking, which belonged to Renaissance times generally, was no doubt influenced by the turbulence in religious and
political affairs following upon the breakup of Christendom. Life
generally and politics in particular seemed to descend into the
"state of nature" envisioned by Thomas Hobbes where "man is to
man as wolf is to wolf", and "sovereigns" (princes) appeared only
able to gain and hold onto power by the adoption of methods
most would regard as immoral.

Thus political science early became divorced from Ethics and
the notion of Realpolitik took over, in much the same way as the
new notion of theoretical science had rejected Metaphysics. This
was the negative side of the modern approach. It was later to be

taken over in both the theoretical and practical fields by the adoption of the new scientific method. The negative side is necessarily a fundamental fault with modern thought but the new "scientific" side as we have noted may be a useful and even a necessary addition (especially its empirical component) provided that it is based on a sound Metaphysics in the one case and natural morality in the other.

Thus it is that we are principally concerned with the restoration of Aristotle's Ethics and Politics (as illuminated by Aquinas) as the necessary basis of political science. This means that an empirically inspired political philosophy is to be rejected so far as it recommends what is immoral, but we can allow that part of it and of more modern works that are based upon acute and astute observation of political affairs. This latter must, however, not be taken as brute "facts" to be indiscriminately used, as at present, to construct a "morally neutral" pseudo-empirico-mathematical science of human and social behavior. Apart from being false to human nature this "scientific" material is readily amenable to being used by the ideological agents in power to manipulate the population to their own perverse ends.

As noted before, however, we can recognize the need to adjust some conclusions drawn by even genial thinkers such as Aristotle and Aquinas in the light of human and social experience gained since their times. This St. Thomas especially allows in regard to practical sciences. As mentioned, the question of slavery has to be looked at closely in this regard. So too we may need to reassess the morality of reliance by the State upon torture and capital punishment, even in the case of convicted criminals.

There is value in the modern emphasis upon the empirical side of science where physical or bodily nature is concerned (including the lower side of human nature). But what we do not need to pay much attention to is the variety of modern philosophies that have sprung up to fill the void left by the exclusion of metaphysical wisdom and natural morality, most providentially given to the world in Aristotle and Aquinas and confirmed as to their essential principles by Revelation. Because of original sin these natural principles and laws may not be sufficient for our understanding of things human and social, but they are necessary. For, by being raised to the supernatural level in grace we do not cease to be human by nature.

Modern political philosophers, from Hobbes to Habermas, have in one way or another absorbed the modern turn from the metaphysical in regard to the object of our intellect and consequently from the spiritual side of human nature. This resulted from the reduction of the range of reason and science to what is sensibly observable and measurable only. This further resulted in science being totally focused on the material world as able to be investigated only according to the physical and mathematical sciences. As we have noted, the modern sciences of human and social affairs have endeavored to apply this scientific method to their practical subject matters, but generally have failed to make much sense of their "findings" for the reasons given above. (Some, by way of reaction against such a pseudo-scientific approach, have resorted to the "anti-scientific" irrationalist under-current in modern thought we refer to)

As noted in regard to the study of Natural Law, the history of political science is, of course, not confined to Aristotle and Aquinas. Indeed, in the late Middle Ages there was much discussion of political theory, as in Ockham and Dante, but it was mainly in the context of the relations between Church and State, with the authority of Scripture being brought to bear on the arguments. This is the beginning of the doctrine of the separation of Church and State that marks the modern era.

Initially, there was a period when some attempted to justify the monarchical structure of government at the end of the Middle Ages by an absolutist political theory. Thus, King James I of England wrote defending the divine right of kings. Interestingly, Francisco Suarez S.J. challenged his thesis, using scholastic arguments derived from Aristotle. We have noted, however, that Suarez is not to be regarded as necessarily following faithfully the thought of St. Thomas.

Thomas Hobbes (1588-1679) was a philosopher of that same time who developed a purely secularist absolutist political philosophy. He was influenced by Descartes and sought to describe human nature and society in mathematical and material terms. His materialism inclined him to see human individuals as liable to war with one another unless they agreed to subject themselves to an absolute ruler. Such a "rational" political solution was essentially a secularist one. This involved a complete rejection of the Aristotelian notion of political science. But it is an initial expression of the tendency to a totalitarian solution that has continued through the modern era.

But, also at about the same time there arose other religiously inspired defences of political absolutism, such as in the case of the works of Sir John Filmer. Then, John Locke, writing specifically against Filmer, divorcing political theory from any scriptural basis, and arguing from a purely "rational" point of view, proposed a kind of contract theory of government. Contrary to Hobbes, he saw the state of nature, before political association, as not necessarily a state of war, but rather as a state of indigence, which inclined individuals to associate for their own welfare. Civil society therefore arose out of a kind of compact made whereby individuals handed over their natural state of liberty to a ruler or rulers on the condition that their common interests would be ensured. This political theory was closer to that of Aristotle, who saw the *polis* as a government of free adult men (and women) for the common good of all.

However, Locke was a thinker in the modern manner, and belonged to the empiricist school of modern thought. His political philosophy therefore joined up with the liberalist interpretation of the nature of human society that came to prominence in the "Age of Enlightenment". As noted with regard to the early modern study of Natural Law, Locke's political philosophy became part of political discussion at an important time in modern history and was influential not only in political but also in economic and moral thinking generally. It too became part of "the intellectual inheritance of the American Revolution and constitutionalism".

We should not however overlook the fact that besides the tension between the liberalist and absolutist schools of thought in modern political philosophy (paralleling in some fashion the empiricist and rationalist trends in theoretical philosophy), there developed an irrationalist stream in the practical study of human nature and society. That we may account for from the fact that, as Aristotle himself noted, practical science is ordered not so much to knowledge or pure science but rather to action. Most obviously with regard to political life and affairs human (free) will has to be taken into account.

Not satisfied with the attempts to account for the political aspect of human life and behavior in purely "rational" terms, whether individualist/liberalist or collectivist/statist, some modern theorists turned to a purely voluntarist explanation. This as may be appreciated had also appeared in pre-modern times, but it took on a particularly virulent (pragmatist) form after the twist that Kant gave to "practical reason". It is to be noted also that it has transcended the limits of politics and taken on "metaphysical" proportions in explaining the deep nature of the reality in which humanity is immersed. Major figures in this regard are Schopenhauer and Nietzsche. There is also an element of this in Marx's concrete notion of humanity (*gattungswesen*). It is this line of "underground" thinking that is what is now called "postmodernism".

So there is plenty that might be taken into account in the study of modern political philosophy. Though it basically rests on the modern rejection of Aristotle, there are partial insights of Aristotle that find their way into some modern practical science. However, as was the case in regard to the modern study of Natural Law, we have not ventured to include this study of modern political theory in this book, as it does not really add anything of moral/legal importance to that of Aristotle and Aquinas. We are only interested here in restoring the fundamentally moral framework in which political science should be viewed. We leave it to others to explore the labyrinth of modern political theory without the thread of Ariadne.

Introduction

There is a certain parallel between the study of Politics as civil society and that of Law as applying in such a political association. As well, the study of Economics or Political Economy, as an aspect of civil society, needs to be incorporated into the study of civil society as a whole, with which Politics is properly concerned. Aristotle also included domestic society, or the family, as an element in the *polis* or civil society. To the family he attached another relationship of individuals to one another, namely, that of master and servant. Finally, he treated of the relationship of human beings to nature below under the notion of property, with which we need to connect the social system of exchange of goods and services. Subject to what we have said in the Preface, we will therefore have something to say about these social institutions as they are part of Politics. It is to be remembered however that much of what belongs here has been covered in my book "Economic Science and Saint Thomas Aquinas".

In our three previous books we have dealt with various issues relating to these particular aspects of civil society (without developing a separate treatment on the family, which is a distinct social order in its own right). It may help to try to bring all these elements together so as to see exactly where political science fits into the picture of human association.

As seen already, there is an insight into the complexity of the social life of human beings that may be gathered by comparison with that of the individual. We expand on this here, as it is something that needs to be firmly grounded in our approach to this subject.

Human life, as is evident, incorporates life as it exists on three levels, the lowest like that of plants, the next like that of animals without reason and the highest that of man, who has reason. These may be called, the vegetative, sensitive and intellectual levels of life. Aristotle had already shown that the highest level is proof of the spirituality of the human soul, the soul being the intrinsic principle of life in a living body. St. Thomas shows that this does not mean that human beings have three souls but that the one spiritual soul, being more perfect than the others, can operate at all levels. Thus, the human being is one living thing, which has actually only a spiritual soul but also is virtually an animal and a plant soul, that is to say like an animal he has a conscious and an unconscious level of life.

Just as we may therefore distinguish the three levels of living operation in the individual human being, so may we distinguish three analogous levels of social life. The individual human being, like the plant, has to nourish itself, grow and reproduce, and, like the animal, has a sensitive life of knowledge. What is proper to man alone is a life of intellectual knowledge.

Animal life, however, may be further divided into lower and higher kinds. Aristotle made such a division on the score of mobility. The lowest level of animal life does not rise above the fixed and immobile state of plant life. As it comes to possess a higher level of sense knowledge the animal takes on the ability to move itself locally. However, there is a further division within animal life that is more relevant to its closeness to human life. That is where the animal takes on the ability to use higher internal senses, such as imagination, memory and instinctive judgment.

St. Thomas notes that in the order of nature there are essential and formal distinctions, such as is obvious in the differences between plant and non-rational animal and the latter and rational animal or human. But, he famously also notes that, in regard to these definitive divisions, "the highest of the lower touches the lowest of the higher". The difference between having sense knowledge and not having it is a difference of worlds in nature. But where the highest of the lower meets as it were the lowest of the higher it may be difficult to discern whether the actual object is animal or plant life only. It is obvious where you have the higher external senses such as sight and hearing, but at the lowest sense level of touch the automatic activity of the plant upon being prodded may seem not much different from the spontaneous reaction of what is in fact a form of sense knowledge.

There is therefore quite a range of sensitivity in the animal world. The generic difference becomes quite clear as we go up that range, but it may not be so clear at the lowest point. So too does this apply in the case of the difference between animal sensitive life and human intellectual life. Applicable here is the fact that life begins at all levels in a generative activity followed by a process of growth to maturity.

Though Aristotle and St. Thomas were prepared to allow in the case of human generation a kind of individual evolution from an initial generation at the level of plant life, passing into another at the level of animal life before the final generation of a human form of life, this seems to have been held precisely because of the empirical difficulty of determining the nature of the life involved. Now that the relevant science has advanced to the stage where the specific nature of the offspring can be identified at the very time of conception there is no need for positing such a graduation of transient souls. Moreover, St. Thomas had already explained that there need be only one soul in the human being because the more perfect form can do all that the less perfect can achieve. It stands to reason therefore that human embodied souls should be capable of producing instantaneously offspring with human embodied souls even though such souls would need time for the bodies to develop for their higher potentialities to become active.

The discovery of this sharp distinction between the genera and species of living things at their origin actually weakens the case for evolution. For it clarifies the distinction between generation and growth. The process of growth can be almost from nothing to everything within a specific or generic form; it is not from absolutely nothing though but from almost nothing of act; with a minimum of act it also has everything of that form of being in potency. Its growth or evolution takes time, whereas generation does not. Generation is a substantial and instantaneous mutation; growth is an accidental motion, which here is of two kinds, qualitative (alteration or variation), and quantitative (growth or evolution). There can be any amount of development and variation within a specific or generic form but it is nonsensical to suggest that something of one form of being grows or evolves into another. Aristotle pointedly compared true species to numbers. One might as well say that the number two can evolve into the number three.

Evolution is a mode of growth and as such ought not to be used to account for the generation of a new form of life. A new genus or species of anything requires it come into existence from the creative activity of an intelligent agent that has it in mind. This is all too obvious in the case of artificial forms. No one but a fool would think that having seen a heap of materials on a building site some time before and then later seeing a newly made house it might be that the materials evolved into the house. Yet this is what is suggested might have happened in the case of natural forms or new species being supposed to have arisen from other specifically different species or forms in the course of past time.

The evolution theorists bring in the process of reproduction to try to account for new species being formed out of the old. But that is another mental sleight of hand. Reproduction as a feature of naturally living bodily reality manifestly only occurs where a living thing (or pair) re-produces its own kind. Trees reproduce trees; elephants reproduce elephants; and time is irrelevant to the possibility of trees reproducing elephants.

Sexual reproduction can account for a vast variety of individual differences within the one species. Such accidental variation may involve such great observable differences that we classify them as quasi-specific. Various empirical tests are devised to classify things so different. But it must be understood that the meaning of "species" in the modern empirical sciences is not the same as that more philosophically considered. Nor is it so significant that the species of things so considered "scientifically", change dramatically over time by reason of changes in environment.

This all has to happen, however, within the range of changeability limited by the specific form of being, philosophically considered. This can only be appreciated if we can make the philosophical distinction between substance, or natural essence, and accident. The modern scientist is handicapped by having dispensed with that distinction so that he does not know if he is thinking in essential or only accidental terms.

Taking everything that happens in nature as accidental, or by chance (nonsensically called "natural selection" – selection being an act that supposes intelligent deliberation), the common interpretation of evolution is that the higher "species", forms of being, have evolved later in the quasi-infinite course of time. But this itself is a surreptitious importation of a mind into the process. For it is like saying that raw materials placed on the building site were "accidentally" prepared so as to be more fit to take the final form of the house. How could this have happened? Well, the weather may have done it, despite the fact that we know that "nature" left to its own devices, the weather, has the opposite effect.

Not only final forms require an intelligent cause, so too does any course of action "designed" to bring them into existence.

Without the other three causes of efficiency, exemplarity and finality, which have to be located ultimately in an intelligent (and sufficiently powerful and loving) agent the influence of the material cause or causes can only be for things to fall apart. It is true that pre-modern science neglected the material causes and the modern resurrection of them was an advance in natural science. But, typically in human affairs, the reformers went too far, virtually reducing natural science to the influence of material causes, or empirical evidence being the only line of explanation to be taken into account.

The materialist evolutionist, relying only on accidental factors, is forced further and further into absurdity as he tries to account for the present settled state of things. What Pope Pius XII was prepared to allow to be discussed was the possibility of the human species being the result of a gradual process of evolution at the animal or bodily level so that God created the first human spiritual soul in matter provided by the animal presumably at the highest level of evolution beforehand. This soul being a simple form (capable of existing outside the body, if unnaturally) can be created in and proportioned to matter but cannot be in any way dependent for its existence upon matter, as a subject.

Accordingly, as Aristotle deduced, the human intellect's dependence upon the body and material reality can only be objective, i.e. as something that provides the material thing out of which comes the intelligible object that is abstracted. This led him to posit the necessity for an agent intellect as well as a potential intellect into which the abstract form or essence is received.

This spiritual soul, as St. Thomas explains, is of such an elevated kind that, with the co-operation of bodily organs, it can operate at the lower levels of animal and plant life, and thus be the vital principle not only of spiritual life and operations (with spiritual powers of intellect and will) but also of material or bodily life, which reaches to the highest levels of animal life.

These lower powers and operations require bodily organs just as they are required in plants and animals. What has to be appreciated, though, is that such organic life can be very refined in the higher animals, "touching" the level of human life at its lowest point. It is, no doubt, this apparent continuum in nature that encourages the evolutionary theorist to rub out the formal lines of natural specific and even generic difference (which can only be detected by intellectual abstraction from individual conditions). Philosophically, he is virtually forced to conceive physical nature as a giant substantial blob, or some amorphous genus of being that differentiates itself in an inexplicable way into a multitude of accidental "specific" differences. It is a metaphysical and logical mess, caused by a lack of the purely intellectual knowledge of Metaphysics and Logic.

Enthused by Pope Saint John Paul II's concession that Evolution, taken so far as the human body is concerned, as supported by scientific knowledge at the present time, is "more than a hypothesis" (scientifically speaking, meaning there is some evidence to support it), some try to envisage how a theistic ordered evolution might have come about. There is the problem that a human person would have come into existence at first without a human mate, unless (against all odds) two of different sex were produced at the same time. In any case a person of opposite sex would have had to be produced in order for the processes of procreation to occur.

This has led some to speculate that there might have been sexual intercourse in the beginning between a human and a non-human. The problem with this is that this would have involved the sin of bestiality, a sin so contrary to nature that God would not excuse it (refer to St. Thomas's classification of sexual sins in II-II, q. 154). It is argued that even on the biblical account there would have had to be at the beginning what normally is a sin, namely, some form of incest. But this difficulty can be overcome in so far as it is contrary only to a secondary principle of the natural law, which God and nature may dispense with in order to serve the higher end of continuance of the human race.

That some could countenance the occurrence in the natural order of gross unnatural offences is hard to believe. It could perhaps be explained by the debasement of modern culture, which has become inured to accepting other unnatural sex acts, such as contraceptive and homosexual intercourse, as morally innocuous and even socially respectable. One shudders at the retribution that this entails even from a natural point of view.

So, even from a preliminary philosophical, i.e. rational, consideration of the theory of evolution, it could only be intelligibly possible if it presupposed a separate agent capable not only of creating the natural forms of being, according to ideas already had in mind, but also capable of directing the whole process (either immediately, or mediately through naturally inclinations implanted in the creatures – as an arrow hits a target only if aimed at it) to the present state of being, and ultimately to some final outcome desired by the agent. Absent any of these causal influences there is no reason why anything should happen in the natural world. That things do happen plainly demands the existence of the Maker of the natural world, God. An atheistic materialism that is proposed as the basis of the modern "scientific" theory of Evolution falls immediately into a plain absurdity. The modern mind is so indoctrinated into ignoring contradiction that it blithely passes over such absurdity.

However, we are not concerned here to go into the details of this modern scientific explanation of life. That may be left to the philosophy of nature, or natural science, as extending to metaphysics where human nature is concerned. We are concerned to relate analogously the distinct levels of individual human life to the levels of human social life, i. e. the life of a civil community. So let us examine a little more closely the levels of individual human life in relation to that of animal life. What ultimately distinguishes the human being is rationality. That primarily refers to the fact that the human being thinks by reasoning. Reasoning is but the third act of the human intellect. It presupposes intellectual judgment and apprehension.

Before proceeding along these lines let us go back to a closer examination of the level of animal life, with a view to noting the difference it manifests in human life as opposed to non-human. The most significant difference within animal life is that between having the external senses and sense consciousness, on the one hand, and the higher internal senses, on the other. Within this general difference there do exist again degrees of animal life.

The sense life of all animals below man has a definite connection with the earth. This is all too evident where the lowest level of animal life exists like plant life, the connection being an inability to move itself locally, though the natural movements of wind and water cause some to be moved from place to place. But this connection is also there if not so evident all the way up to the highest levels of animal life, and as we shall see verified in human beings in so far as they are animal.

For sense knowledge, of itself, though a higher level of life and being in a substantial and essential way, as an activity it is still limited by material conditions and remains at a superficial level. The proper objects of sense knowledge are only the appearances of things. What "is seen", indeed, equates with what is meant by "it seems". The objects are fleeting and evanescent and, even in higher animals, designed to serve the needs of life at its lower but more materially substantial level, namely, nutrition, growth and reproduction. All this is symbolized in the stance of higher animals. Though some approach the fully erect stance of human beings, they always decline to some extent towards the earth in their constant need to feed themselves.

It is only the rational animal that breaks out of this circle of dependence. Chesterton wittily but perceptively put it in the fact that "man is the only wild animal". All other animals (unless "domesticated") spend their lives in an iron-clad routine, in a

"rut", even at the highest animal level. Their actions are spontaneous, which only means having the certain degree of freedom
that comes from knowledge, but they are specifically driven.
Human actions are deliberate, which means "freed from" (liber-
ated from) all material constraints and even finally from nature's
formal determinations, so that the human person seems to have
the capacity to make himself. This, in fact, is what he is morally
(by free will) bound to do, in accord with the spiritual nature he
has been created with and the end he has been created for.

The gulf between human life and all other animal life is therefore infinite, more than physical, metaphysical; the difference is
between the world of matter, change and time, and the world of
the spirit, unending existence and, as has been revealed, the
chance of ineffable divine life.

However, this spiritual life is mysteriously joined to a material body and here below has to work in and with it. The dependence of the spiritual soul upon the body is, as noted, not "subjective", meaning as having to exist in a subject/matter, but "objective", meaning having to have the body as a means to supply the
objects/forms of the soul's knowledge that is intellectual. This
introduces another orientation in human animal life, not so
much at the lower level of the external senses but at the level of
the higher internal senses of imagination, memory and judgment
(natural prudence, called instinct, in animals below man).

St. Thomas notes a strange "spiritualization" of these higher
senses in human knowledge, indicating the subjection of their
functions to the intellectual faculties, bringing about a change in

their names. Instead of having a merely receptive imagination, man has a creative imagination; instead of having a merely recording or collecting memory, man has a re-collective memory, or reminiscence; instead of having a merely natural power of estimating his situation in relation to his environment, an estimative sense, man has a cogitative power, able to apply his universal and necessary judgments to his particular and contingent circumstances. In practical matters this is an essential part of prudence.

These internal senses also have a part to play in those theoretical sciences that are focused on the material order of things, such as the natural sciences, whose conclusions St. Thomas even says need to be verified by "observation", which may be taken for any sensible object of our external senses. It may be noticed that there is a certain parallelism between the three acts of the intellect, apprehension, reasoning and judgment and the three higher internal sense powers, imagination, memory and estimative. In the concrete and particular realm of human understanding and action the human intellect depends upon the co-operation of these internal sense powers. Significantly, so far as modern science is concerned, this connection with sense knowledge applies also to the medial sciences that are a combination of Physics with Mathematics.

It is noteworthy that Descartes, a major figure in the birth of modern science, though primarily a mathematician, attempted to apply his expertise in this regard to explaining the "system" of the physical world. He failed lamentably because of the distrust of the external senses, and was one of the first to wander off in his imagination into a world of science fiction. But not only did he confuse the intellectual concept with the imaginative image, he also apparently did not know the difference between purely intellectual judgment of universals and the judgment of particulars that belongs to the cogitative power as explained above. He equated "thinking" with cogitation. Hence he used his famous dictum *Cogito ergo sum* instead of a purely intellectual *Intelligo ergo sum*. The former accommodates doubt the latter does not. If you understand you do not doubt.

St. Thomas explains an important difference between cogitation and the purely animal activity of estimation. The former is quite fallible, even in a clear-thinking human; the latter is quasi-infallible in a healthy animal (hence the name "instinct"). The reason for this given by St. Thomas is that the human internal sense power needs to accommodate the range and freedom of the spiritual powers. The brute animal has only to deal with situations that are "in the groove" of the range of its species. It acts "naturally", which means with uncanny accuracy. The human animal has to act "rationally", which in the contingent world of physical existence can mean in the extreme by trial and error.

But all that we are concerned with here is to appreciate the fact that there are two uses of animal sense knowledge in human life, the first as with all animals is mainly to serve physical existence itself; the second applying only in the human animal, is mainly to serve the needs of one's spiritual life, whether theoretical or practical, but most evident in the practical/moral order.

In the analysis of modern (human) psychology it is in this activity or behavior at the higher level of internal sense knowledge and appetite (desires, fears etc.) that most confusion obtains. For the notion of being intelligent, or "thinking", is applied to the function of judgment by the estimative power in higher animals, such as monkeys, because of its similarity with human cogitation. Indeed, these higher internal senses of animals can be made to function under the direction of human reason. Materialist scientists committed to proving that animals can talk and think are immersed in this confusion.

Now this divided orientation is reflected in social life. What we are interested in seeing here is the way these two orientations of animal life in individual human nature show up in human social and political life. Social organization necessarily involves intellectual direction and motivation. But we can see the double orientation in a number of ways. Firstly, there is the basic task of serving the material or physical needs of a population, as the life of any animal is oriented to this vital level of existence. This we may specially relate to the preservation of life in individuals and in the continuance of the civil society itself. The whole activity at this basic level may be called the economic order of civil society. The modern political mind, having rejected the metaphysical order of human knowledge and the spiritual order of reality, is almost totally oriented, like the animal, towards the "earth" (which can be taken as the physical universe as a whole).

The civil order is mediated through family organizations as the necessary elements or cells of the living society. This elementary part of society needs to be allowed its natural scope and freedom. This level of society may be found to look after itself, if it is not destroyed in the name of individual liberty or collective welfare.

However, from a broader social point of view we may detect the operation of social institutions that are natural at this economic level, such as property and the exchange market, and also something that is hard to see under modern conditions, and that is the natural institution of master and servant, or employment, not within the household but within civil society. Even in ancient times this was difficult to discern because of the institution of slavery, which was thought even among some Christians to be at least a permanent condition of servility of some because of original sin. This is something to which we will need to give particular attention as it compromises our understanding of the natural freedom of all human beings.

In modern times these natural institutions have been disconnected from the family and are known by the abstract notions of Capital and Labour (with the market being a social means of exchange in regard to the two). This individualistic liberalism has led in its turn to monopolization of capital (property control) and decimation of the "workforce", come now to be institutionalized in a distorted way as the two opposed politico-economic factors of Capitalism and Proletarianism. They are, however, but two sides of the same coin. Chesterton pointed out that a more appropriate name for modern Capitalism would be Proletarianism, because by far the greater numbers of individuals within such a socio-economic system are not capitalists. All can be wealthy (and free) in the natural system of economics; but not all can be rich (or free) in the unnatural modern system of economics.

However, let us continue with our comparison of the levels of social life with those of individual human life. The economic corresponds to the lowest level of life, being concerned with the "health" of society in terms of wealth, recognizing that bodily health depends on an adequate supply of material goods (derived fundamentally from the application of labour to land). One thing to note here is that the best indication of a state of health is the absence of any need for conscious attention. The most certain evidence of something wrong at the socio-economic level is the amount of conscious "regulation" thought to be needed.

Despite the modern condition, where politics is almost totally preoccupied with economics, we should not overlook the higher levels of human life, where its orientation changes from mere continuance of existence to the enjoyment of the better things in life. At first this does not rise above the merely animal. It consists in the lowly activity of play, which may be seen as a natural joy of animals in their very existence. However, among animals below man it seems to be ordered to health and fitness for the continuance of life as such. For, like sense knowledge, sensual pleasure is something ephemeral and insubstantial compared to the animal as some living thing. Play seems to be but part of the round of existence of the species.

In the social order of things, we may relate this to organized sport. There is an aspect of this that is recreation in the sense of restoring the energy needed for workers to continue individual and familial existence. In materialist political systems, as in the former Soviet Union, for instance, sport was seen as ordered to producing a better work force. In the Capitalist West it seems to have the same sort of rationale if more subtly as a form of relief for those condemned to servile work but becomes rather sublated in the majority into a form of vicarious participation, or entertainment.

We wish, however, to bring out the double function of animal life in human social life. There is this bending down to earthly concerns, but at the same time, the internal sense life ought to serve the higher life of the spirit. It is clear in the case of the creative imagination, which is operative in the world of art, music and culture. But culture, as the cultivation of the human being according to his or her fullest potential, is a much broader concept than this (even when we take art to include the liberal arts). Art is an important part of the life of the human spirit, but the practical sciences and theoretical sciences are even more important. For this is where the human spirit clearly transcends the physical side of things and breaks away from the bodily limitations of its nature. The practical sciences take us into the regions of morality and religion; the theoretical sciences find their culmination in metaphysics that reaches the spiritual and the divine.

There is no rupture, however, of soul and body, or reason and sense. The activities of the individual soul extend from meeting the needs and rational wants from the lowest level of bodily life to the highest level of spiritual life. This is reflected in the social order, from economic concerns to the highest cultural. The animal part of human nature joins the two.

But there is an order to be preserved, in the individual and in the civilized nation. First of all, the material needs of man have to be met, not measured by greed and lust but by rational sufficiency or economy, according to the rule of the moral law and personal prudence. So too, firstly at the level of civil society, the economic needs of all within each *polis* must be attended to, not measured by monetary (commercial and financial) avarice or "economic growth", but by sufficiency or economy, according to the rule of natural and positive law and political prudence, with which goes social justice (distributive and commutative).

Thus, passing though the animal level of human and civil life there are the activities of play and sport right through those of the rational pleasures of art, music and culture to the intellectual and purely spiritual work of practical and theoretical science and philosophy up to the level of natural wisdom. Religion is at the pinnacle of practical moral/political wisdom and Metaphysics/(Natural) Theology is at the pinnacle of theoretical wisdom.

So the full human and civic life can be seen as at three levels, but with the plant-like and economic at the one extreme ("of earth") and the properly human and purely spiritual level ("of heaven") at the other, with the animal-like level in between turning down initially to earthly needs and turning up to serve the highest spiritual life. This spiritual dimension then operates within the sensible order as needed in respect of bodily life and in the intellectual order as fulfilling the ultimate desires of the human soul.

How can this way to human fulfillment and happiness become disordered? This happens simply by the exercise of human free will, both in the individual and in the civil society. So we have to bring into this analysis of human nature the role of the will. Obviously, that belongs to the field of practical science and primarily at the spiritual and intellectual level of human life. So we should divide the highest level of human and civic life into two parts, the first being the order of theoretical knowledge and the second of practical knowledge and will (self-control and self-government). For the order that man has to observe in his acts of will flow from the principles of which he finds in his nature, which directs what he freely makes in his will. This twofold aspect of the highest part of human life applies to his individual and social nature. Both are personal orders, the one commanded ultimately by personal prudence and the other by political prudence.

We have therefore four aspects of human and civil life to consider, the highest being divided into what can be called the intellectual and cultural (as a matter of theoretical understanding or reason) and into what can be called the moral and political (as a matter of practical reason and will). So far as civil society is concerned it is this latter that is the object of political science. However, it presupposes the order of things as received (by intellectual abstraction of concepts and "induction" of first principles) into the intellect "theoretically" so that man can make himself good (virtuous) in the way, broadly speaking, that "art imitates nature".

All in all, then, we may look at civil society according to four aspects of life, the economic, the recreational (which covers a number of aspects of animal life as explained above), the cultural and the political. It is the last practical aspect that is relevant to our present study, which is but an extension of the moral order that applies already to personal and family life to civil association, as it is natural to man.

At this point we might look at where Economic Science fits into the picture here. It may seem to be just a theoretical science like biology in the study of human social life at its lowest level. That is how it was taken at the beginning, as a natural science. Firstly, David Hume took Newtonian mathematico-empirical science according to its experimental or empirical side, which his fellow Scotsman Adam Smith applied to "Political Economy", converting it into a new social science that now employed the modern scientific method, and, though his university professorship was in Moral Philosophy, detached his new fact-based social science from any moral principles.

Then later the mathematical form of the new Physics took over and the socio-economic science changed its name to "Economics", at the same time taking on a subjective/psychological form opposed to the old materialist/"objective" form. Karl Marx preferred the former and so stuck with Smith and Ricardo, seeing the socialist potential (as did J.S Mill). Thus, however, with the shift from physics to psychology in the first place was born the new theory of value as utility from an individualist viewpoint and Austrian Economic (marginalist) Theory, which defended the individualist liberalism behind the new science against the socialist communism of Marxism.

When the Capitalist Economics collapsed in the Great Depression J. M. Keynes (a Cambridge don and mathematician with concern to save what he called "classical", but more accurately named at this stage neo-classical, economic science) invented a new theory providing a hybrid semi-socialist solution, come to be called Keynesian Economics, that has lasted if with diminishing influence to today in the division within the "mainstream" science between Micro-Economics and Macro-Economics. Governments liked it because it enabled them to "manage" the economy by "monetary" and "fiscal" means, manipulating interest and taxation rates. It has the additional benefit of enabling the economists and politicians to look as if they are doing something.

Disorder, however, is inevitably introduced into this whole complex principally by human will, as acts of immorality and injustice, though this is not to deny certain accidental factors that may come into play. We know from personal and social experience that disorder of a most fundamental kind has been so introduced right into our lives and has been there from the start of human history. Many have proposed all sorts of philosophical and "scientific" explanations for this – Evolution as applied to human nature makes no sense in this regard. The true cause has been given by Revelation and is called original sin, the *non ser-*

viam of the first man, Adam. Whereas for the angels there is no possibility of salvation after such a rejection of their Maker, for man there is, and God in his mercy had it in mind right from the start.

However, we are concerned here with the philosophical and scientific examination of this order, or rather disorder. As is evident it cannot be adequately dealt with at this lower level, nonetheless it cannot be adequately understood without such a consideration. As Pope Saint Paul VI has said, there are two ways in which our thinking can go wrong in matters where Faith and Reason are relevant, naturalism and supernaturalism. But, even at the level of human nature and reason, we have a complex of the spiritual and the material, logically presented as the rational and the animal.

The modern mind has not only rejected the divine gift of grace but, inevitably, has also fallen into two extreme intellectual errors, spiritualism and materialism, in modern times changed to rationalism and empiricism, and after Kant to idealism and positivism. Overlaid on this division in the practical order is that of intellectualism and voluntarism, adverted to above, become in more recent times modernism and postmodernism.

As stated in the Preface, we are not going to venture into the labyrinth of these deviations. We plan to keep our minds firmly fixed upon the order that is within the chaos of modern political life and try to provide a compass in the storm, relying on the most experienced pilots providentially provided, namely, Aristotle and Aquinas. We acknowledge that they are without the experience of modern times and so we will have to adjust some of their advice in the light of an understanding arrived at by history and experience. It will be seen, however, that the adjustments are in accord with the principles enunciated by our guides, so it may be supposed that they would agree with the adjustments.

The plan of procedure, therefore, is to take Aristotle's *Politics,* assisted where available by the thought of St. Thomas, as the reference point of our study. St. Thomas notes that the science of Politics is like in its principles to theoretical science. Hence, it naturally divides into considerations of the four causes. As well as that, however, since it is practical, there must be additional considerations. "Moreover, political science, since it is practical, shows how individual things can be accomplished, something necessary in any practical science." (Prologue *ad finem*) A further consideration, however, is that it is often the case that the end (civic common good) cannot be perfectly achieved. Just as in medical science the practitioner has often to forgo the hope of perfect health, even more so in political science the government has to forgo the natural hope of perfect justice. So Aristotle said that Politics is the art of the possible.

Given the corrupt state of human nature without grace, the practical aim then may be only to bring the subjects into as good a state of justice as is possible. As in regard to Law we have to consider the role of coercion, so in the study of constitutions we have to consider the impact of revolution. Nonetheless, we must not take our eyes off the end/form that bespeaks the best. This, as Aristotle noted, is achieved by keeping our mind focused on the

natural order. For, properly understood, the natural in anything
is not what it is (its actual miserable condition), but what it was
to be (*quod quid erat esse*).

Let us, therefore, follow the general plan of Aristotle. In his
Ethics he begins with the final cause, the ultimate end of all human life, happiness. But he also deals with this at the conclusion
of his work. For the end to be sought is divided into two parts, as
intended, and as achieved or effected. Being a kind of movement,
human life has a beginning, middle and end. The beginning and
the end coalesce, as explained, the central concern is with the
middle part or the means. This is seen to be the doing of actions
as ordered to the due end. Since the end is a good, so the means
have to be good acts proportioned to the end. Human behavior,
however, is most transitory and even erratic. Aristotle explains
how stability is introduced into this course of human life: by the
acquisition of virtue (called moral because an order to the end
having to be freely adopted).

Thus the central part of Ethical Science is the treatment of
virtue. In order to understand the complexity of the order that
this involves we need to know something about human psychology, which constitutes as it were the matter of the study. Aristotle
had already made a full philosophical or theoretical study of human psychology involving its animal and rational components.
In Ethics he needed only to consider such in so far as it under-
pins the practical ethical order, focused on the core faculty of free
will. Hence, he dealt with the impediments to the free, ignorance

and violence. (Refer to our book "Psychology, Science and Saint Thomas Aquinas", hopefully shortly to be published)

However, we are interested here in Political Science. Aristotle saw this as the completion of Ethics. But we need to appreciate that it is only such from a relative point of view. Absolutely speaking, civil society has the same ultimate end as all creatures, namely, the common good of all, God. In regard to spiritual creatures this is realized in the contemplation of the divine, so far as naturally possible. The common good of the civil community is something secondary. Hence, the State cannot demand of its citizens anything that is contrary to their ultimate happiness (and accordingly contrary to conscience and moral virtue). But it can demand the citizens sacrifice their bodily lives and property if necessary to preserve the civil or political common good.

We have to keep in mind that it is only with Faith that we can see perfectly even the natural moral order. Accordingly, Aristotle's practical and political wisdom will be limited in certain important respects, and this may extend to St. Thomas in his commentary on Aristotle. One limitation appears to have been in the making of the *polis*, civil society, too much superior to the individual members; the other, as we shall deal with shortly, in the making of the intellectually superior part of humanity too dominant over the lower, given rise to the problem of slavery.

This ancient bias, if you like, failed to appreciate fully the relation of freedom to personal dignity, a dignity that belongs to all human beings, regardless of their lowly position within society and regardless of their lesser intelligence, even if true. Aristotle himself had noted that man is by nature political and that the *polis* was a rule of the free by the free for the sake of the free. He clearly distinguished this common quality of natural government (of adults) from that of domestic government, and from that of master over slave. In spite of this, it seems that what he has to say in regard to slavery may be interpreted in a way that treats some human beings unworthily.

It is only in the course of the history of Christian civilization that this has been corrected (and may need further correction), so that today most condemn the subjection of individuals totally to the interests of the State (as in totalitarianism) or of some to the interests of others (as in servitude). We will need to interpret Aristotle's work and if necessary adjust some of its conclusions so as to avoid falling into these two extreme practical/political errors.

We will follow Aristotle, therefore, in his general political philosophy but make the necessary corrections where, contrary to his own general ethical principles, even he has seemed to overstep the mark. He begins with a short consideration of the end (final cause as intended), then he proceeds to consider the civic elements (material cause) of a *polis*, proceeding then to consider the nature/form of political association (formal cause), and on to the consideration of government (efficient cause) in its constitution and devolution; and finally to the consideration of the end again (final cause as effected). In the course of following this overall plan, which has a certain resemblance to a theoretical science, we will have to consider the practical nature of the study of "how individual things can be accomplished".

Aristotle's work is divided into 8 books, these divided into chapters and St. Thomas's commentary follows upon each chapter. We will follow the division into 8 books but will condense the treatment of the chapters and commentary into sections, which may contain only one chapter, but may contain more than one. This will be shown in the headings. St. Thomas commentary ends in the middle of Book III.

PART I

Commentary on Aristotle's *Politics*

BOOK I: SECTION I

Chapter One

St. Thomas begins his main commentary at this point (Ch. 1): "After the comments in the Prologue, therefore, we should note that Aristotle gives an introduction to Book I, in which he indicates the aim of political science, and then goes on to demonstrate what he proposes (chap. 2)".

Aristotle first considers the nature of the good or end that civil association is ordered to. In terms of causes it is the consideration of the final cause, which is the first to be considered in ethical studies. In Political Science Aristotle basically follows the same order as in the Ethics, though it is not so easy to detect.

The treatment of each cause does have a problem that needs to be addressed at the beginning. With the final cause it is having to be careful not to take the notion of common good relative to the human civil community (city) too absolutely. With the efficient cause, ("common") will, with which the subject (material cause) coincides as explained in "Ethics Today", we have the difficult problem of freedom, with the political order having to be seen as a form of self-rule also on the part of the ruled. (Note St. Thomas's distinction of two senses of mastery or domination later). Then, with the formal cause (which is twofold) we have to be careful with the definition of citizen, since there is more than one kind of constitution and they are divided into two basic kinds, good and bad, and the concept of citizen has to be adjusted to each form of constitution.

It is here at the very start that we need to make it clear that when Aristotle says that the common good of civil society is the supreme human good this is not to be taken as of supreme good absolutely, even from the viewpoint of nature and reason. He is talking about "human good" of human associations that are formed for the sake of man's temporal welfare, comparing civil society with domestic society.

We need to bring out something that Aristotle says later on about the relation between the individual person and civil society. What he says is that if man were the highest being *Politics* would be the highest science. According to Aristotle Metaphysics is the highest science, and the divine being is the highest being. In this regard St. Thomas comments that man is not subject to the common good of civil society in all that he is. He also says that the individual person is that which is most perfect in all nature, so that under God the person is perfectly free from absolute rule by any other creature, no matter how superior in nature.

There is indeed a community greater than the civil community to which the individual person belongs. That is the community of all creatures, the author and common good of which is God. Man, as Aristotle himself noted, though bodily and therefore belonging to the material world or physical universe, has a spiritual soul whose happiness even in this life consists in the contemplation so far as possible of things beyond the material order, i.e. the spiritual and the divine. This higher natural/rational order of spiritual life transcends that of any that can be provided by natural human association, whether familial or civil. These societies are meant to enable the human person to have the freedom to enjoy personal happiness, which is not meant to be exclusive of others. So it is that the common good of civil society cannot be used to justify a person acting against his or her conscience, which is a necessary condition of being happy.

The implications of this are very profound and we know from Revelation that even this exalted concept of natural happiness is transcended by the gift of supernatural happiness, which, though it is perfect only in the next life, can be participated to some degree in this life. The existence of this supernatural ultimate end necessarily escaped Aristotle. What it does, indeed, is raise the dignity of human nature to the level of the divine, thus making the transcendent dignity of every individual human person the greatest possible; so much so that Mary, the human mother of Christ, is more elevated in dignity that every other created person, including the highest of the angels.

As for the rest of humanity the way the Church puts it is that every individual human person is to be regarded as if Christ himself. ("Lord, when did we see you hungry …") In the light of this divine revelation, that anyone could disrespect a human person, no matter how small and incapacitated and apparently socially insignificant, let alone that anyone could consider aborting a human person's life at its beginning, is totally abhorrent. For a Christian to do or condone such is incomprehensible.

All this, however, goes to correcting any statements in Aristotle's *Politics* that might be interpreted as putting the common good of the State (*polis, civitas*) above the ultimate personal good of the individual citizen. In the order of human temporal sufficiency or welfare, yes, it may be said. But, in the order of personal happiness, in ultimate terms, no, by a long way. Thus, on a full understanding of his philosophy, to read Aristotle otherwise, readily done when one considers the general Greek worship of the city/state, is to misrepresent him (reading his *Politics* without his *Metaphysics*).

This threefold level of human associated life has to be kept in mind in the whole treatment of civil and political affairs. Even from a natural (rational) point of view the highest level is of universal scope (personal Ethics) and the other two (household or domestic, and civil or political) are of particular scope only. The political science and prudence therefore lies in the middle, perfect relative to domestic science and parental prudence, but not relative to ethical science and personal prudence.

Though all are concerned with practical sciences and moral virtues, which belong to the spiritual order of intellect and will, reason and free choice, the operations (human acts) in which the natural (rational) order is to be examined are complex because human nature is a unity of spiritual soul and material body, and human behavior therefore requires the cooperation of intellect and sense knowledge, and will and sensual appetites. Central to the complexity that obtains is the problem of how the human will can be seen as operating freely in human activity at the three levels of association.

But obviously the child at his or her beginning and early growth has not yet developed the bodily organs to the stage where his spiritual powers can operate and so cannot directly belong to the civil community. So too does Aristotle argue for some men, servants/slaves, which exclusion on the basis of deficient intellect and therefore fully free will, has difficulties we advert to.

Aristotle will identify the political association (city) as of the perfectly free (and hence self-ruling), but then his statements in this regard have to be taken relatively only, since the civil association is not the highest. On this account, though he says that man is by nature political, and hence should include every human person, he excludes a certain section of mankind from the freedom of the city, who are therefore to be categorized as unfree, and is constrained then to qualify their possession of rationality.

True enough he places such servants/slaves in the lower social whole of the household, or domestic society. But so does he place too wives and children, having to qualify their freedom and rationality as well. Clearly there is some basis for Aristotle saying that these categories of human persons are natural and rational. But it is difficult to reconcile the complications and apparent contradictions involved.

We do what we can though in the end we believe that even with the help of St. Thomas's interpretation of Aristotle's thought on this problem it is not resolvable at the level of reason. It certainly was not resolved in human history even in the era of Christendom, which no doubt must be attributed at least in part to the continuing perverse influence of original sin.

We can go some way to mollifying what is in Aristotle's definition of the servant/slave but overall it seems inescapable that some men are denied the dignity of free will and rationality that is their due. However, this problem of limitation on human freedom occurs at the two lower levels of human community. It does not touch the highest and most universal level where true freedom ultimately matters.

So, let us leave Aristotle's attempt to deal with it at the political level as it is, possibly as good as any humanly possible without the help of Faith. At least, it does not fall into the modern error of so exalting individual free will and choice as to promote Man (Humanism) over God (Theism), as to fall (again) for temptation to the first and last sin, like to that of Lucifer), a fall that extends throughout the whole history of human living, and seems to be more prevalent in the modern world than ever before.

In this error we have the liberalist interpretation of individual human liberty (become a Christian heresy, derived from the enhanced appreciation of the dignity of the human person), whose immediate outcome ironically is the greatest enslavement of all, sin.

Let us return, however, to the point that Aristotle makes about the distinction between the common good of a household and that of the State and the tendency in modern times to confuse the government of the civil community with the rule of a household. This comes out most clearly at the economic level, in treating the Government's budget as if it were the community's. At that level the notion of State as Government, which is but part (head) of the whole civil community, becomes clearly equated with the State as the civil society as a whole. This in itself has the seeds of totalitarianism.

The economic is but a level of civil society as a whole, which is firstly to be ordered naturally/morally and only subsequently positively/politically. Fundamentally, then it is the government's role to maintain the politico-economic order (of justice – distributive in regard to property/ownership and commutative in regard to exchange of goods and services as explained in my "Economic Science and Saint Thomas Aquinas").

The rule of the household is not a perfect political rule, the rule of free adults, but the rule of children and, in Aristotle's language, of servants (generally translated as slaves, which we need to deal with). The modern "management" of the economy (euphemistically labeled "macroeconomics") amounts to treating the members of civil society as if they were members of a great household, as children or servants, even if the motives are benevolent (as often they are not). That very system of government in Aristotle's view is a form of despotism. Even Catholic moralists and theologians in modern times have failed to see this basic distinction and have countenanced the need under some circumstances for a benevolent dictator.

From a purely rational point of view, that is radically to offend human dignity. In an effectively oligarchical regime, which is the modern political system of the West (paying lip service to

individual freedom and describing itself as democracy) the majority poor (propertyless) tend to be looked down on as incapable
of rule and fit only (for their own good) to be ruled by the few
rich (propertied), "born to rule".

When "the natives get restless", discontented with their lot, it
is not beyond the effective rulers to engage in using ethnic and
religious differences, such as black vs white, Protestant vs Catholic, Muslim vs Christian and Jew, and indeed any other quasi-
natural social differences, from geographical to sexual, to distract
the oppressed from seeing their real oppressors. At their most
evil those in effective control, including that of the means of
communication/propaganda, will be tempted to try to stir up an-
imosity to the point of extremity that it results in murderous violence. For they have already succeeded in sidelining natural morality, they themselves, however, being the first victims of the
spiritual enslavement that necessarily follows.

An oligarchical political system inevitably then falls into
viewing civil society as a great household in which the few are the
"parents/masters". Aristotle did of course allow for a constitution
of Aristocracy where the few rule. But it was not to be equated
with the rule of a household; it had to operate as a political rule
over free men and women who consented to such a constitution
for the common good. It also is feasible only where these few
people are superior, not in theoretical intelligence, but in practical wisdom, that is in moral excellence or virtue (especially in a
sense of justice – note what St. Thomas says about kingly rule in
the quote in the title pages).

We have then in reading Aristotle at this early stage of his *Politics* to keep in mind the strict meaning of common good as it applies to civil society. It is to be distinguished carefully, on the one hand, from that which is above it, the absolute common good of the human person, and, on the other hand, from that which is below it, the common good of the human household.

It is worth noting here a point of terminology, which is perhaps another reason for the confusion. "Economic" in Aristotle's language applies primarily to the domestic society (from Greek *oikos nomos* the law of the household). In terms of budgets, it is concerned with family budgets, and this notion may be extended to any organization's management of its income and expenditure, including that of the Government itself. This is not to be confused with the social or political economy, which is ruled by justice. In terms of political ideologies that confusion is inherent in the language of Socialism, but also in the oligarchical system of Capitalism. It is the path to totalitarianism.

It is the way of thinking, then, that the modern individualist/liberalist falls into, precisely because he has no concept of common good in any sense, and thus relates good to his own or his party's interest. It is only by a sophistic extension that he speaks of the national interest, or even of humanity's interest – his concept of humanity being, as Chesterton quipped, a concept of himself universalized. If man is not made in God's image, he can only be made in his own image.

The Efficient Cause of the *Polis*

Having dealt initially with the end, or final cause, of civil society (*polis*) Aristotle then moves to consider briefly in Chapter One the institution, or efficient cause, of civil society. Thus, St. Thomas comments: "Then he treats of the institution of the political community, inferring from the foregoing that all human beings have a natural drive for the association of the political community, just as they have for virtues. But as human beings acquire virtues by human activity, as he says in the *Ethics*, so human endeavour establishes political communities. (The English language of the translation here shows the deficient understanding of "natural" we discuss: the natural inclination in this context is in the human free will with rational direction –"drive" and such like terms have too physical/materialist a connotation)

What has to be kept in mind here is that the institution of a political community, though prompted by one or a few has to be commonly agreed to, so that it maintains the character of human will as free, or a form of self rule. As Aristotle puts it the life of the citizen is one of a free man, and what is characteristic of political rule is that it is of the free, by the free, for the sake of the free.

Aristotle is aware that the civil community evolves in a way out of the family, extending to groups of families, or tribes, until the stage is reached where a civil society is ready to be constituted. Put another way, we have first the institution of the household or home, then the group of households or village and then the group of villages or city. Nonetheless, just as the household of the family has to come into existence through human wills, or agreement, so the *polis* or civil society has first to be instituted by the will or wills of one human individual or a small group of human beings. So, St. Thomas comments: "And the one who first established a political community brought the greatest benefits to human beings."(23)

St. Thomas says indeed that civil society is the greatest thing that human reason can know and constitute. It is not the greatest thing that human reason can know, that is the Supreme Being, God. But it is the greatest order of things (persons) that human reason and will can "make", just as an individual man and an individual woman "make" (more naturally but not irrationally) a home.

So it is that every civil society has an ethnic character at its beginning. But it transcends that in its development, just as it goes beyond the character of a household. Nonetheless, these lesser levels of association remain as elements. So it is that this ethnic or tribal (and even family) virtuality can become the source of much division, precisely because without the constraint of civil law it lacks the restraints of reason in dealings with others, which come with civil association. The forces of such division can become extreme. St. Thomas comments upon what Aristotle has noted: "For human beings are the best of animals if they have the complete virtue to which nature inclines them. But human beings, if they should be without law and justice, are the worst of all animals."

Civil society is a work of practical reason in regard to our relations with one another. Love binds us together at a deeper natural level. And love is necessary all along (as it is the fount of the social bond of friendship). But in the natural moral order it needs to be associated with reason in a civil manner if we are not to war with one another.

Thomas Hobbes built his political philosophy on the idea that man was by nature "as wolf to wolf" and needed to be subjected to a sovereign/tyrant to be made peaceable. At the beginning of the modern era the civilization known as Christendom broke down and Europe descended for a time into savage ethno-national religious wars. Hobbes was reading a "state of nature" into the unnatural state of politico-religious affairs of the time. His political philosophy belongs to the absolutist/totalitarian trend in modern political philosophy, which as we have noted above has its roots already in Greek thinking. It exists alongside its opposite extreme, radical Liberalism, the worship of the absolute liberty of the individual, working out today in the war between the two ideologies of Socialism and Capitalism.

The reading of history in regard to religion and civility, so long tied together for more than a thousand years, but then apparently falling apart at the beginning of the modern era, led, by way of extreme reaction, to the era of the "Enlightenment" (still current, but is not the prince of the demons called "Lucifer"?), where Reason was divorced from Religion and even proposed as inimical thereto (symbolized in the enthronement of the goddess Reason at the time of the French Revolution).

One may relate this to the rejection of Metaphysics, and practical wisdom or natural morality, and the adverse consequences from this, all of which are now coming to their nemesis. It has resulted inevitably in the loss of civilized life, a return to what Hobbes called the "state of nature", but more accurately akin to a condition of inhumanity, which Aristotle called worse than animal, a time of internecine wars on a global scale.

This is the very negation of the political philosophy of Aristotle, as St. Thomas comments: "But the political order brings human beings back to justice. And the fact that the Greeks call the order of the political community and the standard of justice by the same term, namely, right order, makes this clear. And so it is obvious that the one who established the political community kept human beings from being the worst and brought them to the condition of being the best in justice and virtues."

Aristotle will come to consider the nature of this right order (formal cause), demanding an understanding of political prudence as "right reason about things political to be done", in Books III and following, and it will become the core of his political philosophy. We have noticed the poor understanding of prudence in our book "Ethics Today". The same unfortunately applies to the understanding of political prudence, even in some of those who profess adherence to St. Thomas.

But before coming to Book III we must examine, in the rest of Book I and in Book II, fortunately with the help of St. Thomas, whose commentary continues into Book III, the associations that are the parts or elements of civil society, out of which, as a material cause, civil society comes to be and is constituted.

These elements of civil society Aristotle links with the natural institution of the family or household. He says it is made up of three basic natural relationships: that of man to woman, parent to child and master to servant. But he goes on to consider other relationships in this regard, firstly that of property generally understood, the relationship of man to nature below. As we shall see, the discussion of the master/servant relationship tends to be coalesced with that of property so understood, which causes difficulties.

From the discussion of property Aristotle goes on to include another relationship in the exchange of goods (the market). Rather incidentally, at the end of Book I, Aristotle has something to say about craftsmen, i.e. those whose services we make use of in the household through the market. This discussion can be appended to that of exchange in chapters 7, 8 and 9.

Curiously, Aristotle begins his treatment of the basic relationships that go to make up the household with the one that is translated as slavery. He then moves on to that of property, since slavery seems somehow related to property, then onto the exchange market, and only then comes back to the family. There are a host of particular issues to be sorted out here. But we should keep in mind that for Aristotle the slave is a tool of action, not production, and something belonging within the life of the family home or household.

Moreover, he insists from the start that whilst some men may be servants/slaves by nature, no women are, for their natural function is that of childbearing and the utility of the slave lies in his brute-like strength or bodily utility. All women therefore, as children when within the home, are apparently subject to the "monarchical" rule of their fathers, but, when married, rather participate in a type of aristocratic relationship with their husbands. As unmarried adults, in civil society they are presumably to be regarded as free citizens on an equal basis with male free citizens. Aristotle's analysis is not, therefore, to be blandly equated with the legal institution of slavery in ancient times.

The modern problem of oppression of workers (men, women and children) in the socio-economic order of production and exchange, wage slavery, as it were (cf. *RN*, 3), is something altogether foreign to the thought of Aristotle. The slave of Aristotle, if taken as true to his thought, is essentially a member of the family. The master/servant relationship is rationally justified on the basis of mutual benefit, the master being relieved of servile tasks, and the servant being directed in greater virtue according to a higher practical wisdom. The relationship is that of a principal cause to an instrumental cause. This causes the good of the relationship, however, to be principally that of the master which seems at times inconsistently to deny any good to the servant/slave.

The discussion is complicated and confused by comparison with the ownership of property and the use of tools. It is further confused in my view by comparing too strictly the master/servant relationship, which is a moral one, with the physical relation of the soul to the body. In this context it is a moral not a physical relationship, such comparisons to be taken in an analogous sense.

We might reiterate here a consideration that is relevant when speaking about human association and relationships as natural. The basic notion of natural in Aristotle is equated with physical. Indeed, the Greek equivalent of the Latin word "natural" is "physical". And this applies right up to the highest level of animal below man. The human being is generically animal and so the generic meanings of merely living and sensing can often apply to him/her at the two lower levels of life we have discussed. "Natural" can even be used in contrast to "vital"(unconscious), and to "psychical" (conscious, if only at sense level). The possibility of confusion in modern discussions is endless.

When speaking about human life as here in rational and moral terms Aristotle will be using "natural" in its most proper sense as meaning rational so far as knowledge is concerned and free so far as properly human action or behavior is concerned. For instance, sexual union of male and female, of man and woman, is called natural by Aristotle, and indeed the institution of marriage is regarded by St. Thomas as a natural institution even before civil recognition.

So too, it is with the institution of property (to which in the political order we can relate distributive justice). Though these two institutions, as we discuss in other places, do not come immediately from the primary principles of the natural law, they do come necessarily/rationally, and belong to what is called the *ius gentium,* which St. Thomas places as secondary principles of the natural moral law. They are natural, but also rational and free relationships, where "natural" can only be understood morally.

There is a deal of sorting out to be done here, which we have addressed in our other books on Ethics and Law. What is to be noticed here especially is that, even though called "natural," marriage between a man and woman has to come into existence in every case by an agreement of wills of the two involved.

So calling some human relationship natural is by no means opposed to it having to be entered into freely in the individual case. Obviously, the parent/child relationship is natural in a strong sense, though even here the human child's conception is (or should be) from a free choice on the part of the parents. This is where Aristotle's use of the language of "natural" can get to be a problem for modern thinkers, who are used to thinking of morality and law in liberalist terms, as a limitation on freedom.

Aristotle seems to say that the servant/slave is such because he lacks the use of reason. Taken literally, however, this would have to equate him with someone insane. St. Thomas quotes the scripture's reference to one who is stupid. I suppose to some extent it is a matter of degree in terms of practical reason. St. Thomas qualifies this lack of reason on the part of the servant/slave as relative rather than absolute, not having "sufficient" reason. Hence, being distinguished from an irrational animal he has to be qualified as human. This means the slave is rational and so also has free will, as much a human person as any other.

The relationship in general then can be called natural but this does not mean that any particular relationship is natural as if, for instance, this man and this woman are somehow necessarily matched to one another, or that any particular human being could subject another to his power.

Aristotle may just be saying that particular unions may be entered into and even on a large scale for the common good of both, or rather of the household, and that is something natural for human beings. The conditions attached to such a relationship, as to length of time and nature of tasks, are not made clear. The issue is simply as to whether such a relationship is naturally justifiable, rationally considered. Being life long (by consent) is not a problem in the case of the natural relation between the sexes. But such a lifelong bond is alien to the modern notion of freedom, as it has indeed become in the case of marriage.

The matter is complicated by the entry of positive law into the determination of the conditions. What Aristotle is saying is not to be confused with the legal institution of slavery of Greco-Roman times. Indeed, Aristotle will point out that much of historical legal practice (as in the condition being based on conquest in war) is not consistent with the natural character of the relation.

A very fundamental problem with interpretation of the master/servant relationship, which Aristotle calls natural, has to do with the treatment of it in terms of the notion of property. To the modern mind, this automatically brings up the image of the relation between human persons and things below the rational, even at the highest animal level called irrational, as in my possession of a horse. The same sort of problem attaches to the use of the words tool or instrument.

But if one looks at the Latin word used by St. Thomas, *possessio*, which is more accurately translated as "possession", that does not as such import the notion of property as possessing something below the human. For instance, a man may have (possess) a car, but he is also said to possess a wife, a child and a servant, all things human without any suggestion it is against the will or exclusive of the good of the possessed. It seems that the English translators are too ready to impose on a word that may simply mean 'have' what is considered to be property as generally taken in modern discourse.

All this is said not necessarily to defend Aristotle's treatment of the master/servant relationship, but to point to the problem of determining exactly what he and St. Thomas mean. This is especially important when we note how such an adverse interpretation conflicts so obviously with what he says elsewhere. This appears most starkly in the English translation. We will examine below the original Latin of St. Thomas where the position of Aristotle can be interpreted more generously, if still problematic.

We do not deny that Aristotle appears to use demeaning language with regard to the servant/slave, equating the rule of the master with that of a despot. He does this to bring out differences in the relationships between kings and tyrants, where tyranny does clearly treat its subjects as servants, or even lesser beings, not as free agents. But the same use of despotic could be used if the citizens are treated in the same way as children.

The traditional English interpretation (and possibly most others in modern times), is flatly contrary to what Aristotle says in other parts of his works. How are we to resolve this problem? Over time it may be that this particular relation, conceived as within the fold of a household, has fallen victim to the individualist concept of human freedom that has all but rubbed out any limits to the exercise of individual free will, particularly with regard to any lesser associations in any way to be considered natural, such as marriage or the family.

However, at this point we simply wish to show the strict limits of Aristotle's position even when taken at its worst. The power allowed to the master of the house may be too absolute, seeming to be the same as existed in the historical legal systems of Greece and Rome. But, when the three levels of human community and the inconsistencies of interpretation are taken into account, this mastery may not be so contrary to freedom as appears. The relationship ought not to be simply described as the same as that of property over subhuman things.

However, we come back to the main point in the examination of Chapter One of Book I of Aristotle's *Politics,* which is to distinguish the political association or civil order of human life from the lesser ones of the household, or ethno-tribal ones. The lack of such a distinction today in political studies is most evident in the treatment of a budget that applies properly to the administration of the government's "household", treating the whole wealth of everyone in the community as at its own disposal.

We have paid some preliminary attention to the master/servant relation, to which Aristotle will compare the condition of subjects in political constitutions whose end in not the common good, but the private interest of the rulers. But we should now proceed to examine more closely the state of servitude as dealt with in Chapters Two, Three, Four and Five of Book One of the *Politics* of Aristotle.

BOOK I: SECTION 2

Chapters Two, Three, Four and Five

St. Thomas commentary on Aristotle's treatment of "slavery" is divided, as is Aristotle's, into four parts, which make up chapters 2, 3, 4 and 5 of his commentary on Book I of the *Politics*. In the first part he says Aristotle establishes the definition of what a slave is:

> And so we can infer the following definition: a slave is a living, separate instrument useful for activity, a human being belonging to another. And in this definition, we posit instrument as the genus and add five specific differences. By the fact that we call the instrument living, we distinguish it from inanimate instruments. By the fact that we call the instrument useful for activity, we distinguish it from a craftsman's assistant, who is a living instrument of production. By the fact that we say that the instrument belongs to another, we distinguish a slave from a free person, who sometimes serves in a household freely or for pay, not as property. By the fact that we call the instrument separate, we distinguish it from a part like the hand, which belongs to something else but is not separate. And by the fact that we call the instrument a human being, we distinguish it from irrational animals, which are separate property.

If this is to be taken as a faithful reporting of what Aristotle says it is most troubling. There is no escaping the conclusion that a human person as a slave so defined is to be regarded as not fully human, not distinguished by being rational. Yet Aristotle calls a slave a human being and distinguishes that person from irrational animals. Somehow or other a human person can be treated as lacking in reason to such a degree that it is appropriate to regard him (not her) as not a free agent and like animals and all things of nature below man as able to be property in the most basic and general sense.

We have already made some comments based on this English definition. In order to examine it more closely we need to set it out as expressed in the original Latin of St. Thomas.

> In qua quidem definitione, organum ponitur tamquam genus, et adduntur quinque differentiae. Per hoc enim quod dicitur animatum, distinguitur ab instrumentis inanimatis: per hoc autem quod dicitur activum distinguitur a ministro artificis, qui est organum animatum factivum: per hoc autem quod dicitur alterius existens, distinguitur a libero, qui quandoque ministrat in domo, non sicut res possessa, sed sponte vel mercede conductus. Per hoc autem quod dicitur separatum, distinguitur a parte quae est alterius non separata; sicut manus. Per hoc quod dici-tur homo existens, distinguitur a brutis animalibus, quae sunt res possessae separatae.

Instrument or organ is to be taken in the most general sense, as something useful to a person. It should not be taken in its usual sense in English as an inanimate tool. This should be clear from the first distinction noted. Here we should keep in mind how property or possession is usually taken in English. These specialised meanings will be excluded by the difference of being human. We may leave aside the distinction from a human hand, as this distinction is obviously not of any consequence.

The first important character is that the servant/slave is ordered to action not production, thereby incidentally excluding workers in a factory or on a plantation, not just as paid employees, but even as forced labour. That excludes much that we look upon as a form of slavery and indeed is closer to the modern "definition" of workers. But the telling part of the definition is the character of being a possession of the master of the household, as opposed to someone employed at a wage (presumed to be a free agent) or as an independent contractor, perhaps to do the same sort of work within the household. This note of being a possession is generally translated as being regarded as the property of the master. But we need to make some comment on the confusion latent here.

The most puzzling character, however, differentiates the servant/slave from irrational animals, meaning he is a human being, by definition rational and free. How is that to be reconciled with being a thing possessed, as if the property of the master, and not free? This problem cannot be solved if we take the English translation literally.

In other works of his St. Thomas will interpret the condition of a slave so as to save his inherent dignity as a human person – the power of the master is not absolute as appears from Aristotle's definition (in English) but limited – the master, for instance, has no power to prevent the slave from marrying, or practising his religion. St. Thomas in his other work mitigates greatly the inhuman condition Aristotle seems to attribute to slaves.

The notion of slavery as in some way a natural institution in this demeaning way was in fact not much challenged until after St. Thomas's time, though chattel slavery had virtually given way to feudal serfdom during the Middle Ages (a condition that bound the serf to a portion of land rather than to a master, representing a significant move towards personal freedom). The apostles appeared to accept the existence of the legal institution of slavery as a fact of life in their times though some of the early Fathers of the Church condemned it and in later times many popes did also.

The abolition of this idea of slavery as a natural and legal condition for some human persons rather than others was the result of a gradual process in the light of its stark contrast with the Christian view of the dignity of the individual human person. Such was the profundity of a social revolution of this kind that it may perhaps be appreciated that it could not have been achieved in any other way, without forgetting that it continues to exist in parts of the world to this day.

Some attempted to justify the servile condition as a punishment for original sin. But, that does not make it natural, as Aristotle appears to have contended. And it is with Aristotle's thought that we are here mainly concerned.

However, because of the qualifications that ought to be put on its interpretation we should pause in coming to any definite conclusions about it, least of all to equate it with the ancient legal system of slavery, with all its cruel features. Still less should we regard the modern system of virtual slavery, which is defended as one ruled by a free contract for wages, as necessarily less cruel than the ancient legal institution. In some respects the modern economic exchange system in the employment of labour, the "labour market", is more cruel, because essentially impersonal. It treats the workers' wages as the price of labour, where the great majority of citizens, being with no or little property, are quasi-commodities in a "commercial" market where supply invariably exceeds demand. Any compassion comes from outside the market.

Then again, the modern system of "employment" does not discriminate between man, woman and child. It applies in a totally impersonal way, outside the confines of a household, where one is generally treated as part of the family.

Though in some ways comparable in law with that of a hired labourer, who works under contract, in actual fact because of their condition of necessity (pointed out by Pope Leo XIII in *Rerum novarum, n. 5*) the modern general labourer is little different from that of a slave, without any bargaining power. He or she is compelled to make a living in a politico-economic system where he or she is but one in a "pool" of workers from which the employers can hire and fire on terms they generally can dictate.

Obviously, employers are human beings with hearts and the welfare of the employee is often taken into account. But, apart from legislation, which the "free market" advocate would regard as "political" interference, the commercial and financial pressures will tend to win out in the end, and are justified by modern economic science. That is because the motive of making money (*philargyria*) tends to dominate in a socio-economic system (called Capitalism) based on the exchange of "commodities" at a price governed by "supply and demand".

Aristotle's is certainly a most strange concept of the master/servant relationship with his remarkable exclusion of women and children There seems to be no reason to conclude that this exclusion does not refer also to the wives of slaves or their children. For, he is only dealing with useful adult males.

Then again, St. Thomas refers to the difference Aristotle makes between the natural condition and that constituted by law, which was a common basis for the ancient institution. The latter could be based on conquest in war with which cruelty would be generally attached. There is again a note of indefiniteness in the interpretation of what amounts to lack of reason. It seems that the notion of lack of reason ought to be based not on absolute, but only relative, lack of intelligence or reason on the part of the servant/slave. St. Thomas puts it in his commentary as a lack of sufficient intelligence or use of reason and that in an adult human being.

This way the relationship comes closer to a more rational notion, one that can be based on agreement and in which "natural" can be taken as not excluding freedom that goes with being rational and human. Indeed, by including being human within the definition Aristotle would contradict himself when he makes the slave unfree in any absolute sense.

There are all sorts of problems with interpreting what Aristotle means. One does not have a human relationship with a tool or anything conceived as non-human property, such as a horse, nor can such be for mutual benefit. One simply uses it for one's own benefit. To do harm to it would be irrational not only from the viewpoint of useless cruelty but also from the point of view of our use of it for our own benefit.

Thus, there is a problem with the use of the word "natural", which in one context is opposed to rational but in another is not. Without trying to justify the language of Aristotle here we might perhaps just point to the fact that such seems to have been the power of the culture of the ancient world that the incompatibility of the condition attributed to slaves with the exalted dignity of their human nature was not clearly seen even by the wisest of men of ancient pagan times.

As for St. Thomas's commentary, made without any apparent dissent, we can point to the problem of distinguishing his role of simply putting the position of Aristotle without indicating whether he agrees with it or not. It is clear from what he says elsewhere that he maintained the essentially rational nature of the person in such a condition of servant and his rights as a human being.

However, we do not need to go further into the arguments that Aristotle brought to bear in putting his position. St. Thomas paraphrasing Aristotle puts it: "Therefore, all human beings who differ from others as much as the soul does from the body, and as human beings do from irrational animals, are, because of the eminence of reason in them and the deficiency in others, by nature masters of the others. In this regard, Solomon also says in Prov. 11:29: "The stupid will serve the wise." (10)

It is not to be denied that some are less intelligent than others and it may be expedient for them to be servants. As Aristotle says, this would be for the benefit of both. But that cannot be taken to the extent of regarding the servants as no more than property as generally understood. One thing to note here is the linguistic practice familiar to St. Thomas of giving to what is in fact the lowest form (species) of something the generic name, as in this very context Aristotle gives the name "constitutional" (the same as "republican") to the rule of the many when the rule of one is called kingship and of the few aristocracy. Here we may note that the lowest kind of possession is of irrational animals (readily equated with inanimate things), so that possession comes to be taken for the lowest kind of possession, when there are higher forms that are not opposed to free will in the possessed, as for instance in having a spouse.

As generally presented by his interpreters today Aristotle's argumentation is full of inconsistency, and that of a blatant kind, which one would have thought would cause pause even in those who are keen to denigrate his philosophy, especially in political philosophy where it runs counter to modern liberalist thinking.

The whole problem of inconsistency is brought out in Aristotle going on to distinguish the servile condition founded on nature, which is good, from the condition founded on law, which is bad, if it is contrary to nature. How can this statement of St. Thomas make sense if one's understanding of Aristotle is not distinguished from the ancient legal institution with which the word "slavery" is invariable associated? "And so it is clear from the foregoing that it is advantageous for slaves and masters fit to be such by nature that one be the master, and the other the slave. And so there can be friendship between them, since the association of both in what is advantageous for each is the essence of friendship. But those who are not related to each other as master and slave by nature but by law and force are disposed in the contrary way. For they do not have friendship with each other, nor is it advantageous for them that one be the master, and the other be his slave." (n. 11)

There is plenty of scope then for the benefits Aristotle assigns to a master/servant relationship being understood without having to exclude mutual agreement. Thus one, no doubt more common in an aristocracy, may take a butler into one's household on mutually agreeable conditions. The association might be life-long and quite agreeable so far as the butler is concerned. In the household it would be something resembling the relationship of master to Aristotle's "slave" without the inhuman connotations, with the benefits expressed in terms of utility, as in his notion of useful friendship.

The master/servant relationship so conceived may be proposed as a natural institution (eminently rational), and it might even be held that some are naturally fitted to be masters and others to be servants. But (like the natural institution of marriage) it seems evident that it could be founded on free agreement on the part of the individuals concerned, and also to be ruled by justice between the parties. No one should be forced to serve the interests of others without at the same time serving his own interests, unless as some sort of punishment for wrongdoing.

It is the general human condition of sinfulness that no doubt complicated the understanding of the nature of dominance of some human beings over others and pushed the pagan mind into accepting the ancient social institution of slavery. It is manifest that this confusion of mind and weakness of will was only overcome through Christian influence. As the world abandons this Christian influence and becomes more and more immoral it is "natural" (as a nemesis) that the evil of slavery, as of despotism, is returning on a global scale.

Aristotle tellingly connected rule by the master of the slave with the despotic (tyrant) kind of government. Strangely, he allowed it as natural and good and just within the household economy, contrasting it with the monarchical and aristocratic kinds of good rule of father and husband. Thus, St. Thomas comments: "And household rule includes despotic rule, since despotic rule is rule over slaves, and household rule governs all who dwell in a household, some of whom are slaves, and others free."

We are yet to notice, however, how the domination of man over his fellow man took a different form in the modern era. Slavery in one form or another was disappearing through the influence of Christianity but with the collapse of Christian civilization, Christendom, and the revolutions that occurred at the beginning of the modern world, involving not just a religious revolution, but also a moral one, especially in the ownership of property, commerce, finance and politics, effective enslavement of the majority of men (later to extend to women and children – the latter more useful than adults as chimney sweeps) was developing on a society wide scale, until the government intervened, despite the cries of "Socialism".

As mentioned in the Preface, the aristocratic or baronic element of the political constitution of medieval Christendom took advantage of the turbulence of the times to oust from power the monarchical element (either totally as it turned out in eighteenth century France, or by enfeebling it as was earlier achieved in seventeenth century England) and at the same time to enrich themselves at the expense of the Church's charitable patrimony and of the lands of the emerging small proprietors (yeomanry). This brought about an effective oligarchical rule hiding at first behind an enfeebled monarchy and then after the French Revolution masquerading as the champion of the poor ("democracy") against the *ancien regime* (with which the Catholic Church was identified).

By the nineteenth century a new system of servitude, not confined to the household but pervading the whole of modern civil societies, had taken hold, dividing society into the owners of "property" (the new Capital) and those forced to make a living by working for them (the new Labour). Needless to say, the political system underlying this economic one was oligarchical. The political philosophy that was used to justify this radical takeover was individualistic liberalism, which set out to eliminate the natural social institutions, such as the family, that were a bulwark against the incipient totalitarianism of an oligarchical constitution. The natural institutions of private property and the free market were paid lip service, but put up as beneficent expressions of a rugged individualism and raw self-interest. Just as in the case of ancient slavery right was identified with might.

Pope Leo XIII in his historic encyclical *Rerum novarum* (1891) put it in these terms: "Hence, by degrees it has come to pass that working men have been surrendered, isolated and helpless, to the hardheartedness of employers and the greed of unchecked competition. The mischief has been increased by rapacious usury, which, although more than once condemned by the Church, is nevertheless, under a different guise, but with like injustice, still practiced by covetous and grasping men. To this must be added that the hiring of labor and the conduct of trade are concentrated in the hands of comparatively few; so that a small number of very rich men have been able to lay upon the teeming masses of the laboring poor a yoke little better than that of slavery itself." (*RN, 3*)

The evil effects of this new politico-economic order did not take long to be manifested. From the start they were in the order of justice, fuelled by the vice of avarice, with the political "authorities" standing aloof in the name of freedom and competition. We will elaborate on this after having considered what Aristotle had to say on Property, Commerce and Finance in the following chapters of Book I. For, in order to understand the modern kind of servitude we need to know how these economic features of civil society have been abused. In recent times, however, the moral collapse has become quasi-total, cynically engineered by the promotion not just of the vice of lust, but of lust of the most unnatural kind, resulting in a generalized and rapid fall into the slavery of sin. This will need to be treated subsequently.

Let us, however, move on to the consideration of St. Thomas's commentary in Chapters Six, Seven, Eight and Nine on Aristotle's treatment of Property in its most general and basic sense.

BOOK I: SECTION 3

Chapters Six, Seven, Eight and Nine

Having dealt with the master/servant relationship as an aspect of household society Aristotle goes on to treat of how property fits into the domestic economy. As St. Thomas puts it: "After Aristotle has determined about masters and slaves, who are a kind of property, he determines here about property in general." (n. 1)

However, the having of possessions or property, by which is intended things below the human, from minerals to plants and brute animals, is necessary not only to households but also to civil communities. For the human being needs materials and means not only by way of food, clothing and shelter but also for various other bodily and spiritual needs. Thus St. Thomas comments: "the things called natural possessions are part of a household life as they are means that serve not only the domestic order but also the political. If not already possessed they need to be acquired and kept for the necessities of life and community use whether of the household or the city, For neither the household nor the city can be governed without the necessities of life".

Deinde cum dicit una quidem igitur etc., concludit ex praemissis quod quaedam naturalis species possessivae de qua iam dictum est, est pars quaedam oeconomicae,

secundum quod pars dicitur esse quae est subministrativa:
subministrat enim non solum oeconomicae, sed etiam po-
liticae; et hoc ideo, quia oportet ad actum politici et oeco-
nomici, (ut existant) aut acquirantur et illae res quae the-
saurizantur ad necessitatem vitae et utilitatem communi-
tatis, tam domus quam civitatis; quia neque domus neque
civitas potest gubernari sine necessariis vitae (Book I les-
son 6, n. 11).

St. Thomas then, following Aristotle, notes that such possessions or means are finite (not sought as if infinite as Solon said)
being what we may call natural wealth or riches needed by both
households and civil communities, because they served to satisfy
natural needs according to what is sufficient not only to live,
which is the object of household life, but also to live well, which is
the object of civil life.

Deinde cum dicit et videntur verae divitiae etc., ostendit
quod praedicta possessiva non est infinita. Et dicit quod
verae divitiae sunt ex huiusmodi rebus quibus subvenitur
necessitati naturae. Ideo autem istae sunt verae divitiae,
quia possunt tollere indigen-tiam et facere sufficientiam
habenti eas, ut scilicet homo sit sibi sufficiens ad bene vi-
vendum. (n. 12)

However, there is another kind of wealth or riches people desire to possess without limit of which Aristotle intends to speak

about below. It is from this kind that Solon got the idea that the desire for material goods or wealth was infinite. It is such kind of wealth whose acquisition Aristotle will call unnatural, but St. Thomas calls artificial, that Aristotle will spend most time on. Suffice is to say that modern economists are ignorant of the distinction and even modern Catholic moralists do not have a clue what St. Thomas is talking about. The nature of the distinction and of the wealth for which desire is essentially infinite, whose name is money, is fully dealt with in my books "Economic Science and Saint Thomas Aquinas" and "Ethics Today and Saint Thomas Aquinas" under the subject of Commutative Justice.

> Sunt autem quaedam aliae divitiae, quarum possessio est infinita, ut infra dicetur; de quibus Solon qui fuit unus de septem sapientibus dixit in suo poemate, quod nullus terminus divitiarum potest praefiniri hominibus: unde tales non sunt verae divitiae, quia non replent hominis appetitum. (n. 12)

Here we come upon an unfortunate error, not on the part of Aristotle, but in a radical mistranslation of the commentary of St. Thomas on this part of the *Politics*, carried over into his discussion of it in II-II qq. 77 & 78, no doubt unwitting on the part of the English speaking translators, but suspiciously concealing the basic fallacy in Capitalism and the economic science that is used to justify it. For the lack of understanding of the distinction between natural wealth and money (artificial wealth sliding into unnatural riches) goes to the very basis of understanding the modern means of exploiting the general population and oppressing the worker majority.

The possibility of confusing the two kinds of wealth comes about from the rational "invention" of money as the common means of exchange of wealth when the exchange of wealth moves from barter (at the village level), through the use of precious metals, to money as a form of social debt, evidence of a promise to pay (bill of exchange) that has become socially universalised, not the same as, but generally needing to be backed by government endorsement. It can take any form, such as officially marked coins or paper notes, and in recent times even an electronic indication on a computer within a banking system.

So, Aristotle's consideration of property aside its acquisition outside of the social exchange system (market), with which he sees no problem, moves subtly to a focus on the acquisition of "wealth" (whether natural or artificial) in a market in which the common medium of exchange is money. The system of "making money" quickly comes into existence on the formation of a civil community and soon takes a significant place in the trade or commerce of a civilized society.

Aristotle was very familiar with it, and genially detected the facility with which it could be abused. In fact, he called the first mode of exchange (CMC), where money served as it was meant to do as the common medium, natural, and the second mode of exchange (MCM), where money was the principle and end of the exchange and it was some "commodity" that was used as the means, unnatural, to "make" money ad infinitum. As I have explained, St. Thomas called it artificial exchange, as he called money artificial wealth, and recognised that it might subordinated and limited to a natural end and so brought back within the moral order of gaining a living. But this is all explained in my other books.

What is important to realise is that this second mode of exchange and its unrestrained dominance in the market is what is central to the understanding of modern Capitalism. For, to the modern mind "capital" virtually means money, though deceptively it is put up as no different from any other kind of wealth. Then, furthermore, we need this understanding to make any sense of the critique of Marx and the attraction of Communism. (ref. to Appendix: "Marx's Small Mistake")

It is the distinction between natural and unnatural wealth-getting, or acquiring "wealth", "capital", "property", "assets" in the context of social exchange, therefore, that Aristotle has brought to light what is able to be hidden in the modern sciences of economics and politics because all wealth in the process of exchange is measured "naturally/rationally" as Aristotle notes, not in terms of positive value (utility) but primarily in terms of negative need (exchange value) and secondarily in terms of money. For because of its function as a common medium of exchange money becomes a measure of exchange value, so that all material goods in the market can be dealt with in accounting terms of credit and debt. Aristotle first noted this basic politico-economic distinction.

Despite being noticed by Adam Smith, the objective significance of it in terms of commutative justice was soon discarded
since the notion of justice was incompatible with the new politico-economic regime of Oligarchy/Capitalism. Conveniently, with
the rise of a new concept of science in mathematico-empirical
terms, the social order could be studied in a way that excluded
any notion of value judgments in moral terms. So was born the
modern natural/physical science of Political Economy, whose
name has changed for reasons given into the more mathematical
Economics.

Being born in a deep-seated deception with regard to the
moral nature of political science, of which the economic aspect is
its lower more material aspect, it is not to be wondered at that the
modern studies of political and politico-economic affairs should
become so complex and obscure that not even those who devoted
much of their academic lives to their studies could make much
real sense of them. Though they affected an ability to predict the
future of things economic, which "scientific" forecasts these were
mostly wrong but conveniently soon forgotten, since in social
affairs we prefer to look to the future than learn from the past.
Such indeed is the profound and long-standing success of this
modern methodological "takeover" in the human and social sciences, infiltrating into all sections of modern Western thought,
including Catholic, that it can only be regarded as diabolically
"driven"..

However, as we have written much on this part of Aristotle's
work and St. Thomas's use of it we will not repeat what we have

already said by way of comment and criticism here. The basic position taken by us can be found in earlier books published, especially "Ethics Today and Saint Thomas Aquinas" and "Economic Science and Saint Thomas Aquinas". Treatments of the subject in more particular respects are placed in appendices to this work.

What we will do here is provide an overview of how the two modes of exchange operate. In natural exchange (CMC) there is no wealth-getting in the sense of an increase in wealth but only a matching of goods to the desires or wants of both parties to the exchange. Such an exchange is unto equivalence in exchange value. What Aristotle is getting at is the apparent acquisition of more wealth, expressed in the twofold use of M, through the very process of exchange (MCM), which he took as not natural. What we will see is how this exchange process is applied to the "buying and selling" of labour as if a commodity (C=L), in a quasi-exchange which starts with "buying" labour (wages) and selling it as materialised in the products process at a profit (at a higher price that the labour value in the products.

Marx saw Aristotle's detection of how more money could be derived from the transaction but unfortunately misunderstood it, precisely because, in the modern anti-metaphysical and anti-ethical mould of thinking himself, he excluded its moral dimension. [The symbolism introduced here is: C means commodity; M means money; so that a complete exchange is in two parts, CM = sale; MC = purchase]

The acquisition of wealth without distinction is already translated by some as "money-making", a description that Aristotle
reserves for unnatural wealth-getting. The relevant distinction is
not simply a distinction between natural wealth acquisition,
which is generally from some form of production, and the acquisition of wealth through exchange. It is within this second mode
of acquisition of wealth, by exchange involving the medium of
money, introduced at the level of civil association ("by law").
There is a distinction between natural exchange where money is
but the medium (CMC) and exchange where money becomes the
beginning and end of the exchange (MCM).

Aristotle seems to identify "money-making" simply with the
acquisition of (more) wealth by exchange involving the medium
of money, and regards it as unnatural. This happens in various
ways, such as when one buys a product at a lower price and sells
it again at a higher price, making a nice "profit", without bringing any new wealth into existence. One has just acquired an extra
claim on existing wealth, not necessarily at the cost of anyone
else, but merely through the accidental differences in the measure
of exchange value on purchase and sale of the same thing.

Here St. Thomas brings out an important distinction that is
not clearly made by Aristotle. For St. Thomas agrees with Aristotle that exchange involving the use of money (MCM) as such has
no natural limit (hence Aristotle's condemnation of it as "unnatural"). On this account St, Thomas agrees that the activity has a
species of evil (*quandam turpitudinem habet*). However, though
the desire for money is of itself "infinite" a limit can be imposed

on it by the one engaging in that sort of exchange, by directing the acquisition of all funds by such means to the satisfaction of natural needs or rational wants, whether of the exchanger (merchant) himself or of his family or even of his community. That is to say the merchant can "naturalize" the otherwise unnatural use of the exchange process by limiting it to serving natural necessities or rational wants.

Thus, it is only "money-making" (MCM) by those in the market who engage in such a mode of exchange simply for the sake of making more money that attracts moral condemnation. When one considers the actual practice of those who engage in MCM it is not surprising that Aristotle tended to condemn the practice outright. It would be a rare bird that could control his desire for more money once embarked on making his fortune this way. Like a drug the desire for more money so made tends never to be satisfied.

In modern times, economic science has no concept of this basic distinction between the two modes of exchange (treating the two as one) and indeed tends to equate unnatural money-making with the very activity of the "free" market. Behind this is the identification of wealth with money, which founds the first principle of modern economic science that the human desire for (material) goods is unlimited, whilst natural resources are limited. The basic economic problem then becomes a psychological one of overcoming a condition of scarcity, a matter of choosing which wants to satisfy – generating the modern psycho-mathematical theories of utility, the most absurd of which is the Austrian theory of "marginal utility".

We will need to consider more closely the relation of this "commercial revolution" to the "industrial revolution" that paradoxically resulted in the impoverishment (and quasi-enslavement) of the industrial producers (workers) in modern times. But, we should complete our analysis of Aristotle's account of property in and exchange of goods. We have anticipated a little here because of the problem of translation.

Aristotle is dealing first with the modes of acquisition of property taken as referring to actual material goods, natural wealth such as satisfy our basic needs for food, clothing and shelter, but it can be extended to all human needs and rational wants in this regard, such as the highly advanced means of transport and sophisticated means of communication in modern times. It really refers to all things of nature of which we can make rational use. These natural resources are generally not immediately usable but have to undergo some sort of production.

That is an important fact to be aware of because it brings in human labour as a factor of acquiring wealth. This then enters into the calculation of the exchange value or price of products. It is not the only factor but the relative difficulty of production is a good index of the relative exchange value of things in exchange (recall Adam Smith's comparison of water and diamonds, not in terms of utility, value in use, but of exchange value, value in exchange).

In the main, then, natural wealth signifies (as with St. Thomas) what man produces for his own use. Another way of putting this is to say that it includes all that money can buy, for money is the rational measure of all useful things, though it is here that things can go awry.

Money is not natural wealth but it is not thereby unnatural; it is "artificial wealth". That is not to be confused with artefacts, which are natural wealth from a moral/political point of view. "Artificial" here has a moral meaning, as based on agreement or convention. That is to say it is a rational invention to facilitate exchange of natural wealth. It is not meant to be a means of increasing natural wealth, but it can be a means of acquiring a proportion of such by reason of the accidental differences occurring in the measurement of their exchange value. As such, desire for the acquisition of wealth in this way has no limit – for it is a desire for the conventional measure (a measure of command) not the natural thing/product – but it can be made moral if ordered to the satisfaction of natural needs or rational wants.

This aspect of the exchange process has to be distinguished from "making money" in this exchange process by fraud and deceit, whether by manipulating others by clever psychological means or by obtaining the compliance (witting or unwitting) of political leaders. With the widespread ignorance and deception caused by modern education in economic "science" there is much of this more egregious immorality that goes on (with devastating effects on the majority poor and society generally), but it has to be carefully distinguished from the radical "scientific" structural sin that lies at the heart of modern politico-economic life, in rejecting the moral meaning of natural in regard to law and the market.

However, we previously concentrate on the meaning of property previous to its use in exchange and its extension to cover money. For, though Aristotle will come to consider "making money" in the strict sense, he first distinguished it from what is obviously making wealth in the sense of natural products. So he begins with food, which though it is natural in origin generally has to be gathered (produced) in various ways, even before being cooked.

Aristotle has described the diverse kinds of property, wealth (products), and the occupations whereby they are acquired. This he does in fairly elementary terms, but the range of property and its acquisition may be extended to all manner of material useful things. What they all have in common is that they are all natural in the sense explained; that they all are part of household management, in as much as they are instruments used for household needs or wants; and that they are limited like any instrument. One can only use so many shoes, even if they have to be replenished from time to time. St. Thomas puts it this way: "But the aforementioned wealth is a tool of the household manager and the statesman, since they use it to govern the household or the political community, as he has said [9]. Therefore, such wealth is not infinite but has a limit." (10)

That is property considered as natural wealth. Its utility is based on nature, if this has to be adapted by labour for human use. Aristotle is plainly speaking of property as the material things that the household needs to acquire. Before going any further we should say something more about the concept of property, as it brings in the application of the Natural Law.

Most strictly taken, the concept of property signifies a right. It is then used to refer to the things that are the object of the right. For proper signifies own; what is my own is what is proper to me. So property means the same as ownership. The car is property not just as a material thing but because it is a material thing that belongs to me. Property then signifies a relation that the car has to me. That is its moral and legal meaning.

Now Aristotle is talking about how households may acquire property, as the natural things/products that they must make use of. In this regard he refers to various modes of production, such as farming. But there is a question presupposed here: how did the farmer acquire the land that he had to farm in the first place? He may have inherited it; he may have purchased it. But this cannot have been the first acquisition. He may have been the first to occupy it. Fair enough, if this occurs prior to the institution of a civil community. On such institution suppose that there was not sufficient land to go around, or that one person occupied more than he could use. Who decides who gets what of the natural resources in any community, lands, minerals, natural vegetation (forests), wild animals etc.? Who is there to ensure a just distribution of such common goods/property?

The answer is fairly clear in general, if not so in particular (it need not be since all practical matters require prudence in final determination). In principle it has to be the civil community as a whole at its inception and subsequently as the need arises. The government, the principal organ of the civil community, has to carry out this obligation in distributive justice on behalf of the whole community. In the beginning this political body will be the founder/s of the political society; subsequently it will be his/their legitimate successor/s.

We can be assured that this fundamental duty will be carried out in accordance with (social) justice in the case where the constitution of the body politic is in the hands of what Aristotle described as good leaders as opposed to bad, i.e. of those who act for the common good, and not for their own party/particular interests. In the latter case, it is well-nigh impossible for those in government to resist the temptation to distribute common goods to themselves and their favourites. In the modern era we have witnessed wholesale "legal" expropriation of great proportions of the common goods of populations by oligarchies that have seized control. These common goods have not been only land and other natural resources but also the whole accumulated wealth of a civilization to that date. It has thus not only been a redistribution but barefaced theft under the cover of legality.

This grand larceny of robber barons (St. Augustine's great robber kingdoms) does in the course of time bring its nemesis and it seems that this is happening in our days. But we are concerned here not so much with the history of distributive injustice but with distributive justice as a natural moral basis of any political order. The right of property in any civil community depends fundamentally on distribution to individual citizens according to "merit" in view of the common good.

This is not personal merit but more like civic standing considering how they might contribute by their use of such property to the common welfare. It gives them exclusive possession and the right to manage the property according to their own reason and free will which includes serving first their own natural needs and rational wants and those of their family. But, as St. Thomas puts it, the use of such property should remain common, and anything surplus to their reasonable needs and wants must to give to others according to their needs and wants.

The modern notion of the right of property has lost this common dimension. It is but an extension of the individualist liberalist philosophy. This says a person should be able to do what he likes with his own body and what he owns. It is sometimes expressed as the right to use and abuse what belongs to one. This is already a misconception of the nature of the freedom that goes with the exercise of a right, taking "power elective of means" by itself as absolute, and ignoring "the due order to end being maintained", which is but a rational elaboration of the notion of means.

But not only does it ignore the relation of the right to its natural end, it ignores the relation of the right to its natural origin. In this regard it worships the status quo, which is very convenient for pirates/emperors. It just takes the fact that a person has something in his possession and does not examine further that "fact" at the level of distributive justice. It is as if someone ripped off another's arm and then claimed it to be his because he now possessed it.

It is of course not as obvious as this in the case of separate possessions as property. But present possession needs to be traced to a right of a human being to a thing of nature. This is in the first place a general right of every human being to access to the goods of earth, which includes all nature below man. This is expressed negatively as that no one is to be excluded from what he needs to survive. However, it is clear that this general right does not determine which of the goods of the earth are to be appropriated by which human being.

Before the institution of civil society this appropriation will be haphazard –first in first served. But on the formation of a political association the institution of private property naturally/rationally comes into being, with it falling on the government, as described, to determine to whom particular lands etc. should be allocated. That this has rarely happened according to perfect justice is beside the point. The obligation in justice does not go away. Even if it is not possible under actual conditions to achieve a system of complete justice that must be the social order to which a conscientious government must continually strive.

Aristotle does not go into this aspect of the right of property here – he has dealt with the nature of distributive justice in his *Nicomachean Ethics*. Neither is the subject dealt with much by anyone in the discussion of the institution of property in Politics. So far as an original or subsequent massive mal-distribution is concerned it is felt to be too difficult to "unscramble the egg". Of course, those who profit from the injustice will argue for stability, that any change would be "bad for the economy". Who is going to provide work for the propertyless if it is not the propertied? Who is going to feed the slaves if not their masters?

So it is that Aristotle moves on to focus on "money-making" as a means of acquiring property distinct from the natural means of production on the basis of an institution of private property. This is a study important in itself and Aristotle makes some politically significant distinctions. As refined by St. Thomas, these distinctions provide the means to understand not just the working of a natural market economy but also of a unnatural one, dominated by the love of money (*philargyria*), which is the modern economy. But, more importantly still from a practical political point of view, it provides the clue to the reason why the modern world is defined politically by a war between Capital and Labour, and modern politics is dominated by the opposed politico-economic ideologies of Capitalism and Socialism.

In these two modern ideologies we might see some comparison with the two political constitutions Aristotle related to the rule of the (few) rich and the (majority) poor, namely, oligarchy and democracy (both corrupt regimes). But there are more distinctions that have to be taken into account before we can make such a comparison. To do this we will need to have dealt with Aristotle's treatment of the different kinds of political constitutions in Book III and following.

For the moment, however, let us stay with Aristotle's Book I and his treatment of that mode of acquitting wealth or property

that is called "money-making". For, the proper understanding of
this part of his *Politics* is critical to the understanding of political
economy in general and modern economic science and practice
in particular.

Aristotle has thus shown that the acquisition of property is
part of household management not as part of the activity proper
but as instruments used by the householder. They are instruments of use in this respect. We should not confuse these instruments with those that are part of the production process (acquisition) such as a tractor on a farm - that constitutes capital in
a more physical sense of instrument. That may be included in the
overall concept of property that is part of household management. But it is not a relevant distinction at this stage – we will
deal with it later in the consideration of the concept of capital.

The important point Aristotle wishes to make in regard to the
natural character of such property (natural wealth) is that it is
limited to needs that are satisfied. This will be contrasted with
property that is not natural (e.g. money) that is sought to be acquired through the process of exchange (MCM). That is money-
making, strictly taken.

It is here that the translators really get things mixed up. Some
translators use "commerce" for "money-making" (MCM), but
"commerce" simply means exchange of goods (Latin *merx* =
wealth) and therefore could be applied to exchange without the
medium of money (CC - barter). But even if we applied it to exchange with money (CMC) it is not yet money-making (MCM)
in Aristotle's language.

The process that Aristotle wants to describe is where one uses money to buy something and then sells it at a profit (more money). Money is then not used as a pure medium of exchange of goods (CMC) but as a means of making more money from the buying and selling of commodities (MCM). It is the trade of the merchant *(negotiator)* who does not bring things into the market to sell for money that is then used to purchase what he needs, but who brings money into the market not to take out something necessary or useful but to take more money out of the market. His business is making money. There are no more goods in existence after his activity, only apparently miraculously more money in the merchant's (money-maker's) possession.

So we have to be careful to sort out the various steps involved. First let us say there is the farm property as land, acquired one way or another and traceable back (in Australia) to an original government ("crown") grant most likely to a political favourite who partitioned it and sold it to others at a great profit to himself and his family. Then there is the produce from that land, say food. The farmer has property in that product, which may have been produced with tractors that he has hired, and labourers that he has paid, and so has only a share in its value in exchange.

But let us leave out for the moment these subdivisions. The farmer takes the products to market and sells them. In primitive societies he may barter them (CC) to directly obtain what he needs. But let us move to the civilized kind of market that uses money. The farmer sells his products for money and then uses the money to buy what he needs. There are then two (half) exchanges to complete this process (CM, MC). What has happened to the money? It has simply stayed in the market (in circulation).

That is the process that Aristotle and St. Thomas call natural exchange (CMC). But this is where Aristotle mentions the entry of a new mode of exchange in the market. Instead of bringing goods or products to the market to sell for money so as to buy what he needs or wants (with the money) a person sees the opportunity of entering the market (with money, however gained) in order to use it to buy products or commodities and sell them at a higher price (MCM). This will require some skill and astuteness in watching the movement of prices. For, prices do move, even without being manipulated, because they depend upon "common estimation".

Indeed, though expressed in an exact amount of money the equality of value rather depends upon a practical assessment that allows for a range within which exchange may be said to be essentially a matter of equivalence. It may be likened to measuring the depth of the water of an ocean with a variation according to the movement of waves. Depending on the exact time of measurement one may be measuring at top or at the bottom of a wave. The difference is small enough to be insignificant in the big picture, but enough to enter into the calculations of one interested in small differences.

Thus, the thing to notice here is firstly that the profiting from the differences is not in itself a matter of social concern. It can be carried on without any essential injustice. The goods or commodities can be bought and sold within the range of a just price that as St. Thomas says is not set *punctualiter*. The differences in value in exchange are from a moral point of view accidental, not substantial.

The moral problem begins at the personal level, for we have an object of desire that has no natural limit. It is a pure means and any goodness it has to be derived from some end. So it is that St. Thomas says it can be saved from immorality (avarice) if a natural end is imposed upon it. Without this fairly difficult exercise in restraint both Aristotle and St. Thomas note that it generates all sorts of other vices ("the love of money is the root of all evil").

This immediately flows over into the social order: deceit and even violence are means adopted to destabilize the market so that profit can be made from the exaggerated differences (waves) created. As Aristotle pointed out, this art and skill prostitutes all other arts and skills, since it is such an easy way to make a fortune. Those engaged in such money-making having lost all sense of morality, the means of communication and political leaders are corrupted brazenly.

All this is invisible to the modern economic scientist, for there is only one kind of exchange and therefore one kind of market, whose freedom needs to be protected religiously. That is the view of the exchange process on the surface, as it were. It makes for a market that is highly volatile, with booms and busts, as bubbles burst when inflated without restraint. The modern economic science that focuses on this central aspect of socio-economic life is now called microeconomics. It is the study of the exchange relationship without any sense of commutative justice. Some even propose that exchange is based on inequality not equality. One can see where that perverse idea came from. It is important to understand this aspect of socio-economic life because it enters our everyday experience, with everyone caught upon a veritable "rat race", going around and around endlessly at ever-increasing speed.

We have not brought in here the other way that money is used in the exchange process. That is in the "lending" of money (really a form of exchange of one amount of money today, by the lender, for a greater amount later in return, by the borrower). This borrowed money may be for the purchase of necessities, or immediate needs, such as food or a house. But we do not wish to focus on this here. This will come into consideration later. What we wish to focus on is the borrowing of money in order to enter the market and profit from the activity we have been describing. That is to say if one does not have money to engage in money-making one can borrow it, and be happy to pay the "price" (interest) when there is (easy) money to be made. But what this does is increase the volatility of the market, and the intensity of the "rat race".

However, this is but an exacerbation of an underlying condition. We wish to concentrate here on this condition, money-making, first as it is opposed by Aristotle and St. Thomas to natural exchange. But remember that natural exchange has already been distinguished from a more basic mode of acquisition of property, generally equated with production. Then we arrived at the distinction between natural exchange (CMC) whose immediate end is the possession of some natural useful good (say, shoes by the farmer) and that other mode of exchange whose immediate end is the possession of (more) money (MCM). Finally, we reached the notion of such a mode of exchange as (morally) unnatural in so far as the end is simply more money. This we saw, whilst initially an issue of personal morality (avarice) quickly involves social consequences. The activity in which it takes place is the social institution of the market.

But, now we wish to move on to a more deep-rooted problem that is not to do with this unnatural condition of the modern economy as it affects the operation of the "free" market alone. Unnatural exchange might be a feature in an otherwise just society. It would lead to much social disruption and economic evils but be more or less self-contained. It could however be a superstructure upon a social system that is already structurally unjust as was the case indeed in Aristotle's Greek economy based on slavery. But this was a case of two separate evils existing in the same civil community, one commercial (in exchange) one industrial (in production).

What we want to bring out now is the way the modern economy has merged the commercial and industrial parts of society so that even without a legal institution of slavery, the factor of labour in the production of wealth or property has been subjugated to the "investment" of money ("Capital"). In the process the concepts of Capital and Labour have been changed to their modern meanings adapted to the roles of money and work in the new economic order.

Capital originally signifies simply wealth devoted to the production of further wealth, like the tractor. It is an instrument of production. It is natural as the products produced are natural in the sense explained above. We will see St. Thomas explain that "interest" paid on the use of such capital is natural, because the use can be distinguished from the thing. This becomes important in the discussion of usury in relation to the payment of "interest" on the use of money. For money is treated as the same as capital, the use of which results in the production of more capital (money). But it is only in the process of unnatural exchange that money appears to be an instrument like natural capital.

What we are concerned with here is the fact that Capital came to mean simply money, which is not natural wealth but artificial or rational wealth, based only on human agreement, like some one's promise. It is only truly useful as a medium in natural exchange. In the modern era its meaning as capital is reinforced by its apparent productivity in the artificial mode of exchange (MCM); that Aristotle clearly saw but tended to associate it with the fundamental vice of *philargyria* (love of money for its own sake). St. Thomas explained its unnatural use more clearly.

Its "productivity" consists in the increase of money in the possession of the money-maker, to whom the name "merchant" (*negotiator*) is specially applied when engaged in the second mode of exchange (MCM). This is not an increase in the amount of products passing through a market but simply a relative greater proportion in one person over others of the claim upon such products gained by skimming off the accidental differences of values in exchange (prices) in the manner described. It is not necessarily an essential disturbance of the market equilibrium, but it can be and generally is because of human moral weakness.

Now what we need to come to is the history of this use of money in the modern era. The rise of the new commercial (and financial) morality may be described shortly as roughly coincident with the disappearance of the social institution of feudal serfdom that the new labour system came to replace. This gradual process of liberation was quite clearly brought about through the influence of Christianity and was all but complete by the end of the period of Christendom and the beginning of modernity. Then a religious revolution occurred. In a way this was a smoke screen for the moral/political revolution that was already underway.

The political scene of the times was a contest between monarchy and aristocracy, in England called kings and barons. Aristotle, as we shall see, regarded these two as the best forms of government. However, if they failed to act for the common good, they descended into the worst forms of government, tyranny and oligarchy. At times it might be the king who tended to be tyrannical, using his power to further his own megalomaniac thirst for power; at other times it might be that the barony tended to be oligarchical, using their power to further enrich themselves. In the contest between the two naturally the one accused the other of so descending.

Indeed, at times it was only the king who prevented the barony from exploiting the general population. Yet, the barony was very clever at representing the kings as tyrants, and holding themselves up as the champions of the people (shades of modern democracy!). We know from modern history that it was the barony that succeeded in the end (in England in the Glorious Revolution of 1688) and the official history that we have has been written from their point of view.

So powerful has this oligarchical regime been, not only economically but also culturally, that it is only in recent times, apart from the work of a few historians outside the "establishment", such as William Cobbett at the beginning of the nineteenth century, that it has been exposed for what it is. Its power was magnified by connection with the religious revolution (Protestant Reformation), where monarchy (and true aristocracy) was identified with the "authoritarianism" of the Catholic Church.

However, we are concerned here with the more particular historical fact of the use of property in the hands of the few, greatly enriched by the spoliation of Church property and of the emerging free landholders, whereby a new servile class was created to do the work formerly done for the masters and lords by slaves and serfs.

Such a "miraculous" solution of the problem of social labour (who was going to support the luxurious lives of the rich to which they had long been accustomed if there were no slaves or serfs?) cannot have been the result of any conscious effort on the part of a ruling minority. It was something that "evolved" out of a breakdown in the system of social justice, legal, distributive and commutative, that had been built up in the time of Christendom. Most fundamentally, it was as natural as human nature affected by original sin, ever coming up with new ways to enslave humanity, with the greater slavery (of sin) being inflicted upon the oppressors.

But, how was it done? Well, firstly the new working class had to be rendered propertyless so that they were absolutely dependent upon the propertied (master) class. The most effective way to do this was to deprive them of any property in land. For, without land and the natural resources that attached to it nothing could be produced by labour. The producers lacked a material cause. One might as well propose to build a house without building materials. Even the remaining serfs were being "cleared" off their lands in the agricultural revolution. So those without property were driven into the towns "to find work" - for others, people who owned or controlled (through the possession of money) the necessary "capital".

These impoverished potential "workers" might find employment in households in much the same way as ancient slaves, or work on some lord's estate in much the same way as medieval serfs. But, the new modern way fast developing was in factories (originally called manufactories) working the new machinery that seemed to have been called up into existence by the new great pool of labour. This gave rise to the new kind of employer/master, the entrepreneur (undertaker in old English). But he was only an intermediary between the real masters and the new servants. He was the steward (overseer) of the combination of machine and men, hired capital and hired labour, put to productive use for the sake of profit, in the form of (more) money – a desire that could not be satisfied no matter how rich one became.

Thus, the new economic system of exchange (effectively MCM) developed under the direction of the men of property (money) using machinery and men as commodities for the sake of making (more money); commerce (Capital) and industry (Labour) became a marriage made on earth. By one stroke two oligarchical aims were achieved: the rich could continue their idle life of enjoyment of the good things of life; just as in the old days of slavery and serfdom; and the poor could survive to serve this end; with this added social advantage, that they were "educated" (by public education) to be grateful to Capitalism for providing them with employment. The State was there to ensure that this modern idyllic economic system was not disturbed.

Compared to the previous kinds of servitude there was another diabolic advantage. The substitution of a commercial (and financial) connection for a quasi-personal one between ultimate masters and servants meant that the workers were completely dispensable without the slightest human feeling. For, there was no difference between machine and man as "commodities" in the impersonal processes of the market.

It was left to the entrepreneurs/employers and those overseers down the line (serving very severe masters hungry for profit from the money they had so astutely "put to work") to deal with the human problems of workers and their families. Later these "owners" of the enterprise would be even more hidden from humanity by the "corporate veil". Everything, no matter how horrible and evil, could be justified as being done in the interests of the anonymous group of shareholders or stockholders.

Here again, there is a supplementary commercial/financial activity that enabled others without money to participate in the profits to be made from the modern economic commercial/industrial complex. It was not necessary for the new industrialists (captains of industry) to be men of property (money). Others (even impoverished) could engage in the process if they could borrow the necessary money, being quite willing to pay "interest" on the loan as a portion of the profit. That became as well a secondary source of profit to the rich and a primary source of profit to those who could set up (with political backing) banking companies, which could "create" money (credit) by issuing bank notes (their own IOUs) on the debts (promises to pay) of their customers/money-makers. This brings in the question of usury, which is complicated under modern conditions, because of the coming into existence of new extrinsic titles, discussed in my book "Economic Science and Saint Thomas Aquinas".

We do not wish to downplay the role of this financial factor in modern economic life but it does ride on the back of the more fundamental "commercial" factor (MCM). A failure to separate it out can distract from the basic commercial/industrial matrix of modern Capitalism: the use of the very market process to make the majority/workers co-operate in their own exploitation – MLM – and virtual enslavement. This financial (tending to usurious) activity does add volatility to the market, and the government works by "monetary policy" to moderate this volatility. Indeed, the tendency is also for this system of indebtedness to increase without limit, making in ancient times the need for jubilees. In modern times inflation of money works to similar effect.

But the root problem is as expressed by Pope Leo XIII in 1891: "... by degrees it has come to pass that working men have been surrendered, isolated and helpless, to the hardheartedness of employers and the greed of unchecked competition ... To this must be added that the hiring of labor and the conduct of trade are concentrated in the hands of comparatively few; so that a small number of very rich men have been able to lay upon the teeming masses of the laboring poor a yoke little better than that of slavery itself." (*RN, 3*)

We have explained above how the conduct of trade has been concentrated into the hands of a comparative few, and the kind of trade whereby the majority propertyless/workers are entrapped in a market system (called Capitalism) that subjugates them to "a yoke little better than slavery" and, if left unrestrained (unbridled), as it was at its zenith in the nineteenth century, would allow those who could not "find work" to perish pitilessly.

Thankfully, the State has stepped in to prevent such systematic murder of its citizens but only at the risk of slipping into Socialism, which is a form of tyranny. The only way seen to avoid the modern system of servitude is a more complete one! Those in the "developed world" should not forget that a well-fed slave is still a slave, even if he is allowed to live without work, a possibility not available to those in the "underdeveloped world".

However, though we have to use the insights of Aristotle and St. Thomas into the functioning of the market and have used them to gain our own insight into the malfunctioning of the modern market we wish mainly to take from here the distinctions that are necessary for understanding firstly that between the natural exchange process (CMC) and the artificial exchange process (MCM) and secondly that between the possible moral use of the latter and its more common immoral use.

This provides the clue to the state of the modern economy, and the understanding of the two ideologies of Capitalism and Socialism. Communism is in fact an interpretation of Capitalism, with Socialism as only a purgative stage towards the realisation of the same vision of man as Capitalism, namely, absolute freedom of the individual from any external authority.

We might mention in ending this treatment of Aristotle on property and money-making that these absolutely fundamental moral/political distinctions that may be found in Aristotle as clarified by St. Thomas will hardly be seen in the English translations of their works. The words "commerce" and "trade", for instance, are in many cases hopeless mistranslations. In the very article in the *Summa Theologiae* (*II-II, 77, 4*), where these critical distinctions are made we have the translator referring to the money-maker (*negotiator*) as a tradesman!

One has to resist the temptation to think that the obfuscation is designed to derail the discussion so that the current economic practice and philosophy/science may not be disturbed. But it is no doubt a consequence of a more fundamental indoctrination in the anti-ethical treatment of economics and politics. This can be seen in the attitude of many Catholic academics and "intellectuals" in asserting that the popes and the Church cannot criticise economic theories and practices because they are not technical economists.

BOOK I: SECTION 4

Chapter Ten

Aristotle's focus in Book I has been on the household as the basic element of civil society. He saw it as composed of three relationships, master/servant, husband/wife and parent/child. The main treatment however was on the first to which he attached the relation of property and from which he entered into the exchange/market relationship that is the first level of social communication (of goods). He now moves to consider the two family relationships of husband and wife and parent and child.

But we should first say that the two most significant treatments are that of master/servant and natural and unnatural exchange. The first is tied up with the ancient institution of slavery and the second with what we have seen is the modern institution of what can be called wage slavery. In both the servant/worker is regarded as property, in the first case as a chattel, in the second as a commodity, the one to be used by the master as he wills, the other to be bought and sold by the capitalist in that secondary process of exchange that Aristotle called unnatural (MCM), which we have described above.

The notion of property, therefore, links the two institutions of servitude (whereby a section of the population is made to do the lowly kind of work necessary to provide the material needs of the community, firstly to support the luxuries of the relatively few rich and secondly to keep alive for the most part the majority poor). But the notion of property concerned has two meanings: in the first case the labour of a human being as *an instrument of use* serving the interests of another human being with (legal) power, and in the second the labour of a human being as *a commodity* in a medium of exchange serving the interests of another human being with economic power (money). In the first case the relationship is personal, which makes it repulsive to many; in the second case the relationship is impersonal, which is more prone to cruel indifference.

We may regard Aristotle as seriously mistaken about chattel slavery (though he limits it to the household and males of lesser intelligence) but as having a genial insight into the functioning of the social market. He develops the critical difference between natural and unnatural exchange, though St. Thomas refined it, as explained in other places. But, it existed in his times as a separate distortion of economic relationships together with chattel slavery.

In modern times with the virtual disappearance of chattel slavery (and serfdom) what we discover is that unnatural exchange still exists as before but that it has also been applied to the buying and selling of the labour of propertyless workers (who are called the proletariat, a term adopted by the popes) thus providing a new form of servitude to provide the same "service" to the "fortunate few" as in times past. Thus, instead of the social division into master and slave of ancient times or of lord and serf in mediaeval times, we have the modern dichotomy between Capital and Labour, the first signifying money and the second commodity in the modern "Labour Exchange" (MLM).

This has solved the modern problem of "employment". There are those that are left "unemployed", described as "surplus to requirements". But this itself works to the advantage of the capitalist. For, it means there is a pool of unemployed willing to take the place of those in employment and therefore (as surplus supply does) provides a constant tendency to push down the price of labour (wages) thus rendering greater the possibility of profit from the overall transaction, when the products of labour are sold.

It is of course a vicious circle. For it means that there is less "demand" (purchasing power) in the community (the majority of whom are workers) for the products and so there is downward pressure on the capitalist's profit on that account. So the whole process is "vicious" and the modern economy lurches from one crisis to the next just in respect of this basic level of human social intercourse. We have had more to say about modern Economic Science and its place in the modern notion of science in our other three books "Economic Science and Saint Thomas Aquinas", "Natural Law – Australian Style" and Saint Thomas Aquinas.

However, we should move on to Aristotle's treatment of the other elements of civil society, husband/wife and parent/child. This we can do shortly. For, firstly, this subject matter is, as Aristotle held, dealt with in a separate practical science, ironically but accurately called Economics. There is a work of the same name attributed to either Aristotle or one of his followers. Secondly, the ancient treatment of marriage and the family is even more removed from Christian thought than Politics.

The matters discussed have to do with the differences (natural) between men and women and adults and children with regard to the use of reason and free will, or virtue and freedom, imperfect in children and supposedly of a lesser degree in women. Aside from the complications introduced into human relationships by grace and then the fall there are the deficiencies of the sorts of arguments employed by Aristotle in regard to freemen and slaves. We have the same inconsistencies as discussed in that context. Women, being human, have essentially no less use of reason and free will than men, and children, being human, are as much persons as adults.

Aristotle relates the relationships to political constitutions, aristocracy in the case of husband and wife and monarchy in the case of parent/father and child/son. Since these forms of political constitution are ordered to the common good, this returns the relationships at the level of nature before grace to something approaching the Christian view of equality of all human persons in origin, dignity and destiny. It has to be supplemented by the most fundamental law of love. For the reasons given before, however, we will not go any further here into Aristotle's treatment of the family in his *Politics*.

Aristotle will take up an aspect of these questions later when dealing (in Book VIII) with education for the best civil society. St. Thomas comments here: "For we should consider in the case of regimes things whose disposition makes a difference regarding the goodness of the political community. But such things consist of the instruction of children and women, how instruction is good for both, since women make up half of the population of free persons in the political community, and boys become men, who need to be stewards of the community. Therefore, we should determine about the instruction of children and wives in regimes." (n. 13) We will make some further comments then.

Aristotle finishes up Book I by discussing the position of "craftsmen" in relation to the household economy (Chapter 11). These were another category of men that could not be classed as slaves. For, they are extrinsic to the household, and work not directly for householders (as for masters) but by selling their products to them.

The discussion here is complicated by the ancient view that manual labour and slaves go together. This would seem to include the blacksmith and the shoemaker. But here they are excluded from the class of slaves. In the era of Christendom the craftsmen were clearly free agents and the distinction between masters and servants in this regard was generally a temporary one as between master craftsman and apprentice. Moreover, the social standing of manual labour rose significantly in that era, partly by reason of the occupation of Christ himself as a carpenter, but also owing to the influence of the Benedictine monks with their motto *Ora et labora*.

In the modern era, however, the standing of labour has again returned to that of the ancient disdain for the servile arts. This can be seen in reference to workers as "the poor people who have to work". The majority of the population, the working poor, have acquired the name of "the masses". As well, the lines between the various categories of master and servant have been further blurred, as the servile condition has been socialized beyond the household. Most workers now depend upon capital in others' hands than their own. There are a number of other factors; the nature of production has changed from handicraft to mass production; quality has been superseded by quantity.

We do not need to go into the many sociological similarities and differences between pre-modern and modern times. Leaving aside the treatment of slavery, we only want to bring out the insights that may be gained from the study of that part of Book I of Aristotle's *Politics* that deals with the subjects of property, money and the market. This has been sadly neglected we believe partly because of the prejudice against him on account of his treatment of slavery and partly because of the combination of the dominance of an anti-ethical modern science of economics and politics and the gross incompetence of the English-speaking translators in regard to this critical section of his *Politics*.

The modern discussion of the remaining books of his *Politics*, which consider matters more formally political rather than economic, does suffer from the same deficient causes, for when we come to consider Aristotle's classification of political constitutions, the modern mind has lost (or deliberately rejected) that most fundamental of all distinctions in relation to practical sciences, the distinction between good and bad. That enables people to talk about democracy without worrying about whether it is acting for the common good or not.

Let us move, however, to the consideration of Book II, keeping in mind that St. Thomas's commentary lasts through to a good portion of Book III.

BOOK II: SECTION 1

Chapters One, Two, Three, Four and Five

St. Thomas opens this second book with the comment: "After Aristotle has determined in Book I about things belonging to the household, which are elements of the political community, he begins here to determine about the political community itself ...". That is to say after considering the material cause of the body politic Aristotle moves to consider the formal cause, namely, that moral order which is the formal principle of unity in a civil society. It is a natural order but a natural moral order, not a natural physical order.

It is not a substantial order, unified in being, but an accidental order of many spiritual substances (persons) unified through relation to one end. When Aristotle says that the human being is by nature social or political, he is referring to the natural inclination in each human person to associate with his fellow human beings in pursuit of a common good. Ultimately this common good is the natural end of each person, but the social order itself is a common good of order, that serves the ultimate personal good of each human member of society. That is why St. Thomas says that the human individual is not subject to the common good of the civil society according to all that he is.

In Book II Aristotle means to consider dialectically other political theories and empirically experiments in civil constitutions, before giving his own understanding of the form or essence of the *polis*. He first of all deals then with what Plato has outlined in his *Republic* and then in his *Laws*. He then deals with two other political theorists Phaleas and Hippodamus. Then he looks at the political regimes of Sparta, Crete and Carthage and finally considers some proposals of others. It is to be remembered that he is believed to have also examined 150 other constitutions including the Constitution of Athens. There is no denying that he was imbued with the empirical spirit even in his practical science.

That material causal approach has been revived in modern times. It is necessarily in large part a historical study, though modern authors such as Machiavelli and Locke were immersed in the politics of their day, and thus could speak from direct experience. The difference between them and Aristotle (and St. Thomas) is that they tend to draw their conclusions from "facts" observed and measured after the fashion of a natural physical science, not a natural moral one as explained above.

Thomas Hobbes (1588-1679), for instance, explicitly compared the body politic (Leviathan) to a physical system. As one reviewer put it: "Hobbes's ambition is to found a political and moral physics". J. M. Chadelat, "For REASON [...] is nothing but *Reckoning*": the Postulates of Hobbes's and Descartes's Rationalism" in Revue LISA e-Journal vol. XII-n°5, 2014. It is a thoroughly materialistic philosophy but it is called rationalism because the physics is mixed with mathematics.

Besides investigating various kinds of existing civil associations, Aristotle considers the views of those political theorists who were considered major thinkers in political thought. Plato is of course a leading figure in this regard, though Aristotle roundly criticises his communist proposals. Aristotle notes that civil society is of its nature a sharing. "For, inasmuch as the political community is an association, we need first to consider whether all citizens should share in everything, nothing, or only some things."

So an examination of it will need to consider the things that citizens should share. More properly this should focus on political rule but Aristotle first looks at the proposals of Plato that there should be a sharing of wives, children and property. This can only be because of the prestige of Plato, for the proposals are obviously ridiculous in the case of wives and children, and also can be shown to be misguided so far as property is concerned.

Nowadays, we would not take Plato's proposals seriously and so need spend little time on Aristotle's arguments against them. It is plain that the things in question belong to the social order of the family, which we have already seen is but a part or an element of the civil order. Plato's proposals would lead directly to the destruction of the family, and hence are destructive of civil society itself. Present day proposals for same sex marriage are an instance of even more insane political thinking in the domestic social order.

This irrationality also applies to the proposals with regard to property, meaning private property, to make it common (though Aristotle will point out it can be in some respect made common). It is something that has to belong to human persons, by whose individual reasons and wills the necessary labour is applied to produce what is needed for such individuals, their families and civil society as a whole. Without the guarantee of exclusive possession no one will willingly produce anything. The whole social order of production collapses.

We have enough experience in modern times of Communism to appreciate that such political proposals are profoundly destructive. Aristotle gives a number of reasons why even in the abstract that is so. As he notes, the proposals are only put up because of an unjust sharing put in place in actual civil societies. But what should be adjusted is not the exclusive possession but the injustice in the distribution. Both modern political ideologies of Communism and Capitalism have been schooled to ignore this obvious root of the problem of property/poverty.

We should move on to Aristotle's summaries and criticisms of the opinions of others with regard to the various ways in which political power is shared in a civil society. But before this let us look at a more fundamental point made by Aristotle in his criticism of Socrates' political theory, as expounded in Plato's *Republic*. It is that it is based on a mistaken notion of unity when applied to human association. "Therefore, he says first that we need to think that the reason why Socrates deviated from the truth about the law regarding common property, sons, and wives is because he assumed a false presupposition. That is to say, he presupposed that the greatest good of political communities was the greatest unity." (cf. Aristotle Ch. 5; St. Thomas comment 1)

Though Aristotle did not put it quite this way we can say that at the level of the lowest kind of bodily beings the parts of the whole are physical and homogeneous. Their unity and strength consist in their massiveness. But as we go up the scale of being this unity and strength consists in holding together parts that are heterogeneous, as in living things. The higher one goes up the scale of living things the more diversity there is in the parts.

When we come to social and political unity then, representing the highest level of human life, the strength and vitality of the whole is manifested in the greatest diversity in the members. Aristotle points to the difference in the unity of political association from that of an army, where power depends upon uniformity. Socrates failed to see this and Aristotle commented that too much unity can destroy a State, meaning the unity that applies where sameness of parts are found at the lowest level of (physical) nature. Indeed, we see this deadly uniformity in the corrupt forms of political association, such as in Communism, which gross notion of unity ends by destroying the political or civil association.

All political theorists who fail to see the moral character of human association, which includes virtually all modern political theorists, tend to make the same mistake. The basic reason for this is in their notion of science. St. Thomas says that every science studies some order, but makes a distinction between a theoretical science, which studies an order found, and a practical science, which studies an order that we somehow make, if following the lead of nature. Now the social order is of this second kind, so politics and economics are practical sciences.

However, as explained above, these sciences have succumbed to the modern "scientific method" (empirical-mathematical), which is not just conceived theoretically but is thought of as a science of a natural physical kind (as in Adam Smith's "invisible hand"). All modern scientists even in ethical/political matters tend then to be materialists, having a gross mechanical notion of the constitution of civil society (of individuals as atoms and the social whole as a mass made up of indistinguishable atoms). This is in spite of them being otherwise religious and committed to natural morality. They simply have to have two separate compartments of their minds, Science and Religion, the former founded on "reason" and the latter on "faith".

Such rationalism/formalism cannot rise above the material order of things. Thomas Hobbes, impressed with Cartesian mechanics, though not its "Metaphysics", was more concerned to adopt a mathematical (geometrical) analysis of the psychological, moral and political order of human life than a purely empirical one. This was but an early indication of the mixing of mathematics with physics that culminated in Newtonian Science.

The formal cause of political association is to do with how such an association is to be ruled, i.e. with the nature of the constitution. Aristotle will address directly this aspect of political philosophy and science in Book III. The preliminary consideration of different political theories and existing states is the object of Book II. In this there is mixed up, as we have seen in the case of Plato, proposals to do not only with the nature of political regimes as such but also with matters that properly belong to domestic arrangements, as to do with wives, children and property.

We should note that in respect of the latter human beings, as slaves, are included in the concept of property. This should be rejected as not only unchristian but also irrational, even though Aristotle and others of high philosophical status have seemed to attempt to justify it. We should note too that Aristotle continues this acceptance of slaves as property throughout the whole course of his *Politics*. It seems just to have been taken for granted in ancient times.

Much of the discussion of political theories and examples involves a mixing of considerations that properly pertain to the order of domestic society in with those that pertain to political. Aristotle has identified this as proceeding from a false notion of the kind of unity that applies to civil society. This is connected with the mistake of thinking of political rule as if it were no different from domestic. The rulers of civil society are tempted to see themselves as related to their subjects as parents to children or worse as masters to slaves.

This affects to some extent not only the proposals of Plato but also those of the others such as Phaleas and Hippodamus, as well as the actual constitutions set up in Sparta, Crete and Carthage. We need to ignore all the theories and experiments that try to manage the individual and family affairs of citizens (they are not only present in ancient society but also in modern society) and focus on what properly applies to political rule, namely, the organisation of public offices and the kinds of political regimes, such as kingship/tyranny, aristocracy/oligarchy and timocracy/democracy, which will be more definitively dealt with in Book III.

It is true that in respect of private property for instance the rulers have a role to play. But it is to ensure distributive justice in the first place, so that individuals and families and other groups within the civil community are allotted exclusive possession of a portion of the common goods according to their ability to serve the needs of the community in the beginning and a just proportionate equality is maintained. Then it should be left to the citizens to manage their property as they see fit – subject only to the common good. The maintenance of justice in this regard will extend to ensuring commutative justice in the exchange of goods in the market. The basic feature of civil rule as Aristotle noted is that it is a rule of the free, which can only be fundamentally a system of moral obligations. Resort to force is a "fall back" position. Unfortunately, those of little practical wisdom, and the self-interested, that is to say the ignorant and the arrogant, tend to see political power, law and government as essentially consisting in the use of force.

Hence, barring the failure of citizens to exercise their freedom justly, there should be no need for "political management" of the production and exchange of goods in order that all in the community will be able to enjoy sufficient wealth and prosperity.

It is enough if the scriptural dictum is observed: "Seek first the kingdom of God and his justice, and all these things will be added unto you". The socialistic effort to match the resources of society to individual needs will only result in a worse state of misery and poverty than what already obtains.

That is all that needs to be said about the various political schemes to limit the ownership of property, manage the population, and so on. These matters that pertain to the particular aspects of civil life will all look after themselves if individual rights are protected, family autonomy is safeguarded and intermediate associations' freedoms allowed proper scope according to the principle of subsidiarity. If the political and economic self-appointed experts paid more attention to the popes in their social encyclicals, they would understand that.

BOOK II: SECTION 2

Chapters Six, Seven, Eight, Nine, Ten, Eleven

and Twelve

Let us move on then to the consideration of matters that more properly belong to the formal aspect of political rule. This will include Aristotle's treatment of Plato, Phaleas and Hippodamus. Here, though, we will still see a paternalistic, and even despotic, attitude intrude itself into the thinking of the best of the ancient authors. Of course, this attitude is not absent in modern authors, whether "progressive" or "conservative" in political ideology, or Democratic or Republican, Labour or Liberal in party loyalty. Smug in their own sense of superiority many seek to make man in their own image and likeness.

Aristotle has begun these more properly formal considerations in Chapter 6 of Book II entitled in Regan's work "The Second Regime of Socrates (1)". Thus, St. Thomas comments: "Then Aristotle, since he has said enough before about common wives and property, describes the things that Socrates said about the organization of the regime. First, Aristotle describes what Socrates said about the parts of the political community. Second, he describes what Socrates said about the education of citizens." (n. 2) The second part referred to, however, will unfortunately be a return to the problem of mixing domestic and political concerns discussed above. It is only corrupt regimes that are concerned to indoctrinate the young in opposition to the educational rights of the family. Aristotle himself is not all that clear on the necessary distinctions in this regard.

But let us concentrate here on the various kinds of rule envisioned by ancient theorists such as Socrates or Plato. However, the only thing of note in this chapter about the nature of political rule is the division Socrates/Plato makes of the members of the civil community into two parts, farmers and artisans on the one hand and warriors on the other. It is out of the latter that the rulers (basically the legislature and the executive) are selected. Politically this leaves the farmers and artisans out in the cold. Aristotle's criticism is that Socrates does not make it clear how they are to participate in civil rule.

This is a fairly primitive picture of how a society is to be ruled and in this chapter Aristotle spends most time on Plato's proposals for education – we can say something more about this when Aristotle takes up the subject at the end of his book. So we will not spend any further time on this aspect of Socrates' "regime", but pass on to Chapter 7, which is entitled by Regan "The Second Regime of Socrates (2)". Here St. Thomas comments: "After Aristotle has argued against the position of Socrates regarding the education in the *Laws*, he here argues against the position of Socrates regarding the organization of the political community. First, Aristotle argues against this position regarding the people. Second, he argues against this position regarding the rulers."(n. 1)

Then, St. Thomas anticipates the division of kinds of regimes or political constitutions that Aristotle sets out in Book III. "And to evidence the things said here, we should consider that there are six kinds of organization of political communities, as he will say later [III, chap. 6, nn. 1–4], since either one or few or many rule every political community. If one person rules the political community, that one is either a king or a tyrant. He is a king if he should be virtuous, keeping as his goal the common benefit of his subjects. And he is a tyrant if he should be evil, turning everything to his own advantage and contemning the benefit of subjects. And if a few persons should rule the political community, those who look after the good of the people will be chosen because of their virtue, and we call such a regime aristocracy (i.e., rule of the virtuous or best citizens). Or a few persons, who will turn everything belonging to the community to their own benefit, will be chosen because of their power or wealth, not because of their virtue, and we call such a regime oligarchy (i.e. rule of the few). And likewise, if many persons should rule the political community, we call such a regime by the general name *polity* if many virtuous citizens rule. But there may not be many virtuous persons in the political community, except, perhaps, regarding military virtue. Therefore, this regime is one in which the men warriors in the political community rule. But if the whole people should wish to rule collectively, we call the regime democracy (i.e., rule of the people)."

What is to be noted immediately is that the first division is into good and bad regimes, and this is made in terms of morality, virtue and vice. Aristotle will highlight this in his discussion of who is a true citizen of a civil community. But we must not confuse here personal morality with political morality, though the second cannot be had without the first. Nor should virtue be taken in a theoretical sense of superior intelligence. For the relevant virtue in the social/civil sense is political prudence, the relevant intelligence/wisdom is practical wisdom.

Though all practical wisdom is based on personal prudence and moral virtue it is not enough to be well intentioned and "innocent" in the case of personal prudence. For prudence requires that one be in touch with the world, and what is going on. The act of prudence includes judgment of the "facts" as well as the "law". For, moral judgment is finalized in the particular and contingent, if it does radically depend upon knowledge of universal and necessary practical principles. To put it in a figurative way one needs to be as wise as a dove and as cunning as a snake. As the Scriptures put it: "Therefore be as shrewd as snakes and as innocent as doves". (Matt: 10: 16)

Practical wisdom therefore has two components: knowledge of the moral law (universal) and of its application to the circumstances in which one finds oneself (particular). They are two kinds of intellectual judgments but being in the order of action and not merely knowledge they are also commands whose motive power comes from the will. The first component of these commands contains a whole order of universal practical principles and laws, from synderesis to the most specific of moral laws (which itself may be a complex of natural and positive laws).

The act of command of prudence, which presupposes the particular judgment of conscience has to involve knowledge of the universal moral law, for it is the application of such to the particular situation concerned. But it also has to involve knowledge of the facts of one's situation, say, being hungry and seeing apples on a tree in a field belonging to someone else. The moral law says one cannot take them without permission, because of the law of property; unless there is another circumstance obtaining, namely, that one cannot do this (either because the owner is absent or refuses) and one is dying of starvation; in this case one can take the food, because of the higher moral law of the universal destination of all goods.

Now, the knowledge of particulars when considered by itself is called astuteness, or shrewdness, or when connoting an ignoring of the law may be called cunning. But, sometimes it is called being wise, as in another version of the expression "be as simple as doves and wise as serpents". What is important to understand is that complete practical wisdom includes knowledge of both the universal law(s) and the particular facts.

This is necessary in all (private) moral decisions. But still more is it necessary in decisions to be made in regard to (public) civil life. Unfortunately, it is often found that those considered experts in politics and economics excel in the second and lower level of knowledge and are deficient in the first and higher level. So what we find in the examination of political theories and the investigation of actual regimes, ancient and modern, is that they are for the most part focused on the false and the corrupt. Aristotle has categorised these into tyranny, oligarchy and democracy. We will need to say something more about the meaning of democracy in modern times, as it does not have quite the same meaning as for Aristotle.

Aristotle observes that some think that the best regime is one that is a mixture of the different kinds of regimes. Clearly such thinkers have in mind what Aristotle would call corrupt regimes, since the reason given for this mixing is that "the admixture of one regime moderates another". Accordingly, Socrates thought the best regime ought to be composed of tyranny and democracy. Aristotle comments: "Socrates perhaps said this because the power of the tyrant would then restrain the power of the people, and the power of the people would restrain the tyrant." (cf. n. 4 in St. Thomas's commentary).

Aristotle well notes that "we should not call the two afore-mentioned regimes, namely, tyranny and democracy, true re-gimes, since they follow the impulse of the will, not the order of reason." (cf. n. 5) So we have the discussion here focusing on theories and regimes that are fundamentally irrational. This defi-ciency applies also to the other authors and examples which are addressed. We can note here that as an unjust law is no law at all, so an unjust regime is not really a regime at all. It is called a re-gime though by nominal analogy, as we have pointed out else-where.

Aristotle's treatments in Book II are therefore limited to not-ing what he can of relatively good features to be found in ancient theories of political rule and actual regimes, but which on the

whole fall into the category of false theories and bad kinds of regimes. This factual political situation bodes ill for an attempt in
modern times to find truth and goodness in a historical examination of modern political theories and a historical and empirical
investigation of modern political regimes.

For the modern efforts to produce a science of practical human and social affairs are handicapped from the start by their
scientific method, as explained above. Nor do they have Aristotle's advantage of the fundamental distinction between true and
false theory and good and bad practice in the study of the "human and social sciences".

BOOK II: SECTION 3

Chapters Thirteen, Fourteen, Fifteen, Sixteen and Seventeen

Let us pass over, therefore, what Aristotle has to say about the regimes of Phaleas and Hippodamus and move on to his discussion of the three major regimes or ancient constitutions of Sparta, Crete and Carthage, with a final few remarks about Solon, the founder of the city of Athens, and a couple of others.

Beginning with Sparta Aristotle first of all treats of the matters we have shown above that belong more properly to domestic society, or the household, namely, spouses, children, slaves and property generally. His critique here is flawed for the reasons we have given already. Then he moves on to more properly formal political matters. St. Thomas puts it this way: "After Aristotle treated of the Spartan regime regarding things possessed by the citizens, namely, slaves, women, and property, he here treats of the same regime regarding the citizens themselves. First, he treats of the rulers; second, of the people; and third, of the warriors. And there were three ruling powers with the Spartans, as he also touched on before [chap. 7, n. 3]. There were ephors (i.e., providers), and he treats of these first. And there were also certain elders, and he treats of these second. And there was also a king in the political community, and he treats of this third." (n. 1 of Chapter 13, 2)

We are not concerned to go into the details of Aristotle's exposition and critique of the constitution of Sparta. It is in line with the procedure he follows outlined above. We are more interested in a consideration Aristotle raises preliminary to his treatment of the regimes in question. St. Thomas says in this regard: "Therefore, he says first that two considerations occur regarding the Spartan and other regimes. One is to consider whether what is legally established in them is fitting for the order of virtue. For this is the end of every law. And so a law will not be a true law if it should not be related to virtue. The other consideration is whether there is anything in the regime ordered according to the presupposition and method of a regime contrary to the one proposed." (n. 1, Ch. 13, 1)

It is the first consideration that is most significant in understanding the whole basis of Aristotle's civic philosophy or political science. Though he spends a great deal of time exposing the ideas and examples from his own time and before, of most importance is the moral basis of such that he directs his attention to: "whether what is legally established in them is fitting for the order of virtue". We need to remember however that the notion of virtue that is relevant in the social/civil order of things is justice. Furthermore, it is not to be forgotten that the two virtues that are most relevant to politics (and economics as an aspect of same) are political prudence and social (including economic) justice and that they are moral virtues. As we shall see they need to be principally in the rulers but also participated in by the subjects in true and good regimes, insofar as civil government, like personal discipline, is self-government.

All governments or political kinds of rule that are not "fitted for the order of virtue" decline in one way or another from this true and good state. Indeed, like with a deficiency within the definition of law itself, they fail to be true modes of political rule, or genuine civic constitutions. They necessarily treat citizens as inferior to the rulers, be it all but the tyrant himself in tyranny, all but the wealthy few in oligarchy, or all but the majority (51%) in a democracy. In other words, the subjects not involved in making the laws are not fully free (which freedom applies only to those who rule) but are reduced to some degree to serving the interests of those who rule. It is only in those constitutions that are ordered to the common good, in Aristotle's language, kingship, aristocracy and "polity", that all citizens are equal and free – for strange as it may seem every citizen participates as well in such regimes (kinds of political rule), as rational and free human beings.

Indeed, as Aristotle puts it, the end of every law, and hence of every legislator, is to lead men to virtue. In the right kinds of constitutions this means to greater virtue, for it is supposed that all citizens are already rational and free, i.e. virtuous or just. Their personal virtue needs to be directed towards acquiring perfect civic virtue. Virtue in this context we may call a proper sense of justice. Sadly, this sense of justice is lacking not only in existing civil societies in modern times but also in virtually all modern political theories, even those which speak of justice. For, generally through a system of compulsory education, the people have lost all moral sense, in recent times indoctrinated to equate immorality with sexual immorality only. Justice, when spoken of, will be thought of in the abstract terms of an individualist liberalist ideology, or in materialist terms of a collectivist egalitarian notion of equality. In the contemporary context, the former is aligned with the Capitalist West, the latter with the Communist East.

We have connected this moral truth about political rule with that of law so that just as St. Thomas says that an unjust law is no law at all but rather a species of violence so too an unjust regime, as necessarily are tyranny, oligarchy and democracy, as defined by Aristotle, is no political regime at all, but rather a species of enslavement. This is said in principle or essentially. It may be that by accident, as it were, an unjust regime rules justly in some particular respect. Often, though, because of the bad will involved, this will be a deceitful device to win people over for a time. For the tyrant and the oligarchs (and democrats in the bad sense) still need to deal with those elements in its/their regime that try to oppose it. That is why such regimes are necessarily species of violence. As noted, legal positivists define law in terms of coercion. (This is not to deny that coercion is consequentially necessary in a good regime so far as those members who are without reason and virtue - "outlaws" - are concerned).

But we will come to the proper definition of political rule given more fully by Aristotle in Book III. We simply need to keep in mind that in his examinations and investigations in Book II the specimens he has to deal with are deformed in one way or another. A medical practitioner friend of the author has commented in this regard that it is like having to study medicine when the only specimens one has to examine are pathological. It has taken Aristotle a great effort of insight to see the normal in the abnormal, the healthy in the pathology. It is no wonder, then, that few if any others have been able to do so, for the state of disorder or disease in the moral/civic life of men and women is much more radical than in the physical/bodily life of individuals.

We will simply note a couple of observations of Aristotle with regard to the Spartan regime. It started out as effectively a kind of aristocracy but degenerated into democracy. There was a king, but his power was weakened by the ephors. There was a council of elders whose membership was made up of "the best men" (men of noble rank) and there was the ephorate in which office all the people shared. Aristotle notes that this constitutional composition did have one beneficial effect, as St. Thomas comments: "For, in order to preserve the regime, all classes of the political community should want it to exist, and any section of the political community should be satisfied to remain as it is. And this happened in Sparta." (2)

St. Thomas explains how such a mixture of ruling power and prestige enabled the Spartan regime to last, even though it ended up being a democracy in which "the ruling power was very great and the equivalent, as it were, to tyranny". "For kings accepted the regime because of the honor they held in it. The best men (i.e., men of virtue) accepted the regime because of their membership in the council of elders (i.e., because of their noble rank). For this ruling power was the reward for virtue, so that none but the virtuous were assumed into it. And the people accepted the regime because of the ruling power of ephors, in which office all the people shared." (2)

As happens in democracies military virtue tends to be the most prized (compare the Second Amendment of the US Constitution). St. Thomas notes Aristotle's comment on this aspect of the Spartan Constitution: "But the Spartans wrongly thought that the virtue whereby human beings are rightly disposed in wars is the best virtue, since other virtues, namely, practical wisdom and justice, are more worthy than courage. And even war itself is for the sake of peace, and not the converse." (11) Thus in commenting upon defective kinds of regimes Aristotle makes many acute observations regarding the notion of virtue that ought to be associated with good political rule.

Aristotle adds little of note when he comes to discuss the political constitution of Crete. He remarks: "the Cretan regime is very like the Spartan;"and goes on to note some differences. It seems that Crete was the earliest of the Greek regimes and came to dominance because of its central position. St. Thomas comments: "And the island seems to be suitable and well positioned to rule over the Greeks, since it dominated the entire Aegean, with almost all the Greeks located around the sea. For the island is not far from the Peloponnese and across from Asia around Triopium, and Rhodes."(3)

The reason why the Cretan regime is very like the Spartan is because the Spartan being later modelled itself on the Cretan. Sparta however improved in many respects upon the Cretan regime. Some wished to argue that the survival of the Cretans without civic unrest was a sign that their regime was well ordered. But Aristotle says that this resulted rather from the fact that "the Cretans dwelt on a remote island very far from other peoples and so did not have wars with their neighbors."

Aristotle then moves on to consider the regime of Carthage. Though not a Greek city Carthage was admired for its seemingly successful kind of regime. Aristotle observes: "For the three regimes, the Cretan, the Spartan, and the Carthaginian, resemble one other in some respects and differ greatly from other regimes. And many of the Carthaginian institutions are well disposed. And an indication of their well-ordered regime is that the people rest content with its institutions, and there is no serious internal strife or tyranny." (1)

However, Aristotle's final verdict on the regime of Carthage is that it was of the corrupt kind, tending more to oligarchy. St. Thomas comments: "First, he shows that it diverged toward democracy in some things and toward oligarchy in other things. Second, he shows that it diverged more toward oligarchy." (n. 4) Aristotle remarks: "For the Carthaginian law makes wealth more valuable than virtue, and the whole political community loves money. Whatever the chief part of the regime esteems valuable necessarily also becomes the opinion of the rest of the regime ..."

(7) Sound familiar, when we think of the cities of the West today? Might not New York be re-named New Carthage?

What Aristotle adds here is an important lead in to his explanation of the true nature of political rule in Book III. He adds: " ... and wherever virtue is not the highest honor, the regime cannot be firmly ruled according to virtue." (7) St. Thomas comments: "And in whatever political community virtue is not the highest honor, namely, that the honor of ruling is not related to virtue alone, human beings cannot unerringly rule according to virtue". (7)

Aristotle ends Book II with some general observations about those who wrote about political constitutions and civic laws (civil law taken in its most general sense to include criminal law). First, he noted that some were not active in politics, but others were. Secondly, some wrote only about particular laws, but others wrote about political constitutions or regimes.

St. Thomas explains: "For some lived as private citizens, not participating at all in political activity, since they were not rulers of any political communities. Such were Plato, Phaleas, and Hippodamus, whom he has mentioned before if there was anything worthy of mention about them [chaps. 1–12]. But others lived politically active lives, establishing laws for political communities, whether their own or foreign. The second difference regards the things they handed down. For some were the authors of particular laws but not any regime. But others established regimes (i.e., constitutions for the governance of political communities) and proposed particular laws. Such were Lycurgus, who established the Spartan regime, and Solon, who established the Athenian regime." (c. 17, n. 1)

Then Aristotle makes some observations about the Athenian regime. This is interesting as Athens has come down in history as the model of democratic constitutions. St. Thomas comments: "Solon abolished a very excessive and immoderate Athenian oligarchy; freed the people, whom the immoderate rule of the wealthy was oppressing; established a democracy in his homeland; and composed the regime (i.e., the governance of the political community) well, giving a share in the regime to the people." (n. 2)

This was an improvement upon what existed, even if democracy is taken in Aristotle' s sense of a bad kind of regime, for it is the least bad. However, things were not as simple as they are sometimes made to appear. It was a mixed constitution, of oligarchy and democracy and Aristotle sees that as better than pure democracy. St. Thomas puts it this way: "And so Solon seems not to have abolished things that previously existed, namely, the oligarchic council and the popular selection of rulers, which was aristocratic. But he newly established a popular ruling power when he constituted the courts (i.e., the juror-judges) from all the citizens."

Here Aristotle brings in a point about the advantage of a regime being a mixture of the three kinds. St. Thomas explains Aristotle's point: "But Solon gave only the most necessary power to the people, namely, the power to choose rulers and correct mistakes, and this shows that he did not intend to give all power to the people. And Aristotle says that the power of the people to choose rulers and correct mistakes is necessary, since the people would otherwise be slaves if they were to receive rulers without giving their consent and could not correct the mistakes of the rulers."

Things did not happen, however, according to Solon's intention. The constitution of Athens did turn into a pure democracy, as Aristotle puts it, "by accident". This was the occasion of the war with the Persians. "And so the people assembled at the time of the Persian wars to choose the naval command (i.e. the admirals) and astutely plotted to take over all power. And the result was that the people had wicked instead of good leaders, and these leaders carried out the will of the people." Not quite the virtuous image of democracy that we have in modern times. We will need to examine more closely the concept of democracy in Book III.

There is a surviving work by Aristotle on the Constitution of Athens. In this Aristotle says of Solon: "The mass of the people had expected him to make a complete redistribution of all property, and the upper class hoped he would restore everything to its former position, or, at any rate, make but a small change. Solon, however, had resisted both classes. He might have made himself a despot by attaching himself to whichever party he chose, but he preferred, though at the cost of incurring the enmity of both, to be the saviour of his country and the ideal lawgiver." (Part 2 Section 11)

Finally, Aristotle says a few things about those who were the authors of particular laws. There is nothing of much note here.

He mentions Draco, who has a reputation for providing harsh punishments for breaches of the laws. St. Thomas comments: "Next, Aristotle says that there are certain laws of Draco, who drafted them for an already existing regime, but that there was nothing particularly noteworthy in these laws except that more severe punishment was to be given when greater harm resulted from wrongdoing." Draco is reputed to be the first to institute a written code of laws for Athens. Solon succeeded him and as may be gathered from what Aristotle says was a superior statesman.

The Constitution of Athens contains much greater detail than Aristotle enters into here. This is to be expected for Aristotle is clearly concerned here with general practical principles of political science, to which he now turns directly.

BOOK III: SECTION 1

Introduction

In Book III Aristotle begins to treat of the nature of political rule or civic constitution according to its formal reason. What is it that "makes" a particular multitude of human beings, or rational animals, civilized beings or political animals? Clearly it flows from them being human, and specifically from them being rational (and therefore free). The *polis* or civil community is a work of human reason, and Aristotle has discussed various kinds of such in Greek social experience.

Here, however, he focuses on the essence or nature of the *polis*, what is the rational order if made as it is meant to be (*quod quid erat esse*). This we have seen requires an effort of intelligence or intellectual insight that is most difficult given the attempts to understand it by previous political scientists and the actual examples of its construction by previous city founders. As we shall see, even Aristotle proceeds tentatively at times to determine the precise notions of things political.

The first thing to note is that the form of civil society is an order made. It is a work of practical knowledge, which involves human reason and will. It is a natural order, not in the sense of a physical nature, which is one by reason of being one in substance, but in the sense of a moral order, which is one by reason of end. So the *polis* has something in common with an (accidental) artificial order, such as that of a house, but the end of an artificial order is not natural. The *polis* has something in common with a natural order only in the way indicated. It is a natural moral order. In that way it can be something that is both rational (made as to its form) and natural (found as to its end). Its construction is from human reason and will but according to natural ends expressed in practical principles.

The second thing to note follows from the first. This rational order is a form put into a matter, which is the multitude of human beings having the characteristics discussed in Book I. But, having to be made by human will, it will involve human beings as individuals. That is why its institution depends generally upon one human intelligence and will, namely, that of the founder of the city, such as Lycurgus.

But, the order has to be made in the human reasons and free wills of the multitude so ordered. They therefore have to participate in some way in the constitution and rule. As Aristotle says, political organisation is a rule of the free by the free for the sake of all concerned. It is the rational solution of the deficiencies had by human beings living as individuals or in households. The city is composed of citizens who are by definition rational and free, only bound morally to a certain essential order.

The third thing to note then is that the form of the *polis* is only had if the ruler acts for the common good and the individual members also co-operate in the pursuit of what is good. That is to say the ruler(s) are virtuous and the ruled are also virtuous, which in the social context equates with being just.

Now, Aristotle makes it clear that political rule is self-government. This applies to the rulers but in a good regime also extends to the ruled, even though Aristotle will make a distinction between the two. What occurs to us now is how even good rule can be limited to those of virtue. For, it is common experience that not all are virtuous, i.e. rational, in their behaviour, and so political rule has necessarily to deal with vicious and irrational elements in any regime. Should not we rather say that such a political situation is ideal rather than real?

But, to understand this we may introduce what St. Thomas had to say about the need for political rule in the state of original justice, or before the fall of Adam and Eve. The question in the *Summa Theologiae* (I, 96, 4) is: Whether in the state of innocence man would have been master over man?

The answer is:

"Mastership [dominium] has a twofold meaning. First, as opposed to slavery, in which sense a master means one to whom another is subject as a slave. In another sense mastership is referred in a general sense to any kind of subject; and in this sense even he who has the office of governing and directing free men, can be called a master. In the state of innocence man could have been a master of men, not in the former but in the latter sense. This distinction is founded on the reason that a slave differs from a free man in that the latter has the disposal of himself, as is stated in the beginning of the Metaphysics, whereas a slave is ordered to another. So that one man is master of another as his slave when he refers the one whose master he is, to his own—namely the master's use. And since every man's proper good is desirable to himself, and consequently it is a grievous matter to anyone to yield to another what ought to be one's own, therefore such dominion implies of necessity a pain inflicted on the subject; and consequently in the state of innocence such a master-ship could not have existed between man and man.

But a man is the master of a free subject, by directing him either towards his proper welfare, or to the common good. Such a kind of mastership would have existed in the state of innocence between man and man, for two reasons. First, because man is naturally a social being, and so in the state of innocence he would have led a social life. Now a social life cannot exist among a number of people unless under the presidency of one to look after the common good; for many, as such, seek many things, whereas one attends only to one. Wherefore the Philosopher says, in the beginning of the Politics, that wherever many things are directed to one, we shall always find one at the head direct-ing them. Secondly, if one man surpassed another in knowledge and virtue, this would not have been fitting unless these gifts conduced to the benefit of others, according to 1 Pt. 4:10, "As every man hath received grace, ministering the same one to an-other."

Wherefore Augustine says (De Civ. Dei xix, 14): "Just men command not by the love of domineering, but by the ser-vice of counsel": and (De Civ. Dei xix, 15): "The natural order of things requires this; and thus did God make man."

Thus it is clear that political rule would have existed in the state of innocence, because it is natural to human beings as rational and free. As Aristotle had put it man is naturally a political animal. In the natural order of things social (grace does not substitute for nature but perfects it) being subject to good political rule is consistent with the freedom of individuals. The virtuous, just, citizens accept it happily and indeed welcome it, being grateful to their leaders.

Now, that is to be understood as the natural and therefore real order of things. It is sin, freely fallen into, that accounts for the political disorder that needs to be corrected, if necessary by coercion and punishment, by good rulers. But, it is a more serious disorder if the rulers themselves direct their efforts not to the common good but to the satisfaction of their own interests and desires, for power, wealth and/or pleasure. After the fall, and even after Christ's redeeming sacrifice, the "political reality" has tended to be that of corrupt regimes trying to manage political disorder and civil strife. That is an unnatural (immoral) disorder not a natural (moral) order.

We should not wonder then that Aristotle had difficulty in sorting out the various aspects of political life, given that he has already faltered in regard to the apparently natural existence of slavery. So, when he comes to discussing the various kinds of regimes he will mix up at times the political and the despotic.

What is also to be gathered from what St. Thomas says about the relationship of master and servant in the state of innocence is that, taken as referring to master/slave, it would not have existed. That means it is inconsistent with human nature, or in other words unnatural and irrational, except as a form of punishment of sin. We can apply this to any despotic regime, which includes tyranny, oligarchy and democracy that is not ordered to the common good. This refutes any suggestion that slavery is natural and Aristotle's political (and domestic) philosophy has to be corrected in this regard.

Thus an important point here is that sin or vice is not part of any right political order even in the subjects of political rule. That is to say that right living or virtuous behaviour belongs in reality to political regimes as such. We may apply St. Thomas's dictum about law and justice to politics and moral virtue (prudence and justice particularly): a bad constitution (despotism) is not a political constitution at all; rather is it a species of political violence, or enslavement of one part of a multitude by another.

However, we still have to deal with Aristotle's language in this regard. He makes distinctions with regard to the good citizen and the good man and the notion of citizen itself applied to the members of different kinds of regimes (good and bad) that seem to go against what he has clearly laid down as a fundamental principle of the nature of the city (*polis*). To deal with this we will have to say something about his use of the notion of analogy which we have already commented upon in our "Natural Law: Australian Style".

For, he plainly uses, as we all do, the words "good" and "citizen" in connection with bad regimes. It will be seen however that it is like the use of the word "good" in relation to a criminal, such as describing someone as a good killer or counterfeiter. So a citizen may be called good relative to a despotic regime, such as an oligarchy; he does what promotes the interests of the rich few. So, too, those in the kind of democracy who promotes the interests of the many poor not for the common good but in a way that is unjust to the few rich may be called in Aristotle's usage a good democrat.

In St. Thomas's language this usage is called *secundum quid,* as opposed to *per se.* Aristotle will make a distinction between the meaning of the word in the primary sense and in a secondary sense. That is what is generally understood to be the use of analogy. But we have to be very careful here because many who claim to be Aristotelians and Thomists have been mistaken about analogy and there is much argument even about the meaning of analogy as used by Aristotle.

What has to be understood carefully is that the doctrine of analogy occurs principally in two of Aristotle's works, *Logic* and *Metaphysics.* Moreover, Aristotle uses many purely logical notions in his Metaphysics as preparatory to his definitive teaching on the meaning of being. So we have to be careful then when Aristotle distinguishes between the primary meaning of a word and its secondary meaning to note whether he is speaking about a word that is secondary within the order of real being, such as the word "being" applied to accident compared to substance, or about a word that is secondary because it is not in the order of real being but in the order of logical or mental being only, such as the word "being" applied to a negation or privation compared to something positive and real.

When St. Thomas says that an unjust law is not a law at all, but rather a species of violence, he is to be taken as speaking according to the real definition of law. The unjust law may be, and is, called a law but only in the same sense that a square circle is called a circle. It is a concept formed in the mind out of two contradictorily opposed concepts. As a concept it is a purely logical or mental one.

We have thus had to draw attention to two kinds of analogy that Aristotle did not always distinguish. There is real analogy and nominal analogy. Concepts may have real content or non-real content and words or names (*nomina*) first refer to concepts. It is clear that when Aristotle says that the meaning of being extends analogously to non-being or nothing, or purely mental being, we are dealing with nominal analogy, but when he says that accident is being in a secondary sense (*secundum quid*) we are dealing with real analogy.

There is, however, a further consideration in regard to practical matters, such as concern us here. The logical opposition is not quite contradictory opposition as in the case of calling negations being, or combining two contradictory concepts. It is more properly privative opposition, like that between good and evil.

Now Aristotle has said that good and evil are "in things". Is not an unjust law therefore real; and so too might we say that a corrupt political rule, such as tyranny, is real? They are, but they are not real orders of things but disorders. Evil is a lack of due good. Evil regimes lack due order to the common good. Evil can exist but only as a deprivation of something good in a subject (e.g. a community) that is otherwise good. The unjust law of the tyrant therefore names such a disorder. It may have some element of the definition of law, such as being from a duly elected ruler, but it fails to fulfil the real definition of law. So too a constitution may have an element of the definition of political regime or constitution, such as coming into existence from the will of its founder, but fail to fulfil the real definition.

There is much involved in the understanding of analogy, but the basic distinction we have used is sufficient for our purposes here. An unjust regime, or a corrupt political constitution, is not really a political constitution, but it is called such by linguistic convention. It is not a product of reason with any real basis, but of unreason. In the order of things human and political such irrationality deprives it of all moral goodness. This analysis of analogy has been necessary to deal with the language of Aristotle where he speaks about the virtue of citizens of oligarchical and democratic regimes and where he seems to oppose the good citizen and the good man.

But, before examining what Aristotle has to say about the proper understanding of the nature of the city and the citizen, let us first outline the division of his *Politics* in Books III to VIII. St. Thomas puts it that in book III Aristotle deals with the nature of political organisation and with the division of regimes in general. In Book IV he deals with each of the kinds of regimes in particular. We may see this discussion as concerned with the formal cause of the subject matter of Politics. However, this discussion, though it focuses on the work of reason necessarily brings in the operation of the will. Hence, there comes into play the efficient cause. Though principally concerned with the will of the ruler it also has to involve the wills of the ruled.

St. Thomas does not relate these aspects of Politics to the further books of Aristotle. But we can say that Book V, which discusses revolutions, deals with change in constitutions through the wilful actions of the ruled (by overthrow of current rulers). Book VI deals with the various mixtures of regimes concentrating on the two most common kinds of regimes, oligarchy and democracy.

St. Thomas does relate Books VII and VIII to the consideration of how the best regime is to be established. This we may identify as the consideration of the final cause as end in effect. Unfortunately, St. Thomas's commentary ends in the middle of Book III. So we cannot use Aristotle's *Politics* beyond Book III as the basis of St. Thomas's political science. However, there is enough in what he has commented upon to provide us with a good idea of the fundamentals of his political science, especially when this is supplemented by his own work *On Kingship*.

For a good survey of the relevant writings of St. Thomas on the subject of politics we refer readers to that part of the Cambridge Texts in the History of Political Thought entitled "Aquinas: Political Writings", by Editor and Translator R. W. Dyson. (2002) [One may however treat with appropriate intellectual contempt the editor's assessment of St. Thomas, a typical prejudice of one who rejects the Catholic Faith, or at least of one who fails to understand its relation to reason. He says: "Ultimately, of course, he [Aquinas] is intellectually dishonest; perhaps it would be more charitable to say that he is innocently tendentious." The reason given brings into full view the editor's anti-Catholic prejudice. "He is committed in advance to a closed system of religious and moral beliefs, and his 'philosophical' arguments are without exception devised with a view to supporting and confirming those beliefs." *(from Introduction p. xxxv)* It is the editor who has the closed mind. He has obviously not read properly Book I of the *Summa Contra Gentes* on the Catholic position on the relation between Faith and Reason].

However, let us now consider in detail what Aristotle and St. Thomas have to say about the nature of a political regime and its kinds in general.

BOOK III: SECTION 2

Chapters One, Two, Three and Four

St. Thomas only gets to chapter 6 in his commentary on this book of Aristotle. Fortunately, this part contains the most fundamental considerations regarding the nature of political order (formal cause). From this foundation we can go a long way to determining the many issues that arise in the discussion by others and in the experience of modern political life, even though most regimes fall short of being considered well formed, and as we may appreciate even fail to qualify as true political regimes according to its real definition.

So Aristotle addresses the question: What is that order or form that makes a community something politically organized? To answer this, he says we should reflect on what makes someone a citizen, for it is in the relation of the individual members of the community to the whole that the political order is shown. He comes quickly to the proper answer: "And nothing determines who is absolutely a citizen more than participation in judicial decisions and ruling. ... For we have no name that we ought to use for what is common to juror-judges and members of the assembly. Let us, therefore, stipulate for the sake of definition that we use the term *unspecified office*. Thus we define as citizens those who participate in this way. Therefore, such a citizen is one who most fits all those we call citizens." *(ch. n. 4)*

We may relate this notion of citizen to participation in one or more of the three aspects of government, legislative, judicial and executive, to which we will come shortly. It is important to appreciate that the citizen in a community has to participate in some way in the government of that community – for true political government is self-government. How this can be reconciled with also being a subject will be addressed shortly.

But this is not the end of the matter. It is in regard to this "definition" of citizen that Aristotle says: "And so the aforementioned definition of citizen most of all belongs to a democracy, in which anyone of the people has the power to decide cases about some matters and be a member of the assembly." We have to remember that Aristotle includes democracy among the corrupt kinds of regime. It is obvious that in the other two, tyranny and oligarchy, that such a definition only applies to one or a few members of the community.

Hence, St. Thomas comments here: "Then he shows that such a definition of citizen is not common to all regimes. He says that it ought to be obvious that, in all matters in which individual things differ specifically, one by nature primary, another secondary, and something else next (i.e., next sequentially), there is nothing common in them, as there is not in the case of equivocal things. Or else there is scarcely anything common in them (i.e., common to a degree). And as he will say later [chap. 6, nn. 1– 4], regimes differ specifically, some primary, and others secondary.

For regimes that are deformed and violate right order are by nature secondary to good regimes, as the perfect in any genus is by nature prior to what is defective. And he will show later how some regimes violate right order [chap. 5, n. 7]. And so there needs to be a different consideration of citizen in different regimes. (*n. 5*)

What is said here is that the concept is analogous. For each regime is specifically or essentially different from the others and there is an order of priority. But note carefully the distinction between the two ways of using analogy referred to above. The three good regimes are really analogous, the order of priority (according to perfection of unity) being, kingship, aristocracy and polity. But the three bad regimes compared to the good are only nominally analogous; for they are related as what is evil to what is good, or as what is deformed to what is well formed. Indeed, from the point of view of reality the comparison is equivocal, as St. Thomas suggests.

Aristotle sums up: "Therefore, these things make clear who is a citizen. For when anyone has the power to share in deliberative and judicial powers, we say that he is a citizen of that political community, and that a political community consists of enough such citizens for a self-sufficient life, absolutely speaking." (n. 6) That means that in bad regimes not all can truly be considered citizens, even on the general (nominally analogous) definition.

Indeed, in the least bad kind of regime, democracy, 49% may be disqualified at the time of any one election (which part of the population may change at the next election). Those politicians elected may of course affect to be acting on behalf of all, including those not in their "constituency". But effectively they are deputies of those who voted for them and no doubt try to reflect their preferences.

In the first chapter of Book III Aristotle considers other ways of defining who is a citizen only to dismiss them, either because they are poetical, such as by virtue of residence only, or as submitting to the jurisdiction as foreigners, or children or others incapable of exercising citizenship rights, or exiles; or because they are only "practical" tests, such as being descendants of known citizens, which definition ironically cannot be applied to the original citizens.

Then in the second chapter Aristotle considers whether a political community can be regarded as the same after a regime change. His short answer is that "it is clear that the political community does not remain the same after a regime change." (n. 6) Here we need the distinction between formal and material. It is not the same formally speaking, i.e., according to its political form or constitutional arrangement, though it may be the same materially speaking, so far as the territory and population are concerned. "And so, when the organization of the regime has been transformed, but the territory and the population remain the same, the political community is different even though materially the same."

Aristotle says the question whether the new regime should honour contracts made by the old regime on the community's behalf is another question that he promises to address later but there is no record of this. We suggest tentatively that the answer might have been that strictly speaking there would be no obligation in justice, but if beneficial there may be an obligation in friendship.

Then in the third chapter Aristotle addresses the question of whether the virtue of being a (good) citizen is the same as that of being a good man or person. Initially, he argues that absolutely speaking they are not the same. But it is clear here that he is using the notion of citizen as applying to all regimes, including the corrupt kind. "Absolutely" here then is to be taken in the same manner as "generally" discussed in regard to analogy. Thus, St. Thomas explains: "And so it is clear that we consider the virtue of a citizen as such in relation to the regime, namely, that a good citizen is one who works for the preservation of the regime ... And different virtues rightly order human beings to different regimes. For example, democracies are preserved in one way, and oligarchies and tyrannies in other ways. And so it is clear that there is no one complete virtue by which we can call a citizen absolutely good. Rather, we call a man good regarding one complete virtue, namely, practical wisdom, on which all the moral virtues depend. Therefore, one may be a good citizen but not have the virtue by which one is a good man, and this is the case in regimes other than the best regime."

In the case of the best regime then the good citizen and the good man are the same. Aristotle will however use the notion of analogy here and state that it is only as a ruler that the two agree. In good regimes in so far as one is ruled the citizen has a different kind of virtue, disposing him to obey. But later on Aristotle will say that the true citizen is one who has both virtues and indeed in human affairs one rules best who knows how to obey. Thus he says: "that a good citizen should know both, namely, how to rule and how to be ruled, sometimes seems plausible."

St. Thomas explains more fully: "Third, he lays out another kind of rule in which the other proposition, namely, that the ruler and the subjects should learn the same things, is verified. And he says that it is the kind of rule in which a ruler rules over persons free and equal to himself, not as a master over slaves. And this is political rule, in which now some, now others, in the political community are constituted rulers. And such a ruler needs to learn as a subject how he ought to rule. Just so, one learns how to command cavalry by having been a subaltern in it, and one learns how to command an army by having been a junior officer in charge of a particular unit (e.g., a company or cohort) and planning attacks at the command of a general. For a human being learns how to exercise great office by being a subordinate and carrying out lesser duties. And regarding this, the proverb says well that one who has not been subject to a ruler cannot rule well." (10)

Aristotle's argument here is quite involved and he is easily selectively misquoted to make it appear that the citizen need not be a virtuous person. Indeed, Aristotle clouds the issue somewhat when in the fourth chapter he goes over it again introducing extraneous considerations such as the existence of slaves in a community and even artisans who in Greek cities were considered not worthy of citizenship, because of the manual kind of their labour.

St. Thomas, however, corrects any misstatements when he sums up for Aristotle at the end of his commentary on the fourth chapter: "Then he sums up in an epilogue what he has said. Regarding the question that he asked whether the virtue of a good man and that of a good citizen are the same, he says that he has shown that in one political community, namely, the aristocratic one, a good man and a good citizen are the same. That is to say, offices are awarded according to the virtue that belongs to a good man. But in other political communities, namely, corrupt regimes in which offices are not awarded according to virtue, the good citizen and the good man are different. Moreover, not every citizen is the same as a good man. Rather, the citizen who is a statesman (i.e., the ruler of a political community) and master, or one capable of being master, of things belonging to care of the community, whether alone or with others, is the same as a good man. For he has said before that the virtue of a ruler and that of a good man are the same [chap. 3, nn. 5 and 11]. And so, if we should understand citizen to mean the ruler or one capable of being ruler, the virtue of a citizen is the same as the virtue of a good man. But if we should understand citizen to mean one incompletely such (i.e., one incapable of being ruler), the virtue of a good citizen and that of a good man differ, as what he has said makes clear."

We may take St. Thomas's use of "aristocratic" as equivalent to his use of "best regime" before, and it may even be applied to that good regime called "polity". The virtuous and only the virtuous are capable of self-government.

BOOK III: SECTION 3

Chapters Five and Six

Having determined who is a citizen in the most proper sense as "the ruler or one capable of being ruler", in which sense "the virtue of a citizen is the same as the virtue of a good man", Aristotle in coming to consider in the fifth and sixth chapters the various kinds of regimes, both good and bad, reverts to the wider sense so as to include "one incompletely such (i.e., one incapable of being ruler), in which is had the more general sense where "the virtue of a good citizen and that of a good man differ".

Accordingly, St. Thomas comments: "Then he shows what a regime is, saying that it is simply the organization of a political community regarding all its offices but especially its highest office, which controls all the other offices. And this is so because the whole governing body of the political community (i.e., its established order) rests in the ruler in control of the political community, and such an established order is the regime itself. And so the regime most consists of the organization of the supreme ruling power, different kinds of which distinguish regimes. For example, the people control in democracies, and the wealthy few control in oligarchies, and this distinguishes these regimes. And we should speak of other regimes in the same way." (*n. 2*)

However, let us endeavour to provide a definition of a political constitution according to its real causes: "(moral) order of reason in the multitude of human acts (and omissions) of a community instituted and ruled by the caretaker of the community (one, few or many) for the sake of the common good of all."

Formal cause: order of reason (constitution)

Material cause: multitude of individual human beings (community)

Efficient cause: caretaker of the community so far as politically organised

Final cause: the common good of the community as a whole.

It will be seen how close this is to the definition of law. Law is but the rule and measure of human acts existing in the mind of the lawmaker. It becomes part of the consciousness of the subjects when promulgated. The notion of regime is but the formal effect of the commands of the ruler, taken in all its generality. We might notice here that the word "regime" is taken from kingship, which is the primary kind of political constitution, and applied to all kinds, even the corrupt.

The most basic difference between regimes is in terms of their order to the common good. But before that human association is desired for its own sake, so that even a bad regime does not totally exclude the benefits of association (except perhaps for the most extreme tyranny). Speaking most generally, Aristotle includes even the association of master and slave as providing mutual benefits. St. Thomas elaborates on this: "Then he shows what the end of the political community or regime is, repeating what he said [I, chap. 1, n. 19]. There he determined regarding household management and a master's rule over slaves that human beings are by nature political animals, and so they desire to live with one another and not alone."

Even where there is no absolute or material necessity human beings seek the company of others. "Even if one in no way were to need another in order to lead a political life, there is still great benefit in sharing life in society, and this regards two things. First, life in society concerns living well, to which each contributes his share, as we perceive that one person in any society serves it in one office, and another person in another office. And so all in the society live well. Therefore, living well is most of all the end of a political community or regime, regarding all persons collectively and each person distributively. Second, common life is also useful for life itself, as one of those sharing common life helps another to maintain life even in the face of mortal dangers." (*n. 4*)

But at the end of this chapter Aristotle makes the important distinction between good and bad, or just and unjust, regimes. In St. Thomas's words: "Then he infers the distinction between just and unjust regimes from what he has said. For, inasmuch as ruling over free persons is directed to the benefit of subjects, it is clear that regimes in which the rulers strive for the common benefit are just regimes in accord with absolute justice. But regimes in which the rulers strive only for their own benefit are unjust and deviations from just regimes, since they are relatively, not absolutely, just, as he will say later. For such rulers rule over a political community despotically, treating citizens as slaves, namely, for the rulers' own benefit. And this is contrary to justice, since the political community is an association of free persons. For slaves are not citizens, as he has said before." [chap. 4, n. 2].

Do not be misled by the description of unjust regimes as "relatively just". Such a description, referring to previous discussion of analogy, is consistent with not really being a constitution or regime at all, as unjust law is not law but a species of violence.

In the sixth chapter Aristotle distinguishes the six kinds of regimes, three good and their opposites. St. Thomas comments: "Therefore, he says first that, since a regime is simply its governing body (i.e., the organization of the rulers in a political community), we need to distinguish regimes by their different kind of rulers. For either one, a few, or many persons rule in a political community, and this can happen in two ways in each of these three cases. It happens in one way when rulers rule for the common benefit, and then the regimes will be just. It happens in a second way when rulers rule for their own benefit, whether there be one, a few, or many rulers, and then the regimes are perversions." (n. 2)

Aristotle then gives the names for the good kinds of regime, which have become classical. St. Thomas comments: "Then he distinguishes both kinds of regimes by their proper names, first the just regimes and then the corrupt ones [4]. Therefore, he says first that, if the regime should have a monarchy (i.e., one-man rule), we usually call it a kingship if the ruler is striving for the common benefit. And we call the regime in which a few persons, but more than one, rule for the common good an aristocracy (i.e., rule by the best people, or the best rule). Aristocracy is so called either because the best people, namely, the virtuous, rule, or because such a regime is directed to what is best for the political community and all its citizens. And we call the regime in which the multitude rules and strives for the common benefit a polity, which is the common name for all regimes." (*n. 3*)

St. Thomas then sets out the three kinds of corrupt regimes: "Then he distinguishes corruptions of the aforementioned regimes by name, saying that they are perversions of those regimes. Tyranny is a perversion of kingship, oligarchy (i.e., rule by the few) a perversion of aristocracy, and democracy (i.e., rule by the people, the common people) a perversion of polity, in which many rule because of their military virtue. And he concludes from this that tyranny is a monarchy (i.e., rule by one man) striving for the benefit of the ruler, oligarchy strives for the benefit of the wealthy, and democracy for the benefit of the poor. And none of these regimes strives for the common benefit." (*n. 4*)

Aristotle raises a point here about the proper definition of the two last kinds of corrupt regimes, oligarchy and democracy. They are distinguished initially simply in terms of rule by the few and the many. But Aristotle says this distinction is really incidental, and happens only because the rich tend to be few and the many poor. But the desired object in a regime of oligarchy is the acquisition of wealth, as a means to political mastery, whilst the desired object in a democracy is the freedom to live as one wishes, to which as noted there is associated a claimed right to possess weapons.

Hence, St. Thomas explains: "… we do not distinguish an oligarchy from a democracy, absolutely speaking, by the large or small number of rulers. Rather, poverty and wealth are what intrinsically distinguish the regimes, since the nature of one is ordered to wealth, and the nature of the other to freedom, which is the end of democracy. "This is the basis of the conflict between these two regimes: "And these two classes quarrel with one another on that account, the few wanting to be in control because of their excessive wealth, and the many wanting to prevail over the few and become their equals, as it were, because of freedom."

As mentioned, St. Thomas's commentary on Aristotle's *Politics* ends here, where Aristotle has outlined the various kinds of regime in general. The rest of Book III and Book IV treat of the different regimes, good and bad, in particular. The contents of Books V to VIII have been indicated above.

However, we have the good fortune of St. Thomas having written a special treatise on kingship. So we can move to expound what he says in that work. As indicated above, kingship is the primary analogate of all in regard to political constitutions or regimes and so serves as the standard, which measures all other kinds of regime. It will take us a long way to completing our understanding of the Political Science of Saint Thomas Aquinas, not only so far as kingship is concerned but also so far as all other regimes, ancient and modern, are concerned, even though the modern world has long since rejected the worth of such regimes as kingship and aristocracy.

PART 2

ST. THOMAS ON KINGSHIP

BOOK I

In the first two chapters of Book I St. Thomas simply summarises the matters about human nature that are preliminary to discussing kingship as one of the forms of political rule. Man is distinguished from other animals by being rational and free. As such he is the master of his own destiny. St. Thomas points out that if he were intended to live alone, he would require no other guide to attain his ultimate end.

This is an indication of the supreme dignity of each individual human person even from a natural point of view. St. Thomas indeed puts it that "each man would be a king unto himself". This personal perfection of each human individual, no matter how otherwise insignificant according to his relationship to others or to the whole world, needs to be kept in mind. It is the absolute refutation of every system of slavery, and in political terms of every system of despotism, whereby one man (or woman) seeks to subject another to his (or her) personal interests. Of course, this unique dignity of the individual human being is only magnified infinitely in the order of Christian grace, whereby every baptized person is given a divine kingship.

Even when it is clear that man is not meant to live alone, but is by nature social/domestic/political these associations do not take away his fundamental individual dignity so that his subjection to others (even to kings) is by way of subsidiarity, that is, it is ordained to assist the individual person towards attaining his personal end. The subordination is limited to only what is necessary to achieve this. As St. Thomas puts it, man is subject to civil society not according to all that he is. Accordingly, the rule even of a king in civil society is secondary to each individual's personal sovereignty, which is not to be taken as isolationist but as membership of a greater community whose common good is God himself. This is the fundamental message of the social encyclicals of the popes.

So St. Thomas moves from this position to show the necessity and naturalness of man having to live in a civil society, that is as a political animal. This naturalness has various levels of social relationship from the lowest level of pure physical or animal need to obtain bodily goods to the highest intellectual goods, the former obtained through trade or exchange of material goods, the latter through exchange or communication of spiritual goods, such as knowledge and science. On top of that though there is just the fact that the friendly society of fellow human beings is something desired for its own sake, for after all we are of the same kind (congenial).

And so the problem occurs of how is such a community to be governed. For, the community has an existence in a way distinct from its members' individual existences. Its end, common good, is not other that the good of its members but what the community can provide over and above that of the individuals acting by themselves has to be unified as the community is one. It is immediately evident to our understanding that there needs to be some leading principle, i.e. a leader within the community.

But for those who demand proof of everything we can apply what is called the henological principle (from Greek *ena* for one); the many are not made one through themselves (for they are diverse) so there must be some one cause of their union. Since the civil society is a work of the reason and will of human beings, and such reason and will only operates in individuals, then there needs to be some one principal individual human reason and will (or a manageable group closely acting in deliberate agreement) who can ensure that the common unity and common good is effected.

So after showing the necessity for civil or political association St. Thomas argues for the need for a person (or persons) whose task is to look to preserving the unity of the association (*polis*) in so far as it is distinct from the diverse interests of the members. Next St. Thomas will argue that this task would be best fulfilled by one person, provided he has the necessary ability or qualifications to do the task.

The discussion had above in Aristotle's *Politics* with regard to the nature of citizenship is presupposed. Though there are many aspects of human life, from bodily to spiritual, and association serves at many levels, the principal human level is that of living according to reason and free will, or virtuously. That means that the principal task of civil association is to assist individual persons to do this. It is the same principal task then that is assigned to the leader or governor.

So St. Thomas in the second chapter brings in the distinction between the right way to act and the wrong way. This applies not only in regard to individual personal behaviour but also in regard to the actions of the governor or leader. Assuming for the moment that is the rule of one person (monarchy) then we have two opposed kinds of rule, that which serves to lead the citizens on the right path, which is ascribed to a king, and that which does not, which is ascribed to a tyrant.

St. Thomas elaborates here on how this comes about. The tyrant is not motivated by evil as such – no one is – but seeks a good that is opposed to what he should, namely, his own interest as opposed to the common good of those he has been appointed to govern. St. Thomas will use here the notion of slavery. For it is of the essence of slavery that the master directs the slave for his own benefit, treating him like a piece of property. We have seen how unnatural this use of other human beings is but it does serve to bring out the unnaturalness of the actions of corrupt rulers.

St. Thomas here takes the opportunity to elaborate upon the different kinds of regime outlined by Aristotle apart from the rule of one, namely, the rule of a few, which is correspondingly called aristocracy and oligarchy, and the rule of many, called polity and democracy.

And so St. Thomas argues for the rule of a king in the third chapter, where the heading is put in the form of a question: Whether it is more expedient (*utilis*) for a multitude of human beings living together (community) to be ruled by one or many? It is evident already that the unity of the community would, barring extraneous considerations, be better served by one rather than a few or many in government. But it is not a simple theoretical question, and we may notice how "politically" St. Thomas puts it.

He is after all writing to a king (of Cyprus). But even from a practical point of view St. Thomas is able to use various persuasive arguments that support the proposition that it is more expedient (better) for a community to be ruled by a king than by the other possible forms of government. Rule by more than one opens up the possibility (and even likelihood) of dissension and disagreement over policies. But the reasons in favour very greatly depend upon conditions that are not easy to realise. For, the king has to be an exceptional person in virtue, that is, in the exercise of the necessary reason required, not in knowledge that is theoretical, but in practical wisdom or political prudence, which goes beyond simple innocence of worldly conditions.

As well, there are many obstacles and dangers that attend to having only one person as the sole ruler. Not the least is the one given by St. Thomas in the fourth chapter, namely, that the king could become a tyrant "which is the worst kind of government". Indeed, in the fifth chapter, St. Thomas observes "not a few rulers exercise tyranny under the cloak of royal dignity". He goes on then to recount the history of the Romans to whom "the royal name was hateful" because of their bad experience. A similar observation may be made about the modern era, in which both monarchy and aristocracy are associated rather with tyranny and oligarchy, and democracy is considered the only appropriate form of government, though this has involved also the loss of the notion of the common good.

In other parts of his works St. Thomas will be in favour of a mixed constitution, which is more likely to be stable given the actual conditions of human and social affairs. The other consideration is that the office of king is not to be contrary to the truth that all civil government is self-government by all members of the community. So the many need to have some part to play in actual rule. The idea of a king is that of a principal part, or head, of a body that is living and thus self-moving, not moved about like something driven, or even unfree. The rule of a king needs to be like that of God, who governs all things in accordance with their nature, which in the case of creatures of spiritual form, which man is, has a will that is free.

St. Thomas's recommendation of kingship, therefore, is qualified and realistic. What it does for us in the modern confusion in regard to political affairs is that it enables us to keep a right perspective in dealing with the nature of political government. For one thing it highlights the dire consequences of having a government not act for the common good, which is difficult to ensure if there is no awareness of what that means.

Aristotle had noted that as a matter of political fact governments tend to oscillate between oligarchies and democracies, to which we may add: with outbreaks of tyranny (totalitarianism) in between. That is to say, we get the governments we deserve. If we wish to obtain good government in any form, as St. Thomas says in the seventh chapter of Book I, "the people must desist from sin".

More than for any other reason this is why the notion of common good has been lost in modern political science. It just does not fit the facts. This is compounded by the all but universal application of the anti-ethical "scientific method" to the investigation of political "facts". Most of the time modern politics is a case of the blind leading the blind and both falling into the ditch. It is only the presence of the Church that saves us from perishing permanently in this world, for as Chesterton remarks there is in it a mysterious principle of resurrection. The blind of course attribute their good fortune in this regard to themselves and their "scientific knowledge".

As Shakespeare has put in "Measure for Measure":

> But man, proud man,
> Dress'd in a little brief authority,
> Most ignorant of what he's most assur'd—
> His glassy essence—like an angry ape
> Plays such fantastic tricks before high heaven
> As makes the angels weep ...

After arguing in the third chapter that in principle the rule of a king is the best he spends the next few chapters in warnings about the risks involved. Chapter Four for instance is headed: "That the Dominion of a Tyrant is the Worst". St. Thomas explains: "Moreover a government becomes unjust by the fact that the ruler, paying no heed to the common good, seeks his own private good. Wherefore the further he departs for the common good the more unjust will his government be. But there is a greater departure from the common good in an oligarchy, in which the advantage of a few is sought than in a democracy, in which the advantage of the many is sought; and there is a still greater departure from the common good in a tyranny, where the advantage of only one man is sought ... thus the government of a tyrant is the most unjust." (n. 24)

St. Thomas then details the various ways a tyrant acts in pursuing his own interest. "... he will oppress his subjects in different ways according as he is dominated by different passions to acquire certain goods. The one who is enthralled by the passion of cupidity seizes the goods of his subjects ... If he is dominated by the passion of anger, he sheds blood for nothing." More damning for the community generally is the fact that there are serious spiritual consequences: St. Thomas notes: ""few virtuous men are found under the rule of tyrants"; quoting Aristotle [*Eth. III, n. 11; 1116a 20*]: "brave men are found where brave men are honoured"; and the Scriptures: "When the wicked reign men are ruined." [*Prov. 29: 2*]

These evils may be attributed proportionally to the other two corrupt kinds of regime, oligarchy and democracy. Oligarchies are more disposed to cupidity, and therefore seize "legally" the property of the people they rule; but even in a democracy minorities are oppressed by "public opinion" and "community standards" that override moral considerations. Passions can also rise in such regimes to the level of violence against those who resist the injustices perpetrated by the ones in power.

In the fifth chapter, as we have noted, St. Thomas recounts the history of the Romans: "worn out by continual dissensions taking on the proportion of civil wars, and when by these wars the freedom for which they had greatly striven was snatched from their hands, they began to find themselves under the power of emperors who, from the beginning, were unwilling to be called kings, for the royal name was hateful to the Romans." He continues: "Some emperors, it is true, faithfully cared for the common good in a kingly manner, and by their zeal the commonwealth was increased and preserved. But most of them became tyrants towards their subjects and vacillating before their enemies, and brought the Roman commonwealth to naught." (*n. 33*)

What is noteworthy is that in the sixth chapter St. Thomas makes an argument that tyranny is more likely to arise from the government of a few (polyarchy) than of one (monarchy), for the reason that among the latter there is bound to be one who plots to promote his own interest at the expense of the common good. This is verified by experience and St. Thomas refers again to Roman history. Thus there is less risk of the rule of a king, who will at least have begun to rule desiring to promote the common good, falling into tyranny than a group of people most likely to fall out with one another. If one can find a good ruler in a king, then it is the best and safest kind of regime.

The problem, however, is in finding such an exceptional person, for he has to be outstanding, an evident champion of the community, selfless and dedicated to the common good. The pervasiveness of sin makes the argument for such a regime weaker. There may be in fact more safety in numbers with their checks and balances. So it is that in modern times rather than even considering the possibility of both monarchy and polyarchy, the first associated with tyranny and the second with oligarchy, political theory has opted to make "democracy" the only good kind of regime. The other two alternatives, monarchy and polyarchy, even when called by their good names, kingship and aristocracy, are necessarily to be rejected precisely because they are "undemocratic".

The confusion of language here is in abstracting from the vital distinction between good and bad, which as we have noted is connected with the loss of the notion of common good. There may be talk about the national interest, but, if it is not reduced to individual interests (Liberalism) or that of the government (Statism), it is equated with a collective notion of individual interests (Socialism). Democracy is naturally associated with individual freedom but here too the philosophical basis is Liberalism. All this is reinforced by a physicalist/atomist notion of science as applied to human and social affairs.

The anti-religious sentiment is only thinly below the surface, designedly associating monarchy and aristocracy with the hierarchical structure of the Catholic Church and the "dark ages". In this even religious people (non-Catholics) join forces to distort history and paint the modern era as one of enlightenment. But the true dark ages are those of ancient paganism and modern materialism, both destined to die a gruesome death. The happier and lightsome times did come with Christianity and is manifest in the era of Christendom (when England was "Merrie"), which prompted a noted historian to call the thirteenth century "the greatest of centuries".

This has some relevance to St. Thomas's lauding of kingship. For, relative to earlier and later times there were good kings and people prospered under their rule in the period of Christendom. St. Thomas himself lived in the time of the king-saint Louis IX of France (1214-1270). He was canonised within 30 years of his death. Such was his reputation for goodness that numerous places have been named in his honour not only in Europe but also in the USA. He is reputed to have banned trials by ordeal, and to have introduced the presumption of innocence in criminal procedure. That last legal measure would be enough to honour his memory in the Western world. Unfortunately, in our own corrupted times the presumption has been greatly weakened in public trials by media, prompted significantly by the desire to defame the Catholic Church.

The political contests of the times leading up to the modern era were mainly between the kings and the aristocracy (barony). Magna Carta is celebrated as a political milestone for civil freedom in English history, but it marks rather a victory of the barons against the king. The king often proved the only bulwark against the depredations of greedy lords (and ladies). When the barons finally won out in 1688 ("The Glorious Revolution") the most significant result of this was that that barrier against oligarchical cupidity was effectively removed (it had been greatly weakened since Henry VIII's time).

So far as St. Thomas's treatise is concerned, however, we should not import into it the bad image that attaches to kingship (and aristocracy) from the history of ancient and early modern times. There is a degree of deviousness involved in disdaining the royal dignity especially. For not a few modern regimes are effectively oligarchical under the cloak of a rule propagated as one of democracy and freedom.

St. Thomas spends the seventh chapter in considering "how provision might be made that the king may not fall into tyranny". There seems not to be much remedy allowed by St. Thomas should this happen other than to appeal to a higher authority, ultimately God himself. St. Thomas sets the saying of St. Peter against cases in the Old Testament that seem to allow otherwise. There is a remedy of course if the tyrant is a usurper. He has no legitimate political authority and may be deposed if that is possible without greater evil being done.

In modern times in the West the problem is not so alive. For, most governments are short term. The nearest thing to a king is a president who is also elected for a short term only (he may for his short term of office try to curb the power of the barons/oligarchs but they are ensconced long-term and can simply work to ensure the election of a more compliant "king" next time). The rise of a tyrant on any long-term basis would therefore have to be by usurpation. We may then leave this question aside and focus on the more positive side of kingship as a possibility, given the existence of a society that is inclined more to virtue than to vice, and of a leader who excels in the requisite political virtues.

In the eighth chapter St. Thomas begins to consider what should be the reward of a king. It is not earthly honour and glory as this passes. In the ninth chapter he identifies it with the same reward of all rational beings, namely those of virtue, which is eternal happiness, but in an appropriately higher degree. In the tenth chapter St. Thomas puts this as the highest. But it is to be noted that we are speaking here in the natural order. Transferred to the supernatural order of grace a simple peasant's reward may transcend that of a king.

In the eleventh chapter St. Thomas moves to consider the case of the tyrant. The thing to note here is the folly of a desire for tyranny or any other corrupt kind of political power. For the very temporal advantages for which the tyrant, oligarchs and democrats abandon justice, whether it be wealth, pleasure, worldly honour and glory, fellow human beings' admiration and friendship, are all lost in their case, whereas if they had but remained just, as does a king, they would have enjoyed all this as something added to their eternal reward. Moreover, the reign of a tyrant is generally short lived. As St. Thomas puts it: "Aristotle in his *Politics* [V 12: 1315b 11-39] after enumerating many tyrants shows that all their governments were of short duration; although some of them reigned a fairly long time because they were not very tyrannical but in many things imitated the moderation of kings."

In chapter twelve St. Thomas makes the point, related to the above, that it is "in seeking to acquire these things [power wealth honour and fame] unduly that princes turn to tyranny. For no one falls away from justice except through a desire for some temporal advantage." (*n. 86*) With a little wisdom and humility they may have seen the futility of this short-sighted course of action. "The tyrant, moreover", St. Thomas adds: " ... brings upon himself great suffering as a punishment".

In chapter thirteen St. Thomas discourses on the duties of a king. Simply speaking, just as it belongs to each individual human being to govern himself by reason so it belongs to the multitude to be governed by the reason of one man. That is the function of the king. He is the principle of unity in society just as the soul is to the body and God is to the world. St. Thomas sums up: "If he reflect seriously upon this, a zeal for justice will be enkindled in him when he contemplates that he has been appointed to this position in place of God, to exercise judgment in the kingdom; further he will acquire the gentleness of clemency and mildness when he considers as his own members those individuals who are subject to his rule." (*n. 95*)

In the fourteenth chapter St. Thomas elaborates upon what he has said about imitating the divine government. We do not need to comment on this. In the fifteenth chapter St. Thomas clarifies the principal role of the king or government as being to lead men to virtue, though this is not to be thought of as the ultimate end. "Yet through virtuous living man is further ordained to a higher end which consists in the enjoyment of God ... Consequently, since society must have the same end as the individual man, it is not the ultimate end of an assembled multitude to live virtuously, but through virtuous living to attain to the possession of God. (*n. 107*).

Nonetheless, the end of political rule is to lead men to virtue rather than to wealth or any other state of material welfare. "If that ultimate end were an abundance of wealth, then knowledge of economics would have the last word in the community's government [as it does in modern times]. If the good of knowledge of truth were of such a kind that the multitude might attain to it, the king would have to be a teacher [the academic idea of living well]. It is however clear that the end of the multitude gathered together is to live virtuously. For men form a group for the purpose of *living well* together, a thing which the individual man living alone could not attain, and good life is virtuous life."

This is something that is not at all understood in modern political science, even though what St. Thomas adds about the nature of law and government makes it clear. "The evidence for this lies in the fact that only those who render mutual assistance to one another in living well form a genuine part of an assembled multitude. If men assembled merely to live, then animals and slaves would form a part of the civil community. Or, if men assembled only to accrue wealth, then all those who traded together would belong to one city. Yet we see that only such are regarded as forming one multitude as are directed by the same laws and the same government to live well." (*n. 106*)

To live well is to be taken in its fully human sense, i.e. in full accord with a rational and moral life. The modern fashion of taking morals out of politics only degrades the function of government and prepares the ground for its corruption and ideological manipulation.

In the sixteenth chapter St. Thomas broaches the question of the relation between secular rule and religious rule, or between that of the king and that of the priest. On an international scale this became concentrated upon that between the emperor and the pope. Now it was clear that in terms of natural religion the priest was subject to the king. But when it came to the Christian dispensation it was generally accepted that in the theory of the matter the roles needed to be somehow adjusted, because of the obvious supernatural status of the Christian priest.

St. Thomas had put it this way in his commentary on the Sentences: "Spiritual and secular power are both derived from the Divine power, and so secular power is subject to spiritual power insofar as this is ordered by God: that is, in those things which pertain to the salvation of the soul. In such matters, then, the spiritual power is to be obeyed before the secular. But in those things that pertain to the civil good, the secular power should be obeyed before the spiritual, according to Matthew: 'Render to Caesar the things that are Caesar's.' Unless perhaps the spiritual and secular powers are conjoined, as in the pope, who holds the summit of both powers: that is, the spiritual and the secular, through the disposition of Him Who is both priest and king ..."

Things are therefore left not so clear. It must certainly be held by a Christian that in terms of power the divine is superior to the human, and so the priestly power is superior to that of the king, or of any civil government. But God rules in the natural order through natures and hence through duly appointed or elected rulers. The priestly power is not going to be used contrary to that. As to what happens if such secular power is abused, especially as aimed against the Church, was it the general view including that of St. Thomas that the Pope could depose the ruler? But against this we have to put the example of Christ himself.

However, we are not concerned here to enter into such theological considerations. We might simply give a quote from a most recent pope concerning the relation between Church and State.

BOOK II

Chapters One and Two

In Book II St. Thomas turns to consider the material conditions that any government or regime needs to give close attention to; this corresponds to concern for what belongs to bodily conditions in an individual. Though preservation in virtue (through prudence) is the principal concern, the care of one's body is part of the care of one's person. At the socio-political level this is what may be equated with the modern concern for the environment.

Many may be surprised to find such a fundamental ecological concern in pre-modern times. But it is a central part of the discussion of the best regime in Books VII and VIII of Aristotle's *Politics*. Here is a sample: "Special care should be taken of the health of the inhabitants, which will depend chiefly on the healthiness of the locality and of the quarter to which the are exposed, and, secondly, on the use of pure water; this latter point is by no means a secondary consideration. For the elements which we use most for the support of the body contribute most to health, and among these are air and water." (*VII, 11 1330b 8-14*)

In the first chapter of Book II St. Thomas gives advice to the king in the very founding of a city. "Now in founding of a city or kingdom, the first step is the choice, if any be given, of location. A temperate region should be chosen, for the inhabitants derive many advantages from a temperate climate." Subjection to extremes of temperature affects not only bodily health and comfort but also can have an adverse effect on the human spirit and even political life. St. Thomas uses an observation of Aristotle here: "Those who live in hot regions are keen-witted and skilful but possess little spirit, and so are in continuous subjection and servitude." (*n. 127*)

This may be an observation that is not so applicable in modern times, when natural conditions can be readily controlled by human inventions. But it does show a keen interest in climatic conditions from the very beginning of human history. In the second chapter St. Thomas develops this concern for the environment to the quality of the water and air: "purity of air is what conduces most to the preservation of men." (*n. 132*)

There is much attention given in current times to the effect of human industry on the natural environment. In order to understand this, we should shortly outline something of the history of modern capitalism. The attention of those profiting most from the commercial, financial and industrial revolutions (intrinsically interwoven with a religious revolution) that marked the end of the mediaeval period and the beginning of the modern was first concentrated on the human "capital" that could be employed to provide opportunities for enrichment to the new class of captains of industry and entrepreneurs that came to be called capitalist. "Capital" took on a new significance, coming to mean money that could buy not only the materials and machines necessary for production but also the men (labour), from the "investment" in which great profits could generally be expected. The "owners" remained in the background, making their money "work" through entrepreneurs and employers. How this was accomplished we have detailed in our book "Economic Science and Saint Thomas Aquinas" and will detail again here shortly.

The adverse effects that this economic system had on the multitude of the working poor, which effects increased in intensity during the nineteenth century, drew a reaction from the oppressed (towards revolution) and concern from social leaders to their plight. This concern took two opposed forms: on the one hand, some, such as Church leaders, were concerned to prevent revolution by persuading the oppressors to moderate the injustices they were perpetrating on their fellow human beings (and even compatriots); on the other hand some, filled with hatred of the capitalist "system", were determined to promote the revolution, by stirring up the working "class" (proletariat), to such an extent that they would rise up and overthrow the oppressive politico-economic system to which they were subjected.

Karl Marx became the theorist of this revolutionary movement. A student of ancient and modern philosophy he discerned something of the modern commercial/financial twist in the notion of Capital and its role in the conversion of the modern worker into a new form of servitude. In this he made use of a distinction that was in Aristotle's theory of the use of money in the market between natural and unnatural exchange, even introducing a symbolism that accurately represents it: CMC and MCM.

However, his basic materialism (imbued from the ancient natural philosophers and fortified by the modern scientific revolution) prevented him from seeing the essentially moral nature of Aristotle's politico-economic analysis. What for Aristotle was the basis of a moral deficiency in the use of the market (MCM), with money treated as capital, became for Marx part of a natural/historical process in human history to be explained in Hegelian dialectical terms. Contradiction for Hegel was the theoretical law of intellectual progress; Revolution in Marx's mind became the practical law of socio-historical progress. Imbibing as well the Darwinian materialist theory of evolution, Marx adopted the Heraclitean Metaphysics: conflict is the principle of natural evolution.

So was conceived the tragic modern story of Communism, a devastatingly false politico-economic theory, but based upon a half-truth that can be traced back to the great Aristotle. In the order of practical political philosophy, it is up there with the genial philosophical work of Kant. Accordingly, it drew and continues to draw within its sphere of influence a multitude of modern intellectuals. Marx identified the unnatural character of the new Capitalism, but he "naturalized" it so as to incorporate it into a fatalistic Hegelian historical dialectic that the proletarian revolution would cancel out and usher in the era of absolutist liberty the modern mind dreamed of. Ironically, Communism was for Marx the natural child of Liberalism, and therefore the twin of Capitalism.

Students of history will know that things have changed radically in recent years and to a certain extent the proletarian phase of Communism is a thing of the past, or at least for various reasons it has fallen from the centre of attention, though its causes remain. In more recent times attention has shifted from the abuse of "human capital" to that of "natural capital". The exploitation focused on now is that of the earth's natural resources – for the sake of profit. "Capital" still has the same commercial significance, meaning the use of money to buy materials necessary for production and then to sell off the products for the sake of "making money", with the productive process being almost an incidental part of a commercial operation. However, it is essentially a parasitical activity and so the natural productive and exchange process underlying it has to be kept functioning.

Now, this economic system having attained global proportions, natural resources within poorer countries are "traded" by impoverished regimes for ready cash, and the materials worked upon in countries where labour is cheap, so that there is great potential for profit from the supply of the finished goods to the apparently insatiable appetite for consumption in developed countries. Such desire for profit, as is evident, if it gives no thought to the welfare of the human beings involved, must give even less to the rational management of natural resources.

It is this "out of control" exploitation of the natural environment together with the related pollution caused by the adoption of the most efficient means of production regardless of the social or environmental cost that has quite obviously reached crisis proportions. To what extent this situation is irreversible is a moot question. But the desire to do something about it, the political will, follows along the same lines as the argument over the exploitation of labour.

There is the desire in those relatively well-off under the prevailing socio-economic conditions to ensure that these conditions are not disturbed, just as in the nineteenth century there was strong resistance to any "interference" in the labour market, bringing to bear the free market assumptions of economic science. Being based on the "findings" of a strictly objective science any fears as to possible adverse consequences, whether in the operations of the market for labour or "capital", have to be illusory. Adverse consequences already evident in the poverty and indebtedness of the workforce, or in the degradation and spoiling of the environment, might be addressed in some way but not in any way that altered the free functioning of the market. That would be like trying to amend the law of gravitation.

The tendency then in this sector is to downplay the disturbing facts with regard to other human beings, and to life outside the insulated compounds of the rich, and to play up the comforting certainties of the official economic science. These capitalist ideologues maintain that the market should be allowed to operate freely as has been the custom in the history of modern times. The economic system works to provide the necessary luxuries to the rich and the necessary work whereby the poor can survive. To interfere with this system will not only hurt "the economy" but will also deprive the poor of work. Everyone will suffer. It is only those who are mad enough to want to bring the whole economic system crashing down who demand radical change to human be-haviour.

On the other side, the concern for the environment is genu-ine, but it takes two forms, as we have noted in regard to the ex-ploitation of labour. On the one hand, there are those, including some Church leaders, who see the evil as moral and therefore its remediation a human responsibility, but as they were concerned to prevent a disastrous revolution on the part of the oppressed workers, in the one instance, they are concerned to avoid an irra-tional reversal of the use of natural resources, in the other, by persuading the capitalists to moderate the injustices they were perpetrating on their fellow human beings (and even compatri-ots), and the damage being done to the environment.

On the other hand, there are those who, filled with hatred of the capitalist "system", are determined to promote revolution, on behalf of man and nature, as before stirring up the working "class" (proletariat), now the poor and otherwise disaffected gen-erally, to such an extent that they might rise up and overthrow the politico-economic system so inimical to Nature herself. Like the Marxist ideology this extreme philosophical position works so as to use the State itself to destroy the politico-economic sys-tem in place.

There is another element and that is the revolutionaries' ap-peal to another kind of science. They had done this in the case of labour, which Marx called scientific socialism. It has the empiri-cist method common to all modern science, with its mathemati-cal component, but the underlying materialist philosophy is the dialectical materialism adapted by Marx from Hegel. In the West it has infiltrated the human and social sciences, particularly Sociology. But it has now been extended to the natural sciences generally, called environmental sciences or ecology.

In assessing the "findings" of these sciences, which have a certain partial validity, one has to be careful of their materialist philosophical underpinnings, both on the part of the Capitalism and Communism. Both political-economic ideologies are errors taken to the extreme. The academic discussion of such matters in the West therefore is mostly a contestation between their defenders, tending to be interminable as the one focuses on the errors of the other. No one in secular academia, and nowadays very few moral theologians unfortunately, sees the possibility of them both being wrong, so powerful is the scientific prejudice that "Economics" (and "Ecology") is a science in which morality has no place. Accordingly, even some Catholic academics, prominent in the USA, regard the Church and the popes as having no competence to adjudicate on socio-economic and ecological matters.

The case for radical change of social behaviour in respect of "climate change", then, relies on the findings of the new environmental science. Admittedly, like trying to predict the weather, especially long term, it is not yet an exact science. But, if it is in any way accurate, the predictions are so dire that not only will everyone suffer, but indeed everyone will perish.

What is common to both parties is the faith in modern science, in one case Economics, in the second Ecology. That the problem and the remedy may lie in the order of practical reason and morality simply does not occur to anyone. The sad thing is that moral theologians in the USA especially seem least of all able to overcome the moral blindness in this regard despite the principles of the moral judgment to be made being clearly set out by St. Thomas not only in the *Summa Theologiae* (II-II, 77, 4c) but also in this work (Book II, ch. 3 following). Such is the ignorance in the consideration of the question, and what renders it more invisible, is the case that the English translations, even by the most respected Thomists, are hopelessly incompetent.

So perhaps we should say a little more about how the modern situation has come about. The political revolution at the heart of this radical social change was the freedom won by the oligarchical element of government from the political power of the king referred to above, so that the last remaining barrier against oligarchical cupidity was effectively removed and a new era of "liberty", to unbridled use of one's economic power, came into existence. As explained before, this changed the whole structure of the social or political economy so that the ancient system of slavery and the medieval system of serfdom were no longer necessary to supply the material needs of the many poor in the community, or, more importantly so far as the instigators were concerned, the luxuries to which the few rich were accustomed.

Perhaps the greatest advantage – for the masters - of the new system of servitude is the impersonality of the relation between master and servant, and the consequent anonymity of the masters. Even the immediate employer can plead that the paucity of the pay and the harshness of the working conditions are nothing to do with him but are demanded by the "market". This reasoning is now extended to the market in minerals and other natural resources as indicated above. Meanwhile, the deluded purveyors of the dismal science (modern economists) laud the efficiency of the free market.

The early economic laws proposed manifested the mechanistic thinking of the modern mind. We had "the iron law of wages" attributed by some to Ricardo. Malthus (who inspired Darwin's materialist theory of evolution) contributed to Economics "the law of population" (of the relation between production and re-production) to explain inexorable poverty under modern working conditions: production increases by arithmetical proportions, reproduction by geometrical. A suggested explanation for the growth of debt under usurious conditions is: the inexorable nature of compound interest.

All this "natural science" (and mathematics) is designed (wittingly or unwittingly) to distract us from the moral cause, the misuse of economic power in the hands of the new people of "property" (money). Later on the science was even more heavily mathematicized, in line with modern science generally, which also gives it an aura of magic and esotericism, trumpeted as immune from error despite the almost universal failure of the predictions of its prophets.

This history of distraction and deceit from the real causes of modern global poverty and injustice continues in the new eco-science. Speaking only of the "developed" world, the human "capital" (working population) in the nineteenth century having been almost decimated and the system moderated and "re-formed" (with the help of globalization and the exportation of capitalism to the East) to a permanent state of comfortable servitude in the West in the twentieth century, the focus of decimation has moved to that of the "natural capital" (land and resources) that is necessary to advance economic growth (oligarchic cupidity).

What damage this has done on the environment and what effect it will have on the climate is hard to estimate. One thing is certain, however, is that the main opponents on both sides of the argument about "climate change" are driven by ideology (the voice of the only ones to preach a rational/moral reform – the popes – is all but silenced by the major contenders, backed up by some pro-capitalist American theologians). Neither extreme ideology will address (for they cannot or will not see) the real villains in the piece. For, the real villains are in hiding, not necessarily consciously or conspiratorially, but for the historical reasons given above. The "hero/villain" proposed (depending on one's ideology) is a (politico-economic) "system" which must be quasi-religiously defended ("America/Capitalism First") or destroyed (to be replaced by "The New World Order").

BOOK II

Chapters Three and Four

In the third chapter of Book II St. Thomas moves from the need for material conditions with regard to the healthiness of the site to its ability to provide the necessary food, which may be extended to all material needs such as for clothing, shelter, transport etc., on the basis of Aristotle's conception of the city (*polis*) as the form of human association that enables the community to be self-sufficient. The idea of the city is still focused on such a multitude where the principal aim is to lead the citizens to a full life of virtue. Accordingly, it cannot be too large. But it needs to be large enough to allow that diversity of talents and interests, from technical skills, mechanical arts, through liberal arts to science and philosophy that will enable the inhabitants not only to live but also to live "well".

Such a concept is not meant to be suggestive of any uniformity. No city will have the same organisation in this regard but will be as individual as human beings themselves. But so far as material needs are concerned the idea of self-sufficiency has a definite limit. Just as an individual needs only so much food to eat, so many shoes to wear, so many houses to live in, so a civil community's need for same will be limited, if needing to be continually maintained and replenished when necessary.

Aristotle had made this point in Chapter 8 of Book I: "… the amount of property which is needed for a good life is not unlimited … But there is a boundary fixed just as there is in the other arts; for the instruments of any art are never unlimited, either in number or in size, and riches may be defined as a number of instruments to be used in a household or in a state. And we see that there is a natural art of acquisition which is practiced by managers of households and statesmen, and what is the reason for this? (*Book I, ch. 8 1256b 31-20*).

It is in the very first principle of human behavior with regard to the desire for wealth that the modern science of Economics goes so badly awry that it vitiates the whole science. Its fundamental principle is the very contradiction of Aristotle's statement.

The modern study of Economic Science begins with asserting that our wants for goods are unlimited. It is the goods that can satisfy them that are limited. The basic economic problem then is that of scarcity, of having to choose which of our wants to meet. It is a basic assumption that we cannot fulfill them all – we must be forever in a state of short supply relative to our reasonable desires for wealth. As John Stuart Mill put it: Nature is niggardly. However, the truth is that nature is limited but nature does not fall short of our needs if we conduct ourselves rationally. Rationally considered, economic means sufficient, not scarce or inadequate.

The modern economist works on the assumption that our desires for economic goods cannot be satisfied, precisely because they are seen as ends in themselves. But Aristotle points out that natural wealth must be seen as means, instruments to the ends of our bodily nature. Food is not an end in itself, but a means to keeping us nourished.

There is one kind of wealth, however, that Aristotle will identify as something that can be, and often is, seen as desirable for its own sake, as an end and not a means. That is money in the process of exchange. It is in the context of contrasting this kind of wealth (artificial) with natural wealth that Aristotle discusses the question of a limit to our desires. He wants to warn us not to confuse the two. But this is precisely what tends to happen, as it did even in his time.

It has happened with a vengeance in modern times. For the confusion has been institutionalized in modern economic science. Wealth has been totally identified with money, and the basic principles of Economics have been adjusted to reflect that fact. In effect this identifies the desire for wealth with the vice of cupidity. That is the modern economist's notion of self-interest, which from Adam Smith has been presented not only as something innocuous, but even as the motive force of economic progress. How more economically disastrous a confusion could there be?

But, perversely, it helps to conceal the injustice of, and even to justify, the other profound political institution that has replaced the ancient one of slavery and the medieval one of serfdom that we have discussed above. Capital (its control in the form of money) is prior to Labour; it feeds it, employs it. The 'investment' of capital is the motive force of all economic activity and "growth" (an illusory profit made by the already too rich which only results in the further impoverishment of the already too poor).

St. Thomas will identify this form of "capital" investment and detail some of the social evils of this system of capitalism. But Aristotle had already listed the abuses it leads to. First he says: "Hence some persons are led to believe that getting wealth is the object of household management, and the whole idea of their lives is that they ought to increase their money without limit, or at least not lose it." (*Book I, ch. 9 1257b 38-41*). Then he explains how men become disposed to cultivate this "art" of making money within the natural exchange system. " ... they are intent upon living only, and not on living well". That is to say, such men abandon the restraints of virtue and morality and succumb to avarice. " ... and as their desires are unlimited, they also desire that the means of gratifying them should be without limit."

There are various ways in which such cupidity is expressed. "Those who aim at a good life seek the means of obtaining bodily pleasures; and since the enjoyment of these seems to depend upon property [money], they are absorbed in getting wealth [money]". "And so there arises the second species of wealth-getting [through exchange: MCM].

Their evil disposition, however, does not end there, in simple employment of the "art". " ... if they are not able to supply their pleasures by the art [alone] of getting wealth [MCM], they try other arts, using in turn every faculty in a manner contrary to nature." They debauch the good natural qualities they have, such as daring or courage [in taking risks]. "The quality of courage for example is not intended to make wealth [money], but to inspire confidence; neither is the aim of the general's or if the physician's art; but the one aims at victory and the other at health."

The cupidity fed by this *philargyria* [love of money] spreads to all pursuits, especially those professional skills [such as law and medicine] which cost much to acquire [buy] but whose price is what one is willing and able to pay for one's health and freedom. Thus, Aristotle concludes in this regard: " ... some men turn every quality or art into a means of getting wealth [money]; this they conceive to be the end, and to the promotion of the end they think all things must contribute." All this is generated by the desire to make money, which is stimulated through the second species of exchange [MCM].

So entrenched has this climate of cupidity become in modern civil or political life that the science of human and social behavior takes it as "natural" and good and the politicians and even moral leaders of the community (especially in the USA) take it in with their mother's milk, unable to conceive of any other way of managing an economy.

But the saddest thing is that those moral and religious minded people who know there is something terribly wrong with society are denied access to the practical wisdom of the greatest minds in history whereby the solution to the problem may be seen, if that does not mean it would thereby be solved. The works of Aristotle and St. Thomas Aquinas which directly address the root of the problem, if the circumstances of their times are not the same as ours, are, as we have attempted to show, so little understood as to be virtually useless to the modern moral philosopher and theologian.

This lack of understanding in large measure flows from the indoctrination carried out under the regime in place, as indicated above. But it is compounded by the deplorable ignorance and incompetence of the translators from the Latin, particularly glaring by those who are generally acknowledged to be well versed otherwise in the thought of St. Thomas, such as Gerald Phelan in the case of the translation of *On Kingship* and the Dominican translators in the case of the translation of the *Summa Theologiae*.

Admittedly, careful attention needs to be given to the distinctions made, which are difficult even in the context of a healthy social order. Moreover, there is much potential for ambiguity in the language used by Aristotle and St. Thomas. But the important distinctions are few and may be seen if we attend to what St. Thomas explains as he goes.

Let us outline the necessary distinctions. We need first to note the two ways of acquiring wealth. By wealth is meant at first what St. Thomas calls natural wealth, such things as food, clothes, buildings and generally all material things that are useful for human living. We have discussed the notion of property where we need to distinguish the right from the thing. But that distinction does not affect the points that follow. Some translators use the expression "wealth-getting" for the acquisition of wealth. But that is incidental.

The first way of acquiring natural wealth we may equate with the various means of production, whether in an original way like farming, mining, hunting, or by subsequent adaptation like manufacturing, transportation, storing.

The second way is by exchange. That is the social way to acquire the natural wealth we need. Aristotle makes the point by saying that "twofold is the use of the shoe". The shoemaker produces the first use, to wear on the feet. But in a society he uses his products in the second way. That is his way of making a living. Notice that at this stage exchange may take place directly by barter (CC). He exchanges a pair of shoes for a bag of potatoes with the local farmer. But soon it becomes obvious that there is a much easier way to engage in exchange with other producers. A product is selected to serve for use in exchange only.

That is the first appearance of money as a pure medium of exchange. It soon becomes evident that the proper use of the product selected is incidental and can even be dispensed with by the use of some token or coin generally accepted at a certain value in exchange. It is this article of no proper usefulness but with the common usefulness of mediating an exchange of useful goods that St. Thomas calls "artificial wealth", as opposed to natural wealth.

This leads to the developed exchange system that we are all familiar with. Notice that today this monetary function may be done by the general acceptance of electric signals on a computer.

Money then is defined as the common medium of exchange in any society.

However, the next distinction is the most important for our understanding of the working of an economy, and for the understanding of economic science. It is to be noticed that money has been developed ("invented") by human reason to facilitate the exchange of useful products. Aristotle accordingly classed it within the concept of natural exchange. This is not to be thought of as unnatural exchange compared with exchange without money, or barter. Barter is imperfect natural exchange. Exchange using the medium of money is the civilized kind of natural exchange.

What tends to confuse matters here is the tendency for us to look at a market from our own individual point of view, thus considering exchange as a sale (CM), which is the exchange of a product (commodity) for money as a completed exchange. But it is even from our point of view only a half-exchange. We do not want money for its own sake but to buy (MC) a product (commodity) that we want. A natural exchange with money as the medium is not completed until two products (commodities) are exchanged (CMC).

The important distinction between natural and unnatural exchange that Aristotle made was to do with using money not as a medium in the manner above but with using it as the principle and term of an exchange (MCM). The object of the exchange was to end up somehow, not with another product, but with more money. This led to the common economic axiom for making money: "buy cheap and sell dear". A completed natural exchange involves selling first and then buying something practically equivalent in value or price. Such is the depth of the penetration of the mode of unnatural exchange into the modern psyche that one famous economist argued that exchange is not based upon equality but inequality of value.

There is a further refinement introduced by St. Thomas. He distinguished Aristotle's "unnatural exchange" into two ways of employing it. Though it is difficult to imagine that a person devoted to making money by astutely using the market will put some limit on the amount of profit he can make his activity, St. Thomas says that the real vice to do with the activity is its lack of a natural limit. Accordingly, he agrees with Aristotle that considered in itself it has "a species of turpitude".

However, though it is something that is essentially lacking due order to a natural end it can voluntarily be ordered to the satisfaction of natural needs or rational wants. So St. Thomas allows a legitimate use of this kind of exchange process if the exchanger (merchant) directs and limits what he makes in money to the natural end of exchange, which is the satisfaction of the reasonable needs and wants of himself, his family and even the needy within the community.

St. Thomas uses the Latin word *negotiatio* (doing business) for this secondary kind of exchange (MCM). It is not necessarily to be condemned, but it is if the making of money is not "moderated" as indicated. The exchanger, generally called a merchant, St. Thomas therefore calls a *negotiator*. He is thus distinguished from an exchanger who brings products to the market to sell and uses the money made to purchase what he naturally needs or has a rational want for. Somewhat confusingly, for it extends to a shoemaker selling his shoes and using the money gained to buy what he needs, Aristotle and St. Thomas call this (natural) exchanger a householder (*economos*), but it may also be the government (*politicos*) in its need to acquire goods for its own public purposes.

We might just comment on the use of the word "rational" here. For it has been abused in modern economics to apply to any engagement in exchange without the distinction between natural and unnatural exchange as explained. Aristotle and St. Thomas would describe the unnatural mode of exchange (for money as such or profit unlimited) as irrational. The modern mind has simply lost the connection between rational and moral. So too the distinction between natural and unnatural in practical moral topics like politics and economics makes no sense to him. The avaricious person is just as rational as the non-avaricious. Indeed he is viewed as more so, because he satisfies his desires as much as he can.

However, let us now deal with the confusions, keeping in mind that they are calculated to obscure an underlying disorder of structural injustice of historical dimensions and of contemporary magnitude. First of all, there is the fundamental confusion between wealth and money. Money is not wealth, but being the common medium of exchange it is also a measure of wealth. That means that it is able to command (demand) wealth in exchange.

It is a kind of social system of credit/debt, a debt owed generally by those in the community who possess wealth (social debtors) to those who possess money (social creditors). In modern society there is a sub system of debt, which may extend beyond the present value of people's possessions/property (wealth) to be paid out of their future earnings.

However, all we are concerned with here is the general tendency to identify wealth and money, or in St. Thomas's language, natural wealth and artificial wealth, with artificial wealth (money) looming more largely in mind. Wealth-getting and money-making are similarly confused, but these expressions need not be of any consequence, as a metaphorical way of speaking, were it not for the confusions we come to.

The important philosophical confusions have to do with the nature of exchange. First of all, "commerce", which is but another word for social exchange of goods and services, (merx: Latin for wealth) does not make any distinction between natural (CMC) and unnatural exchange (MCM), but it is used (by Regan, for instance), to stand for the latter only, suggesting that Aristotle had some nonsensical prejudice against commerce as such (CMC). It is unsurprising that this should be a common misunderstanding, as the modern economic expert cannot understand any criticism of the market or any kind of commerce.

So the unnatural kind of exchange and Aristotle's trenchant criticism of it went entirely unnoticed (very convenient for the oligarchical masters of the new "commercial" servitude of labour). The love of money (philargyria), equated with the profit-

208 *Political Science and Saint Thomas Aquinas*

motive, became the central commercial virtue rather than the root of all evil. At this point none of the modern moralists and theologians (including Catholics and Thomists) could not make any sense of St. Thomas's agreement with Aristotle's criticism of a function of the market.

This led to misinterpretations and mistranslations that in the language of today's young were "off the planet". We know that the English word "trade" equates with "commerce". This too was used in the same ambiguous way, giving the impression that Aristotle and St. Thomas railed against trade. The ambiguity here was bad enough. But the *piece de resistance* appeared in the translation of *negotiator* in the *Summa Theologiae* (*II-II, 77, 4c*), and repeated here in *On Kingship* (*Book II, ch. 3*), as tradesman!!!

This shows as complete an ignorance of the ordinary meaning of English words as it is possible to imagine. It can only be explained as proceeding from a distortion in thinking engendered by a perverse indoctrination in modern economic science. "Tradesman" is a notion that has nothing to do with trade as commerce. The word "trade" in the commercial context comes form the Latin *tradere*, which means to hand over. "Tradesman" comes from a word of Old Saxon origin **trada** ("track") and is cognate with Old English *tredan* ("to tread"). It came to signify a course of conduct and in the economic context a work occupation followed. In modern times it applies to workers such as carpenters and plumbers.

St. Thomas is talking about merchants in the old days and traders on the stock exchange today. So, not only is the word "trade" used ambiguously even when used in the context of commerce, so as to exclude any moral judgment, when St. Thomas wishes to condemn a form of trading that signifies commercial (wheeling and) dealing – *negotiatio* - it is hopelessly mistranslated by Catholic moralists and theologians. How could a person who does not read Latin hope to make any sense of what St. Thomas has to say on what is perhaps the most critical aspect of modern social behaviour? That such mistranslation should pass unnoticed for so long only testifies to the weakness of the modern Catholic understanding of the moral theology of St. Thomas in respect of economic and political affairs. [Does the system of education in the West, especially in the USA, have something to do with producing such a degree of obfuscation that even Catholic moral thought, normally able to be objective, is so badly affected?]

We can illustrate all this by looking at the extract from St. Thomas's *On Kingship*. In the third chapter of Book II in *On Kingship* St. Thomas says: "Now there are two ways in which an abundance of foodstuffs can be supplied to a city. The first we have already mentioned, where the soil is so fertile that it amply provides for all the necessities of human life. The second is by trade, through which the necessaries of life are brought to the town in sufficient quantity from different places. (*n. 135*)

The Latin is: *Duo tamen sunt modi quibus alicui civitati potest affluentia rerum suppetere. Unus, qui dictus est, propter regionis fertilitatem abunde omnia producentis, quae humanae vitae re-*

quirit necessitas. Alius autem per mercationis usum, ex quo ibidem necessaria vitae ex diversis partibus adducantur.

It will be noticed that the word for trade is *mercatio*, which can be taken here for commerce in general and external trade in particular. Then, shortly on, St. Thomas says: "Again, if the citizens themselves devote their life to matters of trade, the way will be opened to many vices. Since the foremost tendency of **tradesmen** is to make money, greed is awakened in the hearts of the citizens through the pursuit of **trade**. The result is that everything in the city will become venal; good faith will be destroyed and the way opened to all kinds of trickery; each one will work only for his own profit, despising the public good; the cultivation of virtue will fail since honour, virtue's reward, will be bestowed upon the rich. Thus, in such a city, civic life will necessarily be corrupted." (139) (highlight added)

The Latin is: *Rursus: si cives ipsi mercationibus fuerint dediti, pandetur pluribus vitiis aditus. Nam cum negotiatorum studium maxime ad lucrum tendat, per negotiationis usum cupiditas in cordibus civium traducitur, ex quo convenit, ut in civitate omnia fiant venalia, et fide subtracta, locus fraudibus aperitur, publicoque bono contempto, proprio commodo quisque deserviet, deficietque virtutis studium, dum honor virtutis praemium omnibus deferetur: unde necesse erit in tali civitate civilem conversationem corrumpi.*

Notice how St. Thomas has introduced the secondary mode of trade [MCM] that he specially calls *negotiatio,* and even describes its special character in exchange. He is talking about a tendency for this secondary mode of exchange to foment avarice and lead to all sorts of vices and ultimately to the corruption of civic life. He is arguing generally about the city remaining as self-sufficient as it can, and to avoid letting in foreign traders, which has its own dangers. But this reliance on external trade he then believes will bring with it the tendency of merchants to engage in the mode of exchange that is most corrupting.

However, what we want to notice here is the translation of *negotiatores* by "tradesmen", which carries the suggestion that tradesmen are profit-hungry operators and liable to corrupt civic life. How ridiculous even on its face! *Negotiatio* (MCM) is also translated simply as "trade", so as not to be distinguished from commerce in general (CMC). *Ad lucrum tendat,* where *lucrum* refers to the profit made from buying cheap and selling dear, is also translated simply as "make money", which can have the general sense discussed above. Confusion is worse confounded.

St. Thomas ends his work *On Kingship* in chapter four of Book II. It contains nothing of particular significance. He simply makes the point that it is important for a city to have pleasant surroundings, but as a good moralist cautions against excess even in this regard: "It is therefore harmful to a city to superabound in delightful things, whether it be on account of its situation or from whatever other cause. However, in human intercourse it is best to have a moderate share of pleasure as a spice of life, so to speak, wherein man's mind may find some recreation." (148)

CONCLUSION

We have surveyed Political Science as far as what may be gleaned from the work of Saint Thomas Aquinas. This work consists mainly in his uncompleted commentary on Aristotle's *Politics* and his own work *On Kingship*. However, we believe that there is sufficient in this body of work for us to assess the fundamental contribution of St. Thomas to the science.

Overall, we believe that one may grasp enough of practical principles to apply them to the conditions of modern political and economic life as well as throw much needed light on the profound moral problems that afflict all societies regardless of the kind of political regime by which they are ruled.

Furthermore, we are confident that Aristotle's and St. Thomas's insights can be used to provide a solid critique of modern economic and political sciences, showing up fundamental errors both in the assumptions used and the method adopted. This has involved a general critique of modern science and in particular the modern scientific method as tried to be applied to the human and social sciences.

On occasion we have used what St. Thomas had to say in his theological works, such as his *Summa Theologiae*. The study of Law is obviously a closely related one. We have dealt with it more extensively in our other published book "Natural Law: Australian Style".

However, it will be noticed that much of the commentary on Aristotle's *Politics* is taken up with what today would be considered Economic Science. In modern times that science, though seen as a related one, is treated as a quite distinct, even separate, science. The nature of this difference of treatment and the reason for it we have explained in our book. It is hard to exaggerate the significance of this difference not just for the understanding of modern political rule in the West but also of all aspects of. social life from economic to cultural. For its roots are religious.

Hopefully, from our bringing into the light of the practical principles of Aristotle's *Politics* with the help of Aquinas's insights the reader may gain some understanding of what has presented itself in modern times as a clash of ideologies in politico-economic terms, as Capitalism and Communism, rather than as a clash of regimes in traditional political terms. The key is indeed to be found not so much in what is contained in Chapter Three (and following chapters) of the *Politics* but rather in Chapter One, though we need to see the link between the economic system of modern Capitalism and the rather hidden type of political rule that is Oligarchy. For reasons that may be appreciated such categories of political constitutions have faded into the background.

The purely political analysis of Aristotle tends to be neglected in modern thought not just because of the change in the meaning of science and its method, as explained, but also because of the switch from a moral to a "realistic" approach to the subject. Looking at the world of politics at the lowest level of Economics seems also to fit in with the real world more that some ideal one. So it was that worrying about differences of political constitutions in Aristotelian terms went out of favour. No need to examine such questions of whether the constitutional rule was ordered to the common good or not. We just needed to take the existing political arrangement as fact, what existed, and see how it worked in terms of power struggles.

Coincident with this went the quite significant historical change of attitude to the classical analysis of political rule brought about in the French Revolution. Any type of rule, by one or few, was identified with the *Ancien Regime*, and so violently rejected that only a republican kind of rule was recognised as having any rational status. Monarchical and aristocratic types of constitutions continued in some countries but tended to retain only symbolic power, both in theory and practice.

The political *coup d'etat* that occurred at the beginning of the modern era was enmeshed in a whole series of social revolutions, from religious to commercial and industrial as well as political, as described in our book. Since it consisted of an exacerbation of the division between the rich and the poor, oligarchy being defined in such terms, all levels of social life came to be focused on the economic and the resulting tangled nature of modern social life quite difficult to untangle. Since the deep causes of this went right down to the personal and religious levels of human life, we must expect that there are strong forces of deception working to prevent us from getting to the truth of things, especially if it has moral implications.

The division of political rule into good and bad, though avoiding any moral judgments, being expressed rather in terms of rational and irrational in theoretical terms, came to result in the only intelligibly acceptable political arrangement being democratic. The notion of ruling for the common good was simply assumed to belong to the rule of the many ("the people") and the pejorative note that Aristotle had applied to democracy disappeared. For Aristotle divided rule by the many into "Polity", as for the common good, and Democracy as not for the common good. So too did the distinctions between kingship and tyranny, and aristocracy and oligarchy, disappear. The only good kind of political rule was democratic, or republican as it implied opposition to monarchical or aristocratic. Any rule other than democratic was called "totalitarian".

On top of that the end of democratic rule was conceived in economic terms, as prosperity for all the people, and its security so far as any external threat was concerned. The notion of common good lost all its moral intent, with which went of course its spiritual and religious content. The main focus was on welfare conceived in material terms.

So it is that we have paid more attention to what Aristotle had to say about the economic level of political life in Chapter One and only sufficient about the essence of political rule in Chapter Three. This is indeed out of necessity when having to apply his principles to the modern political and economic scene. It is critical to a proper understanding of the subject matter not just of modern Politics but also of modern Economics. I have written much on this aspect of political theory and practice and so have added four appendices from articles written over time that hopefully bring the reader to a better understanding of the intricacies of the subject.

In dealing with matters in Chapter One we have paid most attention to the subjects of property and exchange, to which in moral terms are related the questions of distributive and commutative justice treated by us within the context of virtues in our book "Ethics Today and Saint Thomas Aquinas". These are the central matters of concern when we have to apply St. Thomas's thought to modern affairs.

It is only when we have sorted out the issues in regard to these that we can begin to make sense of the political and economic scene in modern times in that area that has been dominated originally by Individualism/Capitalism and then challenged by Socialism/Communism (both variants of radical Liberalism). Both are ideologies whose origin is to be found in what is called the West though the distinction between East and West has all but disappeared these days because of the political dominance of these Western ideologies.

But, in dealing with these matters central to the political order (or disorder) of the modern world, there was one thing, the ancient political/legal institution of slavery, addressed by Aristotle right at the beginning of Chapter One, that posed a problem that could and has for many proved to be an insurmountable obstacle to giving any credibility to his contribution to the study of

political theory and practice. This has spilled over to taking seriously any commentary by St. Thomas on Aristotle's *Politics*.

So, we have had to address this problem first and do our best
to prevent it from derailing the application of what Aristotle had
to say about the natural institutions of property and the market,
which in our view are of the greatest help to understanding political life according to its essential principles, and therefore able to
be applied to modern conditions. For, even if Aristotle is to be
criticised for supporting a social position that is demeaning of
human beings, we should be able to assess the worth of positions
and institutions other than this one.

As examined, what we have found is what Aristotle has to say
about the master/servant relationship is not all that clear-cut and
contains inconsistencies and even contradictions that are hard to
resolve internally. So, in the end in our view we can at least put it
aside and proceed to deal with what we are primarily concerned
with. As we have seen the problem of systematic servitude does
not go away in the modern era even if the legal status of previous
kinds, such as chattel slavery and serfdom, has been universally
condemned and abolished.

We hold indeed that the politico-economic system of Capitalism involved the introduction of an effective servitude, not just
for some, but for the majority of the population precisely
through the institution of a "free market" in labour, able to be
understood by reference to Aristotle's analysis of the nature of
exchange of goods in a civil context (using money as the com-

mon medium of exchange). How this has occurred is fully expounded upon in the text.

Thus the Aristotelian based analysis of the Capitalist politico-economic system enables us to understand not only the way a system of exchange can operate unnaturally and be used for individuals' (or organisations') enrichment, when on the surface it operates in apparent freedom built upon however a hugely disproportionate possession of wealth, and control of money, by a few, protected by law and government; but it also can enable us to understand the way there can be a body of "workers" under a system of employment, on the surface based on contract, in which there is no apparent constraint on them to work (the lie to this has been given by Pope Leo XIII as long ago as 1891), who are effectively bound by a yoke little different than that of servitude. But many a Catholic economist will argue for the legitimacy (moral not legal) of the "labour market", where the rate (price) of wages is but an instance of the operation of the basic economic scientific law of supply and demand.

It turns out then that the features of modern political life, mostly negative, in accord with St. Augustine's assessment of Alexander the Great, quoted in the page after the title, can be accounted for on the application of the practical political principles to be found in Chapter One of Aristotle's Politics. The features of a right political order, on the other hand, may be derived by expanding upon St. Thomas's quote given by us on the same page, taken from his treatise *On Kingship*, where no doubt he had in mind St. Louis (King Louis IX of France who he knew personally). The practical political principles here can be found in Chapter Three of Aristotle's *Politics*.

It is no small task to try to apply the moral principles of political rule and analysis of constitutions and institutions to a modern civil order that has descended into disorder not just by discarding the proper political analysis but also by reducing the notion of the object studied to its lowest level, called economic. The right political order Aristotle proposed was best studied in the best kind of political constitution of the *polis*, i. e. the polity of kingship, which however was hardly ever able to be realised in fact, so one had to be content with the best possible.

By default, as it were, of the power of human reason left to itself, this is a task that the popes of recent times, from Leo XIII to Francis, concerned at the extremity of the times, have taken on themselves. In our next book we will try to interpret what they have done in the light of the moral principles to be found in philosophical part of the work of Saint Thomas Aquinas.

Appendices

Appendix A

The Merchant and the Middleman

(An Insight into Capitalism)

In a natural civilized exchange economy, as understood by both Aristotle and Aquinas, money plays an important part.[1] But the part it plays is in the middle, not at the beginning or at the end of the exchange transaction. No matter how various and flimsy the goods and services provided, nor how diverse and curious the desires for same within any given community, the whole point of the social exchange order is for the multitude of goods and services so introduced into the exchange process to

---

[1] Cf. Aristotle, *V Ethics* 1133 b 10-30; Aquinas *In V Ethics, lectio 9.* The rational necessity for money arises when transactions in goods or services are not able to be completed in the present – *Sic ergo pro necessitate futurae commutationis numisma, id est denarius, est nobis quasi fideiussor quod si in presenti homo nullo indigent sed indigeat in futuro, aderit sibi afferenti denarium illud quo indigebit* (para. 986 in fine). Trade between places widely separated also gives rise to a rational need for money as a medium of exchange. Cf. I *Politics,c. 9 1257 a 35-41* Money's natural role or essential lpurpose is simply to facilitate exchange of the useful goods we have need of. (cf. I-II, 2, 1 c)

somehow end up in the possession of those who want or need them.

Reduced to its simplest elements what occurs is that the shoemaker (making more shoes than his family can wear) sells some of his shoes to the farmer and sooner or later buys some food (provided let us imagine by the same farmer). The farmer has needed money to buy the shoes, but he gets it back when he sells his spuds to the shoemaker. So the full exchange process from beginning to end has been completed and the money, having been introduced to be a medium only, is cancelled out.

Now we know that this rarely happens in a big city. But the mental experiment brings out clearly enough the essentials of an exchange system involving the role of money as a medium of a complete exchange. No rational person wants to end up, like a miser, with only money. No matter how complicated things may become the whole process is evidently designed to begin by providing shoes and spuds or the like and end by the wearing of the shoes and the eating of the spuds. The advantage of the exchange is that the shoemaker not only has shoes to wear but also spuds to eat and the farmer likewise. All can be clothed and fed, relatively easily, if we are willing to cooperate with one another. Money does not disappear only because as our present needs are satisfied new ones arise. So the same money can be made to do service again.[2]

---

[2] Essentially money is conventional, i.e. its utility as money arises from will, the agreement of those in the exchange system. But the ex-

Things of course get much more complicated as society grows. Our needs for basic things, or necessities, expand into wants for luxuries, or non-necessaries. These terms are not to be taken here to imply any moral distinction for they have to be judged in the context of each particular society.[3] But, ideally, all

---

change value conventionally imposed on it (whatever form the money may take) is not arbitrary but is tied to the values of the goods being exchanged. Aquinas, following Aristotle, notes that the value of money is variable as are the goods it measures but being a measure its value ought to be so instituted as to hold its value more so than anything else - *taliter debet esse institutus ut magis permaneat in eodem valore, quam aliae res* .(para. 987) This connection with goods and their values clearly is the case where certain goods are conventionally used as money (e.g. gold and silver). But even where money is pure credit (i.e. based in a mere promise to pay) it takes its value through reference to the values of goods in the exchange system. Even in a relatively stable economy exchange values or prices will fluctuate from accidental factors. Money as well will be affected by such accidental factors. But fundamentally the money in my possession truly reflects over time and in different places the value of goods that I have to offer or promise to offer to others in exchange. The big mistake in monetary theory is to confuse the distinction between money (wealth only in this relative sense) and goods or wealth in the positive sense. This is a mistake to which the merchant mentality is especially prone. We would do well to note St. Thomas' clear distinction between money (as artificial wealth) and natural wealth. (I-II, 2, 1 c)

[3] Though thus to some degree relative to the state of the society in which one lives the distinction is not simply subjective. One has a mor-

our reasonable desires for material things are satisfied by the goods and services generally provided within each society's social exchange system. The trade between the shoemaker and the farmer, as each representing the producers and consumers respectively (since there needs to be at least two for both roles to be fulfilled), is, let us assume, free and fair.

We know that there is more to life than the satisfaction of our material needs and desires. So there is a section of the society that provides higher services which must also eat and be shod. However, these can be provided for, in exchange for what they provide. So this does not greatly affect the basic picture. We know that things do not always go smoothly, and some will try to get something for nothing. This will involve some subtraction from the overall goods and services to be enjoyed and perhaps some disturbance to the social order. We will need a government and will have to make provision for its needs. But we can adjust our thinking to this. Making all necessary adjustments in this regard we still have essentially the simple process we started with.

---

al obligation to make a practical prudential judgment based upon the application of this distinction to one's own circumstances. Cf. RN, 35 "But when the demands of necessity and propriety have been met, it is a duty to give to the poor out of that which remains. "Give that which remains as alms." [13] These are duties not of justice, except in cases of extreme need, but of Christian charity, which obviously cannot be enforced by legal action. But the laws and judgments of men yield precedence to the law and judgment of Christ the Lord, Who in many ways urges the practice of alms- giving."

However, there is one section of the society that we have not yet taken into account. What about the merchant who, unlike the shoemaker or farmer, does not put anything into the social fund of goods and services but, precisely as a merchant, is concerned simply to buy what is already provided or produced by someone else and sell it to someone else again (at a profit)?

Here we have to be very careful and precise, for the merchant may be also on other counts someone who provides a service. He may provide a valuable service by transporting or shipping goods to where they are needed. He may store them safely till a time when they are wanted. He may package them in a form that is more convenient to the buyers. But he does these things as a transporter or shipper of goods, as warehouseman, as a packager of goods, etc., not precisely as a merchant. We may call the shipper, the warehouseman, the shopkeeper or the retailer and the like middlemen, as is the merchant. But the merchant is not a middleman in quite the same sense as the others.

These others are middlemen who provide a real social service to others by reason of the demands of material conditions attaching to things or products in the process of exchange, such as differences of time, place, size, number etc that are interposed between the provider or producer and the user or consumer. The merchant's middle role, however, has got something to do with the fact that money is in the middle of exchanges.[4]

---

[4] This is not to say that it is always easy to distinguish the merchant from the other middlemen for he generally conducts his business of

We may get a clearer picture of the merchant's role in the exchange system by supposing that he employs the services of other
people to do all these things that are subsidiary to his primary
activity of buying and selling. The merchant would be quite dis-
appointed if having met all these expenses he did not still make a
profit, even taking into account some sort of reasonable recom-
pense for his time and effort in coordinating all this. What, then,
precisely does the merchant provide? What service does he contribute? In order to understand this we need to look a little more
closely at the exchange process.

By way of preliminary we can say that the merchant's business[5] is not to make goods or provide a service but to make money. Essentially his activity benefits himself alone. It is an activity

---

buying in order to sell by making use of their services. The transport of
goods wanted from another place, for instance, might be done by the
ultimate buyer (consumer) who would have to count the cost of this in
the cost of the goods to him. Or he may employ someone to arrange
the transport and pay for his services in this regard. Similarly the merchant, in the course of carrying out his business, might do the carrying
himself or arrange for another to do it. In all these cases the physical
transport of the goods, and its cost, are something quite distinct from
the exchange that is taking place. The merchant's role as such, as is
made clear below, relates solely to the exchange.

[5] Though we are talking about the merchant as someone engaged
in a particular occupation what we say applies equally to any act of exchange by individuals that is a case of buying in order to sell again at a
profit [symbolized below as MCM].

that is highly individualistic. That is not to say that is necessarily anti-social, as we shall explain. But essentially his business activity or "enterprise" involves no addition to the wealth of the community, nor, to be quite clear about this, does it involve essentially any addition to the service given to others. Precisely as a merchant, he provides nothing and produces nothing and still makes a profit. How is this possible?

The exchange process that starts with the provision of goods or services by two people (as suppliers) and ends with the goods or services being used or used up by the same two people (as both producer and consumer but inversely related) has money acting as the medium of the complete exchange process. This is evidently the natural or fundamental process involved. Without that we in society do not eat and wear shoes or have any of the multitudinous goods and services we take for granted every day.

Let us symbolize this kind of exchange process as CMC, with C standing for any kind of goods or service and M for money. Aristotle and Aquinas called this natural exchange.[6] This does not signify barter, as is obvious, nor does it mean to refer to

---

[6] The distinction we make here is to be found in II-II, 77, 4c. "As the Philosopher says in 1 Politics twofold is the exchange of things. One indeed quasi natural and necessary, through which there is had exchange of one thing for another, or of things and money, on account of the necessity of life." [translations here and below mine] Note inclusion of monetary transactions in this natural mode of exchange. It is called quasi natural because "natural" is used in this context not in a physical but in a moral sense.

"natural" in any sense of being primitive or uncivilized. "Nature" for Aristotle and Aquinas signifies the intrinsic principle in something that orders it to its perfection. So for them the civilized man is the full realization of the nature of man. It is only after Rousseau that we get the modern sense of the natural state of man represented as socially undeveloped and hardly rational.

Thus this natural exchange process is found in the highest civilizations and is the very basis of all trade. It is human community and communication expressed at the fundamental level of exchange of material goods. It is not the only communication of goods in a society. Nor is it the highest level, for, more importantly, community signifies a communication of ideas and other spiritual goods. But, like the unconscious life of the individual human person, it is fundamental, and society cannot live and function without it. Even the monk and the mystic have to eat, if they may do without shoes. It is natural for humans to depend upon the goods and services provided by others. Those who seem to be able to survive without such society are to be likened, in Aristotle's description, either to brute animals or gods.[7]

But this process of exchange does not progress very far before human ingenuity notices another possible mode of using the money involved. Normally, of course, the shoemaker sells his shoes in order to buy other things he needs. The process of natural exchange begins with a sale and ends with a purchase so that money is first received and then expended and we all end up with

---

[7] Cf. Aristotle I *Politics*, c. 2 1253 a 1-4.

what we need or want. Suppose we reverse the process. Instead of selling some goods in order to buy others, we buy some goods in order to sell the same ones. We may symbolize this as MCM.[8]

---

[8] This is what Aristotle calls "*chrematistic*" exchange and Aquinas in the Summa Theologiae "*negotiatio*". This is the name St. Thomas gives to the second mode or species of exchange. "But the other species of exchange is either of monies for monies, or of something for money, not for the sake of [having] things necessary for life, but for the sake of making a profit." (II-II, 77, 4c) In his commentary on Aristotle's Politics (In I Polit. Lectio 8 Para. 129) St. Thomas uses the terms "*necessaria pecunitiva*" and "*non necessaria pecunitiva*" to make the same distinction as it applies to transactions involving money (pecunia). We should take careful note of the difference between the two considered purely from the point of view of the form of the exchanges. It should be noted that St. Thomas is doing two things here. He is making an important philosophical distinction between two species of exchange, which <u>considered in themselves</u> are opposed as quasi-natural and quasi unnatural. Then he is giving the reason why the first is to be commended (*prima commutatio laudabilis est*) and the second is to be condemned (*negotiatio, secundum se considerata, quandam turpitudinem habet*). The reason is that the first is naturally (i.e. from the very form of it) ordered to, and thus limited by, the needs of living. The second, on the other hand, is not so naturally ordered, but <u>from itself</u> serves only the desire for gain or profit which knows no limit but tends to infinity. (*quantum est de se, deservit cupiditati lucri, quae terminum nescit sed in infinitum tendit*).

Modern moralists (including Thomists) in discussing this question, fail to take sufficient account (indeed generally take no notice) of the

Seems rather a roundabout way to go about things, and all we seem to do is end up at the beginning, if we are after some goods to use or consume.

---

fact that there are two diametrically opposed kinds of exchange (the second *per se* knowing no limit, though a limit can be extrinsically (voluntarily) imposed, thus curing its *quandam turpitudinem*). They discuss commercial morality by treating all kinds of exchange as essentially the same and then try to distinguish them morally purely by reference to the profit motive of the individual exchangers. From a philosophical point of view this completely ignores the formal distinctions (in terms of what is naturally good or not naturally good) that must be made before one brings voluntarily imposed limitations into account (important as they are). In regard to the first kind, though it is naturally good, one may voluntarily use it badly. Conversely, though the second kind considered <u>in itself</u> is not good, one can make it good – by voluntarily subordinating it to our natural needs.

The formal difference is not fully brought out by St. Thomas in the Summa, where CMC is paired with barter (CC) and MCM with pure money-changing (MM), but the distinction clearly relates to the fact that, in the first natural form of exchange, money occupies its natural position as a medium of exchange only (cf. I-II, 2, 1 c), but, in the second "unnatural" form, money (the love of which as such knows no limit) becomes a sort of end of the whole exchange process. ("*dictum est de non necessaria pecunitiva, quae scilicet acquirit pecuniam in infinitum, sicut finem .*" (para 129 cited above). What is most significant in regard to the oversight of this essential distinction in regard to the very "mechanism" of the exchanges themselves is that it prevents one having a clear concept of what Capitalism is.

There would be no point in this second process of exchanging if we did not end up with something we want. What could that be if we have bought something not to use it or consume it but only to sell it? The end of this process can only be money; we end up in the middle. But if we end up with the same amount or value of money what is the point? If the transaction is to make any sense at all there must be some increase of money gained. So what is wanted from this process of exchange is more money (or a monetary profit). From the viewpoint of the social exchange process in which the merchant has engaged, the activity ends with money, and is ordered simply to more money.

To do this, however, it is necessary that the merchant have money to start with. If he has none of his own he will be anxious to borrow it. The shoemaker and the farmer could make an exchange without money (by barter). This secondary mode of exchange is made feasible by the use of money. It supposes someone who has money to spare and is looking for something to do with it apart from expending it on goods or services he might need or want. The merchant is not so much a man of wealth, but a man of money, his own or borrowed for the purpose. Whilst the shoemaker puts his lathe to work, the merchant is looking to put his money to work.

Superficially, then, we might be tempted to think of him as no different from any other craftsman or businessman in the social order of production and exchange of goods. Why single him out? But we are not doing this arbitrarily. He has been singled out from time immemorial and by the most celebrated of thinkers on moral and political matters from ancient times, such as Aristotle.[9]

For the merchant is in a peculiar position in any exchange economy. He does not deal in use values, as every one else in the exchange system does. He deals in exchange values.[10] These are designed to be essentially equal between things in exchange. Essentially, the same thing in the same market has the same price. But material goods are not pure essences so all sorts of accidental

---

[9] Cf. I Politics, c. 10 1258a 38-42

[10] Op. cit. c. 9 1257 b "retail trade [meaning MCM or MM] is the art of producing wealth, not in every way, but by exchange. And it is thought to be concerned with coin [money]; for coin is the unit of exchange and the measure or limit of it. And there is no bound to the riches which spring from this art of wealth getting" Cf. also St. Thomas' commentary on this passage *In I Polit.*lectio 7 para 121: "but that monetary exchange [*pecunitiva*] which is 'retail trade' [*campsoria*] multiplies monies, not in all ways, but only through the exchanges of monies. Hence it is totally about money, because money is the principle and end of such an exchange, when money is given for money." Though it may be thought that St. Thomas' discussion here is with reference to pure money-changing (MM) the analysis can be extended also to buying goods with money in order to sell them for more money (MCM), as St. Thomas in fact does in the *Summa Theologiae* II-II, 77 c. See also *ad* 4. *"non quicumque carius vendit aliquid quam emerit, negotiatur: sed solum qui ad hoc emit ut carius vendit."* (Not everyone who sells something dearer than he bought is engaging in "retail trade" [MCM], but only one who buys in order that he may sell dearer.")

things can occur to affect not only the things utility (use value) but also its price (exchange value). Differences of time and place are obvious reasons for the very same thing to vary in value.

But even without these extrinsic factors there is a reason within the very nature of exchange value that allows a variation in an objective valuation of the same thing. At the same time and place you will often find someone willing to pay more than another for the same thing. The prices of things are assessed according to a practical measure. This does not determine the exchange value of some one thing according to any fixed or mathematical equality. Though the price struck between the parties has to be expressed in a fixed ratio the justice of the transaction may name a range rather than a rigid ratio.[11]

So an astute merchant will almost always be able to sell the same goods again at a higher price, without anyone necessarily feeling that it is overpriced. In itself the transaction does not involve as is clear any injustice. The merchant is simply taking advantage of something accidental that pertains to the exchange of goods. Measuring the depth of the sea we will find a difference at

---

[11] Cf. St. Thomas, II-II, 77, 1,ad 1 "*iustum pretium rerum quandoque non est punctualiter determinatum, sed magis in quadam aestimatione consistit, ita quod modica additio vel minutio non videtur tollere aequalitatem iustitiae*". ("the just price sometimes is not determined to a point, but rather consists in a certain estimation, so that a small increase or decrease is not seen as taking away the equality of justice".)

the top of the wave from the bottom. Ordinarily we are not concerned with this and take the mean between and measure this
relative to the bottom of the sea. In a similar fashion in measuring the equivalences of things according to their exchange values
we (meaning most of us) are not concerned with minor differences. Someone who has an eye for detail, however, may reckon
up the difference between the top and bottom of the waves and
bring them into the calculations. Similarly, an astute exchanger
can "buy cheap and sell dear" and make a handy profit in the
process. This too he can do without being unjust to either the
seller or the buyer he has dealt with (even though there is the
temptation to manipulate the market or "manufacture" price differences if he gets in a position to do so[12]).

As mentioned above there may be all sorts of accidental circumstances attaching to things in the social order of exchanges.
The merchant does not mind which ones apply. He simply deals
in (accidental) price differences whether these are between places
or times or from any other circumstance[13]. That is the reason

---

[12] See notes 20 & 21.

[13] Prices of the same things may be different in different places for
reasons that apply to the places concerned. The merchant may buy
them where they are cheap and sell them where they are dear. He
would expect to make a handsome profit even after the costs of
transport are paid. The transporting of the goods to the place where
they are needed is to be considered a true service and so that cost
should be added to the price paid by the merchant to calculate his true
profit as a merchant. This profit differential then becomes a difference

why it is not necessarily an unjust transaction. So far as the pure secondary commercial process of buying in order to sell (MCM) is concerned this may not of itself do any social good but then neither does it of itself do any social harm.[14] Insofar as it involves

---

purely from the accident of place or distance (involving no idea of service). The same analysis could be done in respect of a difference of time only after the costs of temporary storage (refrigeration etc) have been paid by the merchant. The merchant has not been the one to produce or provide the goods. He has simply bought and sold them. Some might think that at least the merchant has done a service in finding a buyer who needs the goods. But his activity was not needed to do this. Buyers' needs for particular goods are not peculiar to one, as if the seller has to seek out the right buyer. The merchant posed as a buyer to the original seller (who was disposed to sell it to anyone at the same price). The merchant has simply found another buyer who because of the inherent elasticity of the just price is prepared to pay more. It is quite accidental therefore that the goods fulfill the need of this particular buyer and not of another.

[14] Cf. II-II, 77, 4 c "*Lucrum tamen, quod est negotiationis finis, etsi in sui ratione non importet aliquid honestum vel necessarium nihil tamen importet in sui ratione vitiosum vel virtuti contrarium.*" (profit nonetheless, which is the end of 'retail trade' [dealing], though in its objective concept it does not denote anything worthwhile or necessary, yet neither does it denote in its objective concept anything vicious or contrary to virtue." (this translation is deliberately somewhat stilted, to retain the literal sense as far as possible). Note carefully that the notion of profit as used here applies only in reference to the second kind of exchange [MCM]. The farmer's and the shoemaker's monetary profit

certain material differences accidental to the exchange as such, such as of time and place, it can involve the rendering of a service, such as transportation and storage of the goods concerned, but this is not the basis of the merchant's profit as a merchant, i.e. as first a buyer (MC) and then a seller selling on the same goods (CM).

But, as Aristotle and Aquinas point out most forcefully, it is an activity in which it is very hard to maintain one's mental and moral balance.[15] For the immediate end of it is money itself, a purely rational means, that has no natural end or limit to control the desire for same. There is a real and present danger for the merchant to fall victim to avarice or philargyria. This is not to say that the activity cannot be used with restraint and subordinated to rational limits (which St. Thomas identifies in personal family

---

from selling their goods [CM], insofar as it is the means necessary for them to buy [MC] what they need, is something intrinsically good and necessary. The merchants buy in order to sell; all others sell in order to buy.

[15] Cf. Aristotle *I Politics*, c. 9; for which reason St. Thomas, quoting Scripture, would exclude the second kind of exchange from clerics, inter alia, "*propter frequentia negotiatorum vitia, quia 'difficiliter exuitur negotiator a peccatis labiorum'*, ut dicitur Eccli. 26, [28]". To highlight the essential difference between these two kinds of exchange, St. Thomas goes on to say that there is nothing against clerics engaging in the first kind of exchange. "*Licet tamen clericis uti prima commutationis specie…*" (II-II, 77, 4, ad 3)

or community needs)[16]. But it takes a lot of self-control. Though from a social point of view its effects may be neutral, this supposes that the individuals concerned exercise the appropriate kind of rational restraint and those that don't do not become so many as to affect the social economy as a whole.

For what it can do is to introduce into the order of exchanges and society generally a different spirit. Focusing as he does on the monetary gain he individually obtains from the transaction, the merchant or entrepreneur who operates in a similar way very easily is led to believe that that is the very purpose of engaging in all trade and business. The common interest that social exchange naturally serves becomes forgotten. In fact on closer examination, it will be seen that this is what has happened in the modern economy.

The new economy is characterized by the dominance of this secondary sort of "commerce" and the motives that move it. So it has been generally assumed that Adam Smith was right to make "self-interest" the motive force of all socio-economic life.[17] What is worse, this was regarded, at least by the early political economists, as the natural order of things economic[18]. Though this sen-

---

[16] II-II 77, 4 c ad finem.

[17] This fundamental assumption can be verified in any book on Economics from Adam Smith on.

[18] This was the fundamental assumption of the Classical Political Economy from Ricardo to J.S. Mill, many even seriously suggesting that the psychological "law" of self-interest or the "motive of profit"

timent no longer obtains the modus operandi of the merchant has become equated with economic "rationality" and a whole new "science" built upon it.[19]

Certain peculiar characteristics appear in an economy so affected. Artificially great differences of time and distance are created between sellers and buyers. It seems as if they belong to dif-

---

occupied a comparable position in Economic Science to Newton's universal law of gravity in Physics.

[19] The fundamental assumption of modern Economics (if in recent times some economists are at last coming to question it) is that it is pure economic rationality for the individual or firm to "maximize" (monetary) profit without reference to any notion of a limit. For modern Economics it is this infinity of our desire for wealth that creates "the economic problem", namely that of having to choose between the limited resources available to satisfy unlimited wants. Any standard modern textbook on Economics can be consulted to verify this most fundamental of economic assumptions. So entrenched is it that practically all introductory textbooks on Economics begin with the discussion of desire (as unlimited) and scarcity. The standard introductory course on Economics (Econ. 101) in Universities and tertiary educational institutions, notably in USA, begins by asserting that Economics is the study of choices, of the ways we have to deal with scarcity. For the sake of verification of this one can consult the website of the Canadian University of Manitoba, but a search of Econ.101 as offered in any higher educational institution selected at random would generally produce the same result.Yet such an assumption is palpably false and only sustainable by a confusion of wealth with money, and a failure to distinguish the two opposed kinds of exchange.

ferent nations To sell becomes the central problem. Middlemen are accordingly multiplied. Contrast the position of the old style shoemaker, who as an independent craftsman has hardly survived modern industrial "progress". In suburbs and small towns or villages where he operated, he had his shop (with workroom and storeroom) and sold direct to his customers whose needs were obvious and predictable. Take also the independent dairy farmer, in the process of extinction. He was able to sell from his farm to the nearest townsfolk whose "demand" was clear and constant. The shoes could be tailor made and the milk could be consumed fresh without refrigeration.

What has happened in the new money motivated economy? Things seem to be turned upside down. In order to trade we have to buy first, for which many will need to borrow. In order to produce we have to buy (or hire) beforehand both capital and labour. There is a lag time between both purchase of goods and sale (in the new commerce) or between the "purchase" of capital and labour (in the new style industry) and their "sale" in the products. This creates a need for more money. Goods are accumulated with a view to an uncertain sale. A whole new "industry" needs to be created – advertising – to induce people to buy what we have produced or have on hand to sell. Money splits the process of sale and purchase, rather than unites it.

The commercial and industrial enterprises that operate according to the new commercial spirit (thankfully not all do so; the society could not support it) are divorced from their customers not only in time and space but also more radically[20]. There is a loss of a sense of community and even of common humanity.

---

[20] This becomes exacerbated by the tendency to monopoly. The merchant and the modern entrepreneur are ever on the lookout for ways and means of increasing the differential between the buying price and the selling price of the goods they deal with. The "natural" way for them to achieve this is by using the advantage that (the increase in) their money power gives them in (the increase in) their buying power, relatively to others in the market for the goods. Being a larger buyer than most, means that they can "bargain" with other sellers or producers on more favourable terms and achieve a price lower than otherwise. On the other hand, monopoly in any degree gives them the power to sell at a price higher than a truly competitive one. The only restraint upon this process of maximization of the price differential (which determines the level of monetary profit) is a quasi-physical one, in that the "traffic" in the goods, i.e. the initial suppliers or sellers on the one hand, and the ultimate buyers on the other, can only support a certain minimum and maximum price respectively. Thus the trick is to obtain the "optimum" price overall considering the amount of goods that can be sold at a certain price of the individual units.

More sophisticated methods of maximizing profit have been devised in more recent times, in (graduate) schools of management devoted to improving the "bottom line" of commercial and industrial enterprises. One very effective way of doing this is by cutting the cost of human "resources" that one is required to buy in the business of making a profit. One needs of course to be quite ruthless in this exercise for it is after all a matter of economic efficiency (read "maximization of profit").

The nexus of the natural trading community has been fractured. This trade, rather than uniting the seller and the buyer separates them; for it constitutes the seller as someone who is not also a buyer in the same exchange system. Like the traveling salesman he comes to town as a seller only, seeking the buyers' money and nothing else. His (the seller's) buying has not been done as a cooperative effort with his customer whose goods he will in turn buy. The merchant has come to market to sell only. He then moves on, or back into a secure, and secluded, life among those like himself.

This spirit if allowed to dominate spoils community relations, alienates rather than associates the diverse sections of the community (most relevantly the rich and the poor). It engenders in those who profit the spirit of the miser enjoying his wealth in private; it engenders in those who are sold the goods an uneasy sense of being pawns in a game of moneymaking. The whole process promotes in all an individualistic outlook.

The extraordinary thing is that we have the "advantages" of modern industry and commerce so drummed into us that we forget what we have lost. We are told that now we benefit from "economies of scale", that there are more products to choose from, that the modern economy has resulted in the miracles of new technology. These technological advances are not to be denied but they are mainly mechanical and material, in no way compensating for the human and social cost. Take the means of communication, it does not seem too paradoxical to say that the media is the message, so empty is the content.

As for the advantages of economies of scale, let G.K. Chesterton's opinion be listened to, for he was living at the end of the nineteenth and the beginning of the twentieth centuries, in the very heyday and triumph of this spirit. "The big commercial concerns of to-day are quite exceptionally incompetent. They will be even more incompetent when they are omnipotent. Indeed, that is, and always has been, the whole point of a monopoly; the old and sound argument against a monopoly. It is only because it is incompetent that it has to be omnipotent. When one large shop occupies the whole of one side of a street (or sometimes both sides), it does so in order that men may be unable to get what they want; and may be forced to buy what they don't want. That the rapidly approaching kingdom of the Capitalists will ruin art and letters, I have already said. I say here that in the only sense that can be called human, it will ruin trade, too." (*Utopia of Usurers and other essays*)

That is to say, improvement by economies of scale, except where mechanical uniformity rather than human diversity is concerned, is essentially a delusion. Talking of the monopolist[21]

---

[21] We have had occasion to refer to the association of this secondary mode of exchange with monopoly. It is connected with the fact that there is no natural limit to the desire for monetary profit. So "growth" for its own sake is a basic idea of business for the merchant and the modern entrepreneur. "Greed is good" may not be something that they consciously subscribe to, for that is too crass. But most would subscribe to the belief that growth without limit is good. Monopoly, most literally taken, which means "one seller", where one has most control over the

millionaire of his day, Chesterton says: "Now, the chief of the
fairy tales, by which he gains this glory and glamour, is a certain
hazy association he has managed to create between the idea of
bigness and the idea of practicality." (*op. cit.*) But there is no real
connection here – the opposite is rather true regarding our real
and important needs.

The same holds for the argument for greater choice. There is
a multiplication of goods, principally of uniform make, that suits
a mechanical mode of production, not the precise needs of the
users; more shoes can be made but it is hard to find one that fits
(so we take the nearest fit). A more inefficient and wasteful system of production and exchange would be hard to imagine; not
to speak of the throw away economy. It is only be reverting in
some fashion to the economy of the "small" craftsman that any
useful quality is returned to goods.[22] The necessity to expend

---

price of one kind of goods (so one is in the happy position of being able
to charge "all that the traffic will bear"), perfectly realizes the dominance of this secondary mode of exchange over the whole economy.
Such total dominance in respect of too many kinds of goods, however,
cannot be achieved without bringing about the end of exchange altogether.

[22]Cf. CA, 36 " In earlier stages of development, man always lived
under the weight of necessity. His needs were few and were determined, to a degree, by the objective structures of his physical make-up.
Economic activity was directed towards satisfying these needs. It is
clear that today the problem is not only one of supplying people with a
sufficient quantity of goods, but also of responding to a *demand for*

huge sums on advertising is an admission of failure to be able to provide or produce what people want. A large part of the commercial and industrial effort (and budget) has to be expended on manufacturing not goods but wants.

How the modern economy's need for advertising has affected art is thus described by Chesterton: "I should say the first effect of the triumph of the capitalist (if we allow him to triumph) will be that that line of demarcation [between art and advertising] will entirely disappear. I do not necessarily mean that there will be no good art; much of it might be, much of it already is, very good art. You may put it if you please in the form that there has been a vast improvement in advertisements ... But the improvement of advertisements is the degradation of artists. It is their degradation for this clear and vital reason: that the artist will work, not only to please the rich, but only to increase their riches which is a considerable step lower ...and ... the artist-advertiser will often be assisting enterprises over which he will have no moral control, and of which he would feel no moral approval. He will be working to spread quack medicines, queer investments ... and to this base ingenuity he will have to bend the proudest and purest of the virtues of the intellect, the power to attract his brethren, and the noble duty of praise." (*op. cit.*)

---

quality: the quality of the goods to be produced and consumed, the quality of the services to be enjoyed, the quality of the environment and of life in general."

Indeed, this is not the only human virtue that may be bent to "this base ingenuity". As Aristotle noted long ago of the spirit behind this "commercial" mode of doing business, any natural virtue, moral as well as intellectual, e.g., courage,[23] may be similarly bent. "Nevertheless some men turn every quality or art into a means of getting wealth [money]" *(Polit. I, 9)*. What distinguishes the modern from the ancient economy in this regard is the extent of the domination of the social exchange system by this moneymaking spirit and the success of the propaganda of those who benefit from it.

The infinite desire for money, which is by that very fact disordered, and a personal and social evil, is subtly shifted by the new Economic Science to being the supposed motor of economic prosperity and progress. The fundamental principle stated at the start of practically every modern textbook of Economics is that our wants are unlimited.[24] Hence, the fundamental economic fact is that of the "scarcity" of goods. Here the notion of wealth is confused with that of money. The desire for money for its own sake cannot be satisfied, for it knows no natural limit. The desires for natural wealth, i.e. the useful goods to which exchange is naturally ordered, are readily satisfied in a civilized society that is

---

[23] With regard to moral virtues we are talking here not about them strictly taken, which virtues cannot be badly used, but about the natural disposition that underlies them.

[24] Cf. note 19

rightly ordered. Following on this confusion the two opposed modes of exchange are not able to be distinguished.

Though, of course, the distortion of the exchange process is not the only evil in human and social affairs, nor the only evil that in our times is called good, it is perhaps the one with regard to which we as a society have in modern times been most deceived. Even today after the devastating exploitation wrought by it in its heyday, and the even worse oppression arising out of the violent social reactions blindly lashed out against it, its propagandists are hard at work preaching its virtues and treating anyone who would oppose it as obscurantist and unscientific.

To what then should we attribute the evident economic benefits we do enjoy in spite of the heavy incubus of this species of evil? We underestimate the power of natural exchange and the great good that it naturally generates. With the growth of society so also grows, to an amazing degree, the benefits of socialization and solidarity. The progress and development of production and trade has occurred because of the natural exchange process; not because of the unnatural process, but in spite of it.

Indeed, there may appear to be a real connection between the new commerce and industry and certain advances in science and technology. Thus it would seem to be incontrovertible that the technological advances in transportation and communication grew out of the new economic spirit. The demands of the new commerce and industry led to, or at least contributed to, many new discoveries and inventions. But on closer examination, and from a properly rational consideration, it will be seen that these "demands" were only the occasion of, not the cause of, these advances in human science and technology.[25]

The "revolution" in commerce and industry that has taken place in modern times names only a socially significant turn to the alternative way of using money in the exchange process. This is not of itself unnatural or immoral, as explained above, though it inevitably degenerates into such where men lack a clear commercial moral code. Unfortunately, this has turned out to be

---

[25] The rapid rise of the United States of America to a position of economic superiority over every other nation on earth may be attributed to the natural productiveness of a society endowed with a rapidly growing population freed from the restrictions of old and defective human institutions, and from the restraints of not so old social divisions based upon privileged wealth and position. Unfortunately, however, it was not too long before America fell victim itself to the same malaise that all human flesh is prone to in this regard. Indeed, it adopted not only the practice (MCM) but also the theory with alacrity, even crediting its good fortune to this new "commercial" spirit, and becoming its champion.

Thus, it is still said that America is the land of opportunity where anyone might become a millionaire, as if one could do that by dint of hard work. But this rather applies to the fact that in America one has the greatest license to engage in a moneymaking venture (with money borrowed for the purpose) where it is possible, if one is astute (and perhaps unscrupulous) enough, to make a lot of money even today. It is also the case too, sadly, that the social, including the economic, disorders that inevitably flow from such commercial license are there most manifest.

the case and it is reflected in the "liberation" of economic thinking from morality with the development of a pure or value-free
"economic science". This new intellectual position on the nature
of the exchange economy has therefore tended to free rather than
restrain men in their pursuit of profit for its own sake. We have
to contend, then, not only with a moral problem but also with an
intellectual one, which tends to obscure the seriousness of the
moral.

We are, of course, not passing judgment on individual
merchants, or on particular commercial modes of operation,
even in their secondary sense. There is a place for them in a naturally based economy, though they deal in accidental differences.
Still less are we passing judgment on the (other) middlemen and
their roles in the modern economy, whether demanded according to the ordinary (accidental) requirements of production and
exchange or because of the artificial "distance" created between
commercialized providers (merchant sellers) and consumers (final buyers) in modern society.

The fact that middlemen tend to be multiplied in the modern
economy does not mean that they do not provide an "essential"
(indispensable) service. Even where the need for them is from a
"diseased" state of the social economy, they may be as necessary
and valuable as a coronary by-pass.[26]

---

[26] The producers and original suppliers to the great merchant companies of today may be heard complaining that it is the middlemen
who get the lion's share of the price paid by consumers for their goods

We do want, however, to distinguish this kind of middleman from the merchant in relation to the whole process of the exchange of goods. That is so we can isolate the role of the merchant and relate it to that of money in the exchange process. His is a legitimate role, provided he controls it by reference to the needs of the community, or of himself and his family within it. Everyone else, including middlemen, is naturally controlled by those to whom they provide their goods or services. In the natural order of exchanges the benefit or profit is mutual and consists in goods or services that satisfy; hence it is something eminently social. In the other exchange process the profit is solitary and consists in more money that as such cannot satisfy; it is essentially individualistic. In the exchange process, it is the merchants, and their industrial entrepreneurial counterparts, who alone employ the secondary mode of exchange (MCM). Everyone else, including all other middlemen, can be represented as employing the primary and natural mode (CMC).

---

or products. But this comes from a confusion regarding the notion of middlemen. Those that provide a real service are as much at the mercy of the monopolistic merchant corporations as are the original providers and ultimate consumers. The "independent" or small business long distance hauliers hardly get it easy.

Appendix B

The Business of Business

The main difficulty with the philosophical and moral discussion of matters in Economics lies in the lack of proper definition of the terms in which the discussion needs to take place. For practically all the relevant terms, and especially those which are more fundamental, are taken from human life in general. These need to be contracted to the context of socio- economic activity until one reaches the strictest application of the terms in question. Only then can one make a judgment about the precise nature and morality or otherwise of the activity being considered.

Without this it is easy for the most pernicious of exploitative practices and the greatest of injustices to be covered up and even presented as being "good for the Economy". For, by talking in generalities, the economic activities that involve such exploitation and injustice are able to be defended as simply examples of what are basically good features of human behaviour.

Nowhere is this problem more in evidence than in the discussion of BUSINESS. Even in the economic context its meaning can be as broad or as narrow as one likes thus making it difficult to follow any discussion in which the word is used.

Let us then try to determine the various ways in which it can be used. For there is a sense in which it is used quite specifically about which both Aristotle and St. Thomas had some quite important and most relevant things to say in their ethical and political writings.

Its most general meaning, indeed, is taken from the adjective "busy", whose meaning hardly needs to be defined, so basic is it to our understanding. It signifies activity as opposed to inactivity. Indeed, its Latin equivalent *negotium* signifies this sense by negating its opposite *otium*, inactivity or ease.

Even at this most general level, however, it is to be noted that being busy is not necessarily a good thing. For, philosophically and finally considered, ease or rest is not primarily a state of inactivity but a higher state of being.[1] Relatively to this human life,

---

[1] We have here a particular case of a word that signifies something that stands in the middle of two states, one below and one above the level of ordinary human life.

Movement, for instance is a sign of activity and life. What is immobile therefore is generally taken for what is inactive and lifeless. But when we need to refer to something above the world of physical mobile things, as in talking of the spiritual and the divine, we are constrained to contrast it with the moveable and changeable. We thus describe God's existence and activity in terms of immobility, not meaning to signify something inactive but rather super-active. So the rest and peace belonging to eternal life is not a lack of activity but the perfection of same.

Similarly in the practical order, as in economic matters, we find that price and value are the central notions, but something that is priceless and invaluable is not thereby reckoned as cheap and valueless. Busyness, therefore, is to be considered good relatively to the lack of it that signifies inactivity or idleness, but it is inferior to the absence of it that signifies the perfection of peace and tranquility. In the natural and rational order of things, we are busy in order to be at ease. The modern worship of business and efficiency, treating these things as economic

however, being busy or active is preferable to being inactive or idle. Within this perspective, then, that of the active life, business, i.e. being busy in the abstract, connotes something generally good.

This general sense as we shall see carries over into the economic order where it can be further narrowed down. However, we should not forget that the most general notion of business (*negotium*) has an application wherever there is any occasion of human activity serving some purpose or end, whether it is practical or purely intellectual.

St. Thomas himself uses the terms *negotium, negotiatio* and their related forms in ways that range from the most general to the most specialized and by following his usage of the word we can obtain the precise definition of business that we are seeking.

Firstly, he applies the noun *negotium* (business, or more elementally busyness) and the verb *negotiatur* (to busy oneself with, or to be occupied with) to the very activity of the mind concerned with reasoning on matters theoretical or practical; "speculative reason occupies itself [*negotiatur*] with the necessary ... practical reason with the contingent ...";[2] "from the essence of things ap-

---

ends or good in themselves, is but another example of taking notions that have a good sense in the right context but are then used absolutely to cover up a situation that is in fact unjust and exploitative.

[2] Cf. Summa Theologiae I-II, q. 94 a. 4 co: "Aliter tamen circa hoc se habet ratio speculativa, et aliter ratio practica. Quia enim ratio speculativa praecipue **negotiatur** circa necessaria, quae impossibile est aliter se habere, absque aliquo defectu invenitur veritas in conclusion-

prehended the intellect is busy [*negotiatur*] with reasoning and enquiring in diverse ways".[3]

The usage of this term in the most general sense is to be found when St. Thomas is discussing not only the natural sciences but also sacred theology so that he refers both to "the business of science"[4] and to "the whole business of theology" [*totius theo-*

---

ibus propriis, sicut et in principiis communibus. Sed ratio practica **negotiatur** circa contingentia, in quibus sunt operationes humanae, et ideo, etsi in communibus sit aliqua necessitas, quanto magis ad propria descenditur, tanto magis invenitur defectus". (my trans. "Regarding this however theoretical reason is had in another way to practical. For, because theoretical reason is especially occupied with necessaries, in which it is impossible for things to be otherwise, truth is to be found without any defect in proper conclusions as in common principles. But practical reason concerns itself with contingencies, amongst which are human operations, and so, although there is in regard to common matters some necessity, so much the more one descends to proper concerns so much the more deficiency is found.")

[3] Cf. De veritate, q. 1 a. 12 co: "Sed ulterius intellectus ex essentiis rerum apprehensis diversimode **negotiatur** ratiocinando et inquirendo".

[4] cf. Sentencia De sensu, tract. 2 l. 5 n. 11. "Deinde cum dicit unde citissime manifestat praemissum modum per duo signa. Quorum primum ponit dicens, quod, quia ex priori motu propter consuetudinem venitur in sequentem vel inquirendo vel non inquirendo, inde est quod citissime et optime fiunt reminiscentiae, quando incipit aliquis meditari a principio totius **negotii,** quia secundum ordinem quo res sunt sibiinvicem consecutae, secundum hunc ordinem facti sunt motus eorum in anima: sicut quando quaerimus aliquem versum, prius in-

logici negotii].[5]

So there is no limit to the generality in which the term may be used. It is able to be applied wherever there is any human activity involved. However, it is more specially applied to the discussion of practical human affairs. In the religious context, when these affairs are contrasted with attention to the divine, they are qualified generally as mundane or secular [*negotiorum saecularium;*[6] *a mundanis negotiis*].[7]

---

cipimus a capite". (The quotations in this note and in the following notes 5-9 are not thought necessary to translate. The particular words that are relevant to the point made in the article have simply been highlighted).

[5] Cf. Summa Theologiae III, pr. "Quia salvator noster dominus Iesus Christus, teste Angelo, populum suum salvum faciens a peccatis eorum, viam veritatis nobis in seipso demonstravit, per quam ad beatitudinem immortalis vitae resurgendo pervenire possimus, necesse est ut, ad consummationem totius theologici **negotii,** post considerationem ultimi finis humanae vitae et virtutum ac vitiorum, de ipso omnium salvatore ac beneficiis eius humano generi praestitis nostra consideratio subsequatur."

[6] cf. Summa Theologiae II-II, q. 184 a. 3 co. "Quae omnia, sicut et praecepta, ordinantur ad caritatem, sed aliter et aliter. Nam praecepta alia ordinantur ad removendum ea quae sunt caritati contraria, cum quibus scilicet caritas esse non potest, consilia autem ordinantur ad removendum impedimenta actus caritatis, quae tamen caritati non contrariantur, sicut est matrimonium, occupatio **negotiorum saecularium,** et alia huiusmodi".

[7] Cf. also Summa Theologiae II-II, q. 81 a. 1 ad 5. "Ad quintum dicendum quod quamvis religiosi dici possint communiter omnes qui

Indeed, the word "business" which as we have seen has been contracted to refer more specially to practical matters is again further contracted to be associated more particularly with secular or worldly affairs rather than religious or other worldly. But a further process of specification or narrowing has to be noted.

With regard to secular human affairs the word "business" can be used in a relatively general sense covering both the business of caring for the common good or general utility of the community and also the management of concerns regarding proper goods or particular utilities pursued by individuals. Thus St. Thomas, in speaking of military affairs, makes the point that other kinds of business [*negotia*] in society are ordered to their own particular goods, but military business [*negotium*] is ordered to the safety the whole common good.[8]

The virtue relevant to the ordering of our activities, so far as they impinge upon our ultimate (moral) good, is prudence. So, all human activity or business needs to be exercised with prudence. But when our concerns descend to the achievement of more particular ends or utilities, which are of themselves indifferent to the ultimate end or common good, prudence has to be

---

Deum colunt, specialiter tamen religiosi dicuntur qui totam vitam suam divino cultui dedicant, a **mundanis negotiis** se abstrahentes. Sicut etiam contemplativi dicuntur non qui contemplantur, sed qui contemplationi totam vitam suam deputant".

[8] Cf. Summa Theologiae II-II, q. 50 a. 4 ad 2. "Ad secundum dicendum quod alia **negotia** quae sunt in civitate ordinantur ad aliquas particulares utilitates, sed militare **negotium** ordinatur ad tuitionem totius boni communis."

supplemented by art. Morality and prudence come into play only according to the good or bad use of such art. The moral person, however, can be quite inexpert in such arts.[9]

It is with the contraction of the notion of business to the exercise of the various arts whereby we make a living that we come to the notion that is most closely associated with the economic concept of business. For we pass over from the one necessary business of living (well) to the multifarious businesses of making (good) things, i.e. making a (good) living, according to the various talents and tastes of people. Here we are close to the usage of the term "business" that is most familiar. Thus we talk of the businesses of shoemaking and farming where the economic context comes clearly into evidence.[10]

Before we elaborate on this, however, we should note the close connection there is between prudence and art, especially where the management and ordering of other people is con-

---

[9] Summa Theologiae II-II, q. 51 a. 1 ad 3. "Requiritur enim ad bene consiliandum non solum adinventio vel excogitatio eorum quae sunt opportuna ad finem, sed etiam aliae circumstantiae, scilicet tempus congruum, ut nec nimis tardus nec nimis velox sit in consiliis; et modus consiliandi, ut scilicet sit firmus in suo consilio; et aliae huiusmodi debitae circumstantiae, quae peccator peccando non observat. Quilibet autem virtuosus est bene consiliativus in his quae ordinantur ad finem virtutis, licet forte in aliquibus particularibus **negotiis** non sit bene consiliativus, puta in mercationibus vel in rebus bellicis vel in aliquo huiusmodi."

[10] The notion of business so far discussed has not brought in the modern usage of the word which seems to oppose it to labour. See discussion at end of article.

cerned. The business of political leaders (including military) involves moral prudence insofar as the common good is directly concerned but declines to art in regard to the manifold concerns that are subordinated to this end. Hence St. Thomas talks both of military prudence and the arts of war.[11]

A similar situation applies in regard to the management of the social economy. The overall supervision of the economic welfare of the community is a matter for political prudence and is a moral responsibility of governments, who must ensure that everything is ordered to the common good of all. That most definitely pertains to the "business" of government. However, the satisfaction of the manifold concerns of individuals and groups within the community are matters for their own skill and art, though none should act contrary to the common good.[12]

Hence the economy is a complex order requiring the exercise of politico-economic prudence and a number of subordinate arts of managing people, in both the political and economic contexts, as well as a multitude of arts of production and exchange. It is to be remembered, however, that leaving each individual and organization to manage its own affairs as freely as possible is part of the common good. The proper exercise of political prudence is in no way inimical to the true freedom to produce and exchange that belongs to individuals. The business of politics is not only to promote solidarity, but also to help the members of the commu-

---

[11] Ibidem.

[12] All arts are of course also subject to prudence and the moral law. In the political and managerial contexts it is sometimes difficult to discern the difference between art and prudence.

nity retain their independence (in accordance with the principle of subsidiarity).

In contracting the notion of business, then, to all these various arts of production and exchange, to the multifarious ways in which people make a living, we have come down to the properly economic context of the notion of business. Though the economic context ought not to be divorced from its material base the notion of production should not be taken too narrowly here. There is virtually no limit to human ingenuity in this regard.

The notion of business thus is contracted further from that of living well to the business of making a good living. Insofar as this involves dealing with other people one has to be careful not to treat others as mere means to one's ends. Unfortunately, this happens too often, as people tend to focus more on the success of their art at the expense of their obligations in prudence.

There is, however, a further step that can be made in the contraction of the notion of business. In the developed society, all economic activity is ordered to exchange or the market. Hence part of the art of making a living involves making a good exchange or sale and purchase. Thereby one satisfies one's natural needs and rational wants in a social way. In a well-ordered society there is no great art involved in this; the necessary transactions are made naturally provided one observes justice in one's dealings with others.[13]

---

[13] Cf. Summa Theologiae II-II, q. 77 a. 4 co. "Una quidem quasi naturalis et necessaria, per quam scilicet fit commutatio rei ad rem, vel rerum et denariorum, propter necessitatem vitae. Et talis commutatio non proprie pertinet ad **negotiatores,** sed magis ad oeconomicos vel

Hence, we have the notion of business limited to that activity, whether of production of goods or provision of services, as ordered to the satisfaction of the needs of others through exchange. The notion of business thus takes on a social dimension. A person exercising the art or crafts of producing shoes or farming simply to satisfy his own needs or that of his family, is not engaged in business in this precise sense. In the social context one in business makes one's living by selling what one produces and buying what one needs.

But in the processes of exchanges there arises scope for the exercise of a new and special art which we may call the art of making money. That is a most special kind of business that is focused exclusively on the processes of buying and selling rather than producing or engaging in some particular art or craft. Doing business in this sense means making profitable exchanges, by buying things already made or provided by others and selling them at a higher price. St. Thomas, indeed, reserves the use of the term *negotiatio* without qualification for this artificial mode of exchange.[14] But here we have obviously a most specialized sense of "business". It is precisely from here that we get the expression "business is business"; for *per se* no other consideration except

---

politicos, qui habent providere vel domui vel civitati de rebus necessariis ad vitam". (translation included below in note 17).

[14] Cf. Summa Theologiae II-II, q. 77 a. 4 co. "Alia vero commutationis species est vel denariorum ad denarios, vel quarumcumque rerum ad denarios, non propter res necessarias vitae, sed propter lucrum quaerendum. Et haec quidem **negotiatio** proprie videtur ad **negotiatores** pertinere." (see note 17 for translation).

the making of money is to be taken into account in assessing the purpose of the activity, least of all any moral consideration.

So we have arrived at the notion of business in its most narrowly contracted and specialized sense. It is a notion that requires careful and close examination as regards its moral implications. Fortunately, St. Thomas has done this in a masterly and comprehensive way,[15] though what he has said on the matter seems to have been lost upon modern thinkers on such matters, including theologians. Though an activity of the most narrow and derivative kind, like a parasite it has the capacity to become all pervasive in any particular economy. This proclivity was pointed up long ago by Aristotle.[16]

It is, unfortunately, the notion of business that has come to dominate our thinking in Economics. Indeed the whole science of modern economics may be seen as an effort to make some scientific sense of "the business economy" in this derived sense, i.e. of a society where the particular arts of making a living are completely subordinated to this seemingly general art of making money.

Already in Aristotle's time the idea of business as the activity exclusively occupied with "making money" was felt to be somehow disreputable. The picture Aristotle paints of this kind of business is one of people subjecting all to the acquisition of money. Prompted by the profits to be made through the use of money

---

[15] The essentials of the question are dealt with in II-II, q.77. However, St. Thomas addresses the issues involved in many places throughout his works.

[16] Aristotle Politics, Book I, c. 9-10

in this way, they not only enslave themselves to a false god, but also they pervert their own good qualities and arts, and generally have a deleterious effect upon the society in which they live and do business.

St. Thomas goes so far as to say that this mode of business "considered according to itself, has a certain turpitude, insofar as there is not within its notion any reference to a fitting or necessary end." St. Thomas, quoting Scripture, would even exclude the second kind of exchange from clerics, inter alia, "*propter frequentia negotiatorum vitia, quia 'difficiliter exuitur negotiator a peccatis labiorum', ut dicitur Eccli. 26, [28]*" (my trans. "*on account of the frequent vices of dealers, because 'the dealer escapes with difficulty from sins of the lips*"). To highlight the essential difference between these two kinds of exchange, St. Thomas goes on to say that there is nothing against clerics engaging in the first kind of exchange. "Licet tamen clericis uti prima commutationis specie...".[17] (my trans. "it is lawful nevertheless for clerics to use

---

[17] It is not to be thought, however, that St. Thomas condemns it outright. We need to read the whole of his argument in II-II, 77, 4 c in order to fully appreciate his position. Firstly, he gives a full exposition of the two species of exchange: "Ut autem philosophus dicit, in I Polit., duplex est rerum commutatio. Una quidem quasi naturalis et necessaria, per quam scilicet fit commutatio rei ad rem, vel rerum et denariorum, propter necessitatem vitae. Et talis commutatio non proprie pertinet ad negotiatores, sed magis ad oeconomicos vel politicos, qui habent providere vel domui vel civitati de rebus necessariis ad vitam. Alia vero commutationis species est vel denariorum ad denarios, vel quarumcumque rerum ad denarios, non propter res necessarias vitae,

sed propter lucrum quaerendum. Et haec quidem negotiatio proprie videtur ad negotiatores pertinere. (my trans: "As the philosopher says in I Politics the exchange of things is twofold. One indeed is quasi natural and necessary, by which namely occurs exchange of thing for thing, or of things and money, on account of the necessities of life. And such exchange does not pertain to dealers but rather to householders or statesmen, who have to provide the necessities of life either for the home or the city. But the other species of exchange is either of money for money, or of whatsoever things for money, not on account of the necessities of life but for the sake of the profit sought. And indeed this business seems properly to belong to dealers."

St. Thomas then goes on to explain how the second derived mode of exchange is "rightly censured": Secundum philosophum autem, prima commutatio laudabilis est, quia deservit naturali necessitati. Secunda autem iuste vituperatur, quia, quantum est de se, deservit cupiditati lucri, quae terminum nescit sed in infinitum tendit. Et ideo negotiatio, secundum se considerata, quandam turpitudinem habet, inquantum non importat de sui ratione finem honestum vel necessarium. Lucrum tamen, quod est negotiationis finis, etsi in sui ratione non importet aliquid honestum vel necessarium, nihil tamen importat in sui ratione vitiosum vel virtuti contrarium. Unde nihil prohibet lucrum ordinari ad aliquem finem necessarium, vel etiam honestum. Et sic negotiatio licita reddetur. Sicut cum aliquis lucrum moderatum, quod negotiando quaerit, ordinat ad domus suae sustentationem, vel etiam ad subveniendum indigentibus, vel etiam cum aliquis negotiationi intendit propter publicam utilitatem, ne scilicet res necessariae ad vitam patriae desint, et lucrum expetit non quasi finem, sed quasi stipendium laboris. (my trans: "According to the philosopher, however, the first [kind of] exchange is praiseworthy, because it serves natural necessity. The second, however, is justly condemned, because, as regards itself it the first species of exchange ...").

This adverse judgment about this second kind of commercial business was not because it involved one in secular affairs rather than religious. Such an explanation for St. Thomas's strictures can be seen to be quite false from what has been said above. It belies such a confusion of mind that it is hard to dissociate it from crass anti-religious prejudice.

Nor is this derived mode of exchange criticised because thereby one is immersed in merely economic concerns about material things, how one should eat, drink, and even be merry, etc. Though moderation is demanded of all in this regard, and even severity on occasion recommended, to kerb one's inordinate desires for material things, nowhere does St. Thomas or any theologian endorsed by the Church describe the satisfaction of one's

---

serves the desire for profit, which knows no limit but tends to infinity. And so dealing, considered according to itself, has a certain turpitude, insofar as there is not within its notion any reference to a fitting or necessary end. However, although profit, which is the end of dealing, does not contain in its notion any reference to a fitting or necessary end, nevertheless neither does it contain in its notion anything immoral or contrary to virtue. Hence nothing prevents profit from being ordered to some necessary or even fitting end; and thereby the dealing may be rendered licit; as when someone directs a moderate profit, which he pursues by dealing, to the sustenance of his home, or even to the succour of the poor or even when someone in dealing looks to the public welfare, so that the things necessary for one's country be not lacking, and he seeks the profit not as an end but as a kind of payment for labour."

desires for material things as such as affected by baseness.

Nor even is it said of commercial business as such, i.e. selling and buying goods as a means of making a living. For as Aristotle pointed out there are two kinds of exchange or commercial activity. And it is only in regard to the second and derived kind that St. Thomas, following Aristotle, makes his adverse judgment.

It is only because today we fail to see the distinct character of this special kind of business to which both Aristotle and St. Thomas are referring that many think they both are railing against "retail trade" or commerce as such. This confusion is compounded by the fact that we even tend to think of commerce as such in terms of this derived and money driven sense, as if the only reason why anyone would go into business would be to make money.

Nonetheless, the association of the word "business" with this secondary and derived commercial activity is only one reason why business has in a certain respect a bad name. In the precise sense referred to it has had a bad name from the beginning of civilization, as evident in Aristotle's and St. Thomas's criticism of it. But in modern times it has acquired an additional opprobrium for reasons that apply particularly to the kind of economy we have inherited, which goes by the name of Capitalism.[18]

I mean to leave the discussion of this modern meaning of business that tends to identify the businessman with the capitalist to a later article. It can be noted here though that it derives from

---

[18] Marxism gained most of its appeal from this more modern aversion to business, though Marx also made much use of Aristotle's more fundamental criticism. But this will be taken up in a further article.

an opposition between the business person as employer and the ordinary non-business person as an employee. It may have been noted that in the treatment so far no reference has been made to this relationship of employer/employee or master/servant.

In the above discussion of the meaning of business it may be assumed that we are talking about independent contractors or the self-employed. The relationship of employment, or the modern notion of Labour, introduces another consideration into the discussion.

Appendix C

Chesterton and Capitalism

Just as the other article "Chesterton's Mind and Method" was directed to defending Chesterton's general philosophy and method against the intellectual culture of his and our day so this is intended as a defence of his social philosophy, which he called Distributism. His social philosophy seems to have been inspired by the Church's social doctrine and in particular by Leo XIII's famous encyclical *Rerum Novarum*. As is the case with this doctrine, Chesterton's social thought, which owing to the particular condition of modern society focuses upon the politico-economic aspects of social life, is looked upon with disdain by the academic social scientists, and especially by professional economists.

The first thing to be noted about this is that such a focus is already a sign of possible abnormality in the consideration of the subject matter, which the Church has adverted to in more recent times. That is to say the object of investigation, namely social life and behaviour, needs to be looked at as a whole. A consideration of a partial aspect of society, such as the economic, though a legitimate abstraction, cannot be isolated from the consideration of the whole (which is ultimately a moral one, i.e. the consideration of individuals within society as persons). The very attempt to resolve social issues or address social injustices at the economic level alone is in a way to fall into a distorted vision of society.

There is more to society than economics and politics, especially as studied in the modern scientific way.

It may be said, then, that the nature of the social problem that had arisen in early modern times gave rise to the kind of ideologies that came to dominate the field of social thinking, namely, individualistic liberalism followed by collectivist socialism. The most visible social effects that ensued after the Reformation, centred in the wholesale expropriation of the Church and people by the already rich and powerful, were and are in regard to the possession and control of the lands and wealth within society, i.e. of a material kind. The modern ideologies which attempted to give an explanation of the new economic order, whether to justify and laud it or to condemn and curse it, are by their basic materialism and utilitarianism locked into such a distorted vision.

It became necessary, however, in order to counter them, to focus on the economic ills of modern times. "Social justice" came to be particularly associated with the question of property and the injustice of systematic oppression of the propertyless, which in moral terms is specially a matter of theft upon a grand scale. But there are of course other and indeed more serious kinds of social injustice, which have come to the fore in our own times, as for instance the slaughter of innocent human life in the ever-increasing practice of abortion, the most heinous of social injustices, worthy to be classified in modern terminology as crimes against humanity.

Even divorce is a more serious social evil in principle than theft, not just because it attacks the more important natural social institution of marriage, but also because it involves a system of serious injustice against the abandoned spouses. Because the principal promoters of these injustices (consciously or in ignorance) are those in power, or if not directly in government at least in effective control (for the main part by virtue of previous acts of economic injustice) the cries of the victims of these crimes go unheard or unheeded.

All these modern social evils are interrelated forms of immorality and injustice.

For the widespread breach of one commandment, when legally condoned, inevitably leads to disrespect for all morality. If this occurred first by reason of the greed of the rich and powerful elements of society, who were able to obtain political control by virtue of their excessive wealth and power (thus constituting the regimes oligarchies, if in more recent times they masquerade under the name of democracies), this disrespect and even contempt has, in the course of time, had a significant effect upon the culture and moral sensibilities of the society as a whole.

In Chesterton's time these flow-on effects of the first modern-style social injustice were just beginning to become overt. But the immediate peril in his day was from the extremity of the economic perversity that divided society into two opposed classes. Not that such a divide is not to some extent inevitable. As Pope Leo pointed out the possession of wealth within society is not meant to be equal. There are all sorts of reasons for such inequality (not necessarily indicative of injustice), including individual differences in intelligence and talents, that mean that some will have more and others less, and that only a few can have much more, whilst a great many will have the least.

This disparity of wealth, if well used by its possessors, works to the overall good of all. As St. Thomas puts it, in words adopted by the popes, it is good and natural that the possession of goods (i.e. property) remain private or in the individual, but their use should in some way be made common.

None should forget that his or her superior talents, and consequent greater wealth, are God-given. So they should be used in the way intended by God – that is for the common good. It is of course in the interests of those possessing inordinate wealth to argue for the right of private property as if it justified their absolute claim to the free and exclusive use of what they have (unjustly) obtained. Chesterton tried valiantly to bring home the necessary distinction between the right of private property always supposing a right distribution within society and the spurious right to property ignoring that question of due proportion. The socialist's mistake is to accept the same spurious definition of property as the capitalist and then argue for an egalitarianism and against the right of property itself. This confusion has been the bane of the whole discussion.

Moreover, by reason of original sin there has been, and will continue to be, those of inordinate great wealth, "the rich", and those undeservedly of little, the "poor" (the poor will always be with us), But what characterised the time which spanned the lives of Leo XIII and G.K. Chesterton was the enormity of the extent to which one relatively small section of society had, and had been allowed by law (since they had usurped the legal power in the process), to dispossess the rest. These dispossessed then became obliged to obtain their living by their labour alone. Hence the divide that was traditionally recognised as that between the rich and poor, came to be identified with that between those who possessed practically all wealth or capital (the propertied or "capitalists") and those who possessed virtually no wealth (the propertyless or "workers"). This rendered the great mass of citizens virtual slaves (under "a yoke little better than slavery" Leo XIII), a condition that in some ways was much worse than the ancient (pagan) slavery (cf. Chesterton's essay entitled "Sex and Property").

So we can come to the precise question that Chesterton faced in his day. It is fundamentally the same today but there are many features of it that are different, the most significant being the moderation of the poverty of the poor or the improvement in working conditions because of State intervention (prompted in large part by the Church's speaking out). This intervention brought its own problems. At present we are witnessing a worrying push to return to the earlier conditions of pure liberalism or "unbridled capitalism". A further complication is the extension of this flawed economic system to the whole world ("globalisation") making the divide of extreme riches and desperate poverty a feature to be found not only within nations but between nations.

This too it seems has allowed the poor of the more developed nations to enjoy to some extent a higher standard of living at the expense of the poor of the underdeveloped, leading to a general problem of "consumerism" within those "developed" nations. Hence, the sense of injustice in the "rich" nations is not so acute as it otherwise might be. The language employed in this regard is significant. The poorer nations are referred to as "underdeveloped". No one thinks of referring to the richer nations as "overdeveloped". For that would identify a defect in them (but in such eyes no one can be too rich).

More poignantly, within nations, the poor are referred to as "underprivileged" as if the normal condition is to be "privileged". Part of the reason for this may be that Capitalism and the modern economic science that is designed to defend it promote a concept of wealth as money where it is considered normal to desire to be wealthy without limit. This will be examined further below – as it is a distinctive feature of modern capitalism that is not brought out fully even in Chesterton and the social encyclicals (though it is hinted at in both) despite being to the forefront in both Aristotle's and St. Thomas's analysis of commerce.

However, as noted above, this economic form of social injustice has been overtaken by much more serious social issues. Nonetheless, that is not to say that the question of economic injustice belongs only to the past. It is very much a live question today. When we turn to examine the question of social justice (or injustice) in the sense of economic justice we will find that Chesterton's insights are as valid as ever.

But, the understanding of the issues depends greatly upon keeping in mind Chesterton's definition of Capitalism. It is a good definition and enables what is wrong with Capitalism to be easily identified. But it has the disadvantage of defining what is a condition of something (and a bad condition at that) rather than the thing itself. We might compare it to a medical definition of abnormally high blood pressure. This can only be understood in relation to what is normal blood pressure. So it supposes some knowledge of the norm. For Chesterton, "distributism" is simply the name for this normal social economy, expressed in terms of the distribution of property.

Confusingly, the word "Capitalism" is used both for an economic system that has an abnormal condition in regard to the distribution of wealth or property, and one where the distribution of wealth is not an issue. Both are systems that are based upon the institution of private property, in the one case in a condition that is normal, in the other abnormal.

The distinction between the two meanings of Capitalism is in fact made in the social encyclical (1991) *Centesimus Annus (para. 42)*. And the difference made there comes down to that between the normal and the abnormal. The encyclical is considering whether we can say that Capitalism is good or bad. "If by "capitalism" is meant an economic system which recognizes the fundamental and positive role of business, the market, private property and the resulting responsibility for the means of production, as well as free human creativity in the economic sector, then the answer is certainly in the affirmative, even though it would perhaps be more appropriate to speak of a "business economy," "market economy" or simply "free economy."

But if by "capitalism" is meant a system in which freedom in the economic sector is not circumscribed within a strong juridical framework which places it at the service of human freedom in its totality and sees it as a particular aspect of that freedom, the core of which is ethical and religious, then the reply is certainly negative."

The former sense plainly refers to the notion of an economy based upon private property and free exchange of goods and is concerned to oppose these characteristics to their socialist denial. It is thus defending Capitalism in so far as it is opposed to Socialism. But it is to be noted that the word Capitalism is not perhaps the most appropriate name for this economic system. What is evidently intended is simply a social exchange system that is functioning normally which ultimately means justly or morally.

The encyclical itself suggests that the second usage of the word "Capitalism", which clearly refers to an abnormal condition from the point of view of justice is the one more appropriate. It is in fact the one used in earlier encyclicals where Capitalism is severely criticised. This is also clearly brought out in other parts of the 1991 encyclical. "In this sense, it is right to speak of a struggle against an economic system, if the latter is understood as a method of upholding the absolute predominance of capital, the possession of the means of production and of the land, in contrast to the free and personal nature of human work. In the struggle against such a system, what is being proposed as an alternative is not the socialist system, which in fact turns out to be state capitalism, but rather a society of free work of enterprise and of participation. Such a society is not directed against the market, but demands that the market be appropriately controlled by the forces of society and by the State, so as to guarantee that the basic needs of the whole of society are satisfied." (CA 35)

And speaking of the conflict between Capital and Labour in another place the encyclical refers to "a conflict which sets man against man, almost as if they were "wolves," a conflict between the extremes of mere physical survival on the one side [subsistence-wage labour] and opulence on the other [concentration of capital], the Pope [Leo XIII] did not hesitate to intervene by virtue of his "apostolic office." (CA 5 Insertions in square brackets mine)

Chesterton's Distributism comes within the description used by Pope John Paul II: "what is being proposed as an alternative is not the socialist system, which in fact turns out to be state capitalism, but rather a society of free work of enterprise and of participation". And the Church speaking of socialism and capitalism in the same terms (socialism as "state capitalism") is fully in line with Chesterton's point that Socialism is simply the monopoly system of Capitalism adopted by the State itself. Both are regimes based upon a monopoly over the processes of the production and exchange and an effective denial of property rights to the majority of the population. Their basic affinity can be seen, moreover, in the fact that the advocates of both hypocritically present such a monopolistic take-over of the economy as being the best way of ensuring the prosperity and freedom of all. Both claim to be ardent supporters of "democracy".

Chesterton was aware of the ambiguity in the use of the word "Capitalism". So he says "The word… is used by other people to mean quite other things. Some people seem to mean merely private property. Others suppose that capitalism must mean anything involving the use of capital." These other uses generally denote the exchange economy operating in a just way without the huge disparity in wealth which puts one of the parties at the mercy of the other not just in regard to employment but also in regard to all types of exchange.

Chesterton's definition of Capitalism then falls fair and square within the second meaning given in the encyclical. "When I say 'Capitalism,' I commonly mean something that may be stated thus: 'That economic condition in which there is a class of capitalists roughly recognizable and relatively small, in whose possession so much of the capital is concentrated as to necessitate a very large majority of the citizens serving those capitalists for a wage.'" (from "Outline of Sanity")

This in fact is an accurate description of the economic system existing in the nineteenth century ("early capitalism" from the perspective of the late twentieth century) and has application even today despite the alleviation of the extremity of the condition of workers for various reasons, including initially by the united action of the workers themselves, then by legislative regulations imposed to restrain the more blatant exploitations within capitalism and by a general social welfare program to supplement the income of the poor and "disadvantaged" or "underprivileged". It is only in the social encyclicals that such re-distribution of wealth is described openly in terms of distributive justice, or treated as a matter of right.

There are many aspects to a normally functioning social economy but the widespread distribution of property is the most fundamental requirement. For it operates at the most basic level of justice, distributive justice, and it is here that social injustice in regard to property begins. For the lands and other common goods (natural resources) of any society belong to no one in particular in the beginning (or as they are discovered) and have to be allocated by the community through its leaders. It is not hard to imagine the temptation of those with the responsibility of dispensing the common goods to favour themselves and their friends in this regard.

It is noteworthy that Leo XIII was prepared to speak of distributive justice in the context of this question of social justice. He even applied it to the question of the just wage, which ordinarily is a matter for commutative justice. But what he noted is that the demands of justice are not to be confined to a contractual or mutual relationship between individuals. They presuppose, as do all relationships of exchange within society, a freedom and equality which it is the society's duty to ensure for all, to which every individual has a natural right.

In his time the disparity between the bargaining power of employers (capitalists) and employees (workers) had reached such a level that not only did the workers have no property to fall back on (having missed out altogether generally) but their parlous position enabled their employers to drive such a hard "bargain" that the wages they were virtually forced to accept were less than enough to support themselves and their families. The unnatural injustice of this, whether from the point of commutative or distributive justice, was plainly criminal. But not only the direct employer had a responsibility in this regard; it was a matter of social responsibility, of "social justice".

Part of freedom and equality depends upon each individual having his or her just share or proportion of the social wealth or common goods of a particular society. Any disproportion in this regard must affect the equality and freedom of the individual members of such a society in their dealings with one another. It is the duty of those who have the care of the community to ensure that there is no original disproportion and that the necessary laws and institutions are in place to prevent such a disproportion occurring as a society develops. Sadly, these responsibilities have been more honoured in breach than in performance.

As for how this distributive justice or proportionate equality is to be achieved, it is not a matter of mathematics but of practical measures. Such a spirit of distribution is not opposed to the institution of property but in fact is a matter of converting common "property", or common goods, into private property. The land for instance of any society originally belongs to no one in particular. But it can only be properly utilised by individuals. It is necessary, therefore, even before any form of production from the land, that there be some kind of institution of "property" in land. But all should be able somehow to share in this common property. There should be no favoritism or system of privilege in the distribution, as is sadly too often the case historically (with the blessing of "law"). The object of distributive justice is to ensure that no one misses out in the distribution of such social benefits. It does not mean that everyone gets an equal amount. It is a question of proportion considering the common good of all.

A just distribution of common goods, however, is not to be thought of only in material terms, as is the case with land and natural resources. As pointed out in *Centesimus Annus*, there is now much social "capital" in things of the mind (such as "know-how") enjoyed by the members of the community that can be considered community generated, through improved education, systems of communication and so on. These kinds of common goods can also be monopolised by the already "advantaged", whether within nations or between nations. They should not be able to be appropriated by the few at the expense of the many.

The proponents of Capitalism, as defined by Chesterton, see nothing wrong with such (mis)appropriation provided the mechanisms of the market are left "free", in an open exchange process. This is what is called "free competition" and "free trade". That is to say, in their eyes there should be no control over the prices of things - apart that is from that control which already belongs to the (long) established monopolistic structures.

A significant social good is the society's recognition of an individual's contribution to society (honouring its citizens). This should not be thought of simply as something going to a privileged few. But it gives a good idea of the notion of proportion in distributive justice. Some may be given more on account of their greater ability to use things (such as land) or on account of some other special civic quality. The distributor, however, should be always looking towards the common good and not to the private enrichment of the individuals. And with the distribution comes the obligation to apply it to common use as much as possible (this does not exclude one's own use within reason)

As noted above the notion of distributive justice can be applied in the case of wages. Ordinarily it is a matter only of commutative justice, but a worker reduced to a condition of extreme poverty and consequent economic impotence (lack of bargaining power) may be deprived not only of what he is entitled to according to commutative justice (a fair return to his labour) but even according to distributive justice (when what the underpayment takes from him is his natural right to a livelihood). This latter does not so much apply to the employer as an employer but as a member of the exploiting part of society (as a capitalist).

So it was that, in the extreme conditions applying in his time to the "workers", Pope Leo XIII used the language of distributive justice in the very context of the just wage. If necessary, as a matter of distributive justice, the State must set a minimum wage which the employer is obliged to pay. "The Pope attributed to the "public authority" the "strict duty" of providing properly for the welfare of the workers, because a failure to do so violates justice; indeed, he did not hesitate to speak of "distributive justice." " (CA 8) Because this goes beyond contractual or commutative justice, this aspect of justice came to be given the name simply of "social justice".

This necessity for fair distribution of common goods extends into the sphere of exchange. Indeed, generally speaking, the market should not be the property of any one (not even of the State – as public property). There may be occasion, however, in exceptional circumstances, for the setting up of a monopoly (state or otherwise) if required for the common good, but only to the extent that it is necessary for the common good (in the case where a certain kind of necessity would otherwise not be effectively provided for). Apart from this exception free entry of all to a line of production or market is a common good and no one should be given property in such by way of privilege or legal protection.

Any control over the market or the prices of things is in effect a form of privileged property (hence it has a monetary value, and an inordinately high one at that). One cannot exchange goods according to commutative justice if the other party has such a monopoly of the means and materials of production that he is able to dictate the terms. The test of a free exchange or free market is that both parties have no control over the price: they have to take it; they cannot make it. But the very definition of a monopolist is one who is able to make the price.

The capitalist wishes to define monopoly only in terms of state monopoly (socialism); price fixing is seen only in terms of the state regulation of prices. But that is taking the meaning of monopoly at its extreme (sole seller). There need not be total control by one. There need not even be collusion between a few so as to act as one. The very advantage that attaches to being one of a few where there ought to be many (especially in regard to necessities, in which work itself may be included) gives those few a power over the "market" (meaning the consumers).

The very difficulty of obtaining otherwise the goods desired expresses itself in a price elevated above the norm (the true market price). Indeed, up to a point the (oligopolistic) supplier can withhold its goods until it gets the price it wants. For it has control over such a large part of the supply that other suppliers cannot fully meet the "demand". Other oligolopistic suppliers (its major "competitors"), having a common interest in keeping up prices, will be inclined to keep close to the highest price possible given the overall "demand" even without express agreement or collusion. That is to say they will watch the "competition" and keep prices generally at an artificially elevated level, all the time devising all sorts of ploys (including a temporary drop in "their" prices) to steal some part of the "market" from the "competition". One may perhaps appreciate how the very language of exchange is perverted.

Without any concept of distributive justice the ownership of goods and their exchange is discussed entirely in the context of contract and an artificially abstract notion of commutative justice, as if all exchanges were necessarily between equals. In such a mind set there is little or no acknowledgement of anything systematically wrong in the social economy. But the encyclicals make no bones about this. "The crisis of Marxism does not rid the world of the situations of injustice and oppression which Marxism itself exploited and on which it fed." (*Centesimus Annus* 26)

Moreover, the encyclicals explicitly speak of injustice in the distribution of wealth (cf. *Centesimus Annus* 12: "To remedy these wrongs [the unjust distribution of wealth and the poverty of the workers] ...") and the remedy must include a restoration of justice in the distribution of wealth. This is precisely where Chesterton's Distributism is rightly to be regarded as a major part of the answer to "the social question".

This working for the restoration of distributive justice is an obligation resting on all, i.e. the community as a whole, and primarily upon the government. It is not so much a matter of passing new legislation as dismantling old legal privileges and bad institutions so that they do not continue to support social injustice. "The State, however, has the task of determining the juridical framework within which economic affairs are to be conducted, and thus of safeguarding the prerequisites of a free economy, which presumes a certain equality between the parties, such that one party would not be so powerful as practically to reduce the other to subservience." (*CA 15*)

Chesterton's social philosophy, therefore, correctly identifies what is basically wrong with the modern economy, and with modern economics. Outside the encyclicals this social philosophy is practically the only one which gives a proper definition of Capitalism. This in itself is a major achievement, for wrongdoers depend greatly upon ambiguity and euphemism, using names which belong to what is normal for what is abnormal, such as "free exchange", "competition", "private property" etc.

The very name which he gives to the social remedy, "distributism", is felt to be quaint or strange only because of our complete lack of familiarity with the notion of distributive justice in this context. This is not to be wondered at given that the reality has been missing from almost every society and especially in modern times. Not even the moral theologians have paid much attention to this dimension of justice, practically the whole of the moral theology of justice being focused upon commutative justice. In discussing the notion St. Thomas himself confines himself to the example of the dispensation of honours. Yet it obviously applies to all common goods, material or rational, that can be distributed from the whole (community) to the parts (individuals).

Chesterton's insight in this regard is, as in most things modern, genial. He saw clearly that the root of the modern social problem of poverty was man made, that the condition of impoverishment of the worker was not something necessary or natural, but a radical failure of justice, not because of a deficiency in the institution of property but because of a deficiency in the institution of government, which had failed and was failing in its obligations in distributive justice.

The word "Capitalism" as applied to the actual economy is another evil euphemism, for it suggests an economy characterised by people who have capital or property. But in fact in such an economic system the great majority have little or no capital, but depend for their livelihood on the wages of labour. We should be honest enough to call things by their proper names. "The truth is that what we call Capitalism ought to be called Proletarianism." (from "Outline of Sanity")

It is reasonably clear, then, that Distributism, as championed by Chesterton, is the social philosophy that best articulates the alternative explanation of the social economy that is necessary for us to have in answer to the false ideologies of Liberal Capitalism and Radical Socialism. It is also the social philosophy that most closely accords with the teachings of the social encyclicals and Catholic moral theology, especially with regard to the right of property and the rights of those dispossessed of property. For the key to these is an understanding of justice, and particularly distributive justice.

A NECESSARY ADDENDUM

But we have yet to understand why academic intellectuals specialising in the study of the social economy (the economists) regard Distributism with such disdain. Part of it can be put down to the anti-catholic culture discussed in the previous article "Chesterton's Mind and Method" with its underlying materialist and/or atheist philosophy. This would account for the academic intellectuals' preference for Liberal Capitalism or Radical Socialism as socio-economic philosophies. But the professional economists seem generally to regard both Distributism and the teachings of the Church on economic matters as altogether unrelated to the real world.

In order to explain this and defend the reality of Chesterton's social philosophy (and the Church's moral theology) in relation to the subject matter of Economics it is necessary to examine further the condition of the modern economy.

There is another disorder of the exchange economy which if not properly understood inhibits the full understanding of the social problem and of how Capitalism works its injustice. Chesterton seems to have intuited it without clearly making the distinctions necessary. It is a disorder that exists within the sphere of exchange or commerce itself. It has to do with the notions of trade and profit. Its understanding requires a careful distinction of money from wealth and of the twofold meanings of trade and profit.

The errors of modern economic science, whether in the older rationalist mode (Political Economy) or according to the newer mathematico-empiricist methodology (Economics), which take capitalism as the "natural" or real order of things economic, are founded in the confusion of the notions of wealth and money.

St. Thomas, following Aristotle, distinguished between natural and artificial wealth, of which latter money is the prime example (cf. *I-II, q. 2, q. 1.*) Shoes, for instance, are natural wealth. It is to be carefully noted that "natural" here is not taken in a physical but in a moral sense. For what makes things such as shoes natural wealth is their natural utility for satisfying a human need, in this case the protection of one's feet.

Natural wealth is characterised by the fact that there is a natural limit to our need for them. We do not desire them without limit.

Money, on the other hand, is artificial wealth. Again the term "artificial" does not have its primary meaning (for shoes are works of art) but is also taken in a moral sense, being defined relative to its end (which is the facilitation of the exchange of natural wealth – a purely rational end). It signifies something conventional, whose utility is not something natural in things so used but arises purely from social convention or agreement. The important difference for our purposes here is that there is no natural limit to the desire for money itself.

According to a rational view of things and goods, our natural wealth is sufficient for the satisfaction of our needs. This is subject to a condition: "Seek you first the kingdom of God and his justice"; that is to say even our material welfare depends not only upon our productiveness, but also and more so upon our observation of the social moral order. Our desires for material goods are however not infinite.

However, the desire for money does not have in itself any reason to say "enough".

For it has no character at all of an end. It is a pure (rational) means. One can see the importance of the distinction in this regard when one looks at modern economics. For it imputes to the desire for wealth of any kind an infinite character. Our wants are unlimited. The "economic problem" in fact is seen as one of "choice", of selecting which of our numberless wants to satisfy in a world of limited resources. Our natural wealth can never be sufficient to satisfy our desires for material goods. The economic condition is inevitably one of "scarcity". Such a viewpoint makes no distinction between wealth and money; indeed, the concept of wealth is equated with money, and the desire for wealth with the desire for money.

This changes our whole perspective on matters economic. It shifts our attention onto trade or commerce, and most importantly to the use of trade or exchange in which money becomes an end instead of a means. Such an economic world becomes entirely focused upon its commercial (and financial) aspects. But, in order to follow this, we need to employ a distinction from Aristotle with regard to the notion of trade, or exchange, or commerce (they all here mean the same thing – except in English "trade" is also used in another sense, not relevant here, of a productive occupation).

Aristotle distinguished exchange into two kinds or modes, which he called "natural" and "unnatural" (cf. *Politics, 1, 8 1236b 27-39*). Following St. Thomas's commentary it would be better to call them "natural" and "artificial", which distinction is related to the one above to do with wealth. As we shall see there is a place for using the term "unnatural". But, the essential distinction between the two kinds of exchange is determined by reference to their ends. The appropriate exchange being considered is one involving the use of money. A natural exchange is simply one in which money is the medium of the exchange of two goods between two parties to the exchange. It is called natural because the end or purpose of the exchange on both sides is natural wealth.

Money fulfils its purpose as the rational and conventional instrument or medium of the exchange.

An artificial exchange, on the other hand, is one in which

money (artificial wealth) is the immediate end or purpose of the whole process of exchange (selling and buying). We can symbolise each process by CMC in the first case and MCM in the second (using C to signify natural wealth or goods and M to signify money or artificial wealth). As St. Thomas notes, this second kind of exchange (MCM) can again be divided into two, for though it has no natural end it can voluntarily be and ought to be ordered to the natural end of exchange which is the same as that of the first kind of exchange (CMC), namely, the obtaining of a sufficiency of material goods. However, if it is not so ordered, and money is sought for its own sake (i.e. without end or limit) it becomes an irrational activity or unnatural exchange.

Thus, in any exchange involving money (or trade or commerce) we have to be careful to identify if it is natural in the first sense (CMC), or artificial (MCM) but not unnatural and hence natural in a secondary sense, or if it is artificial and unnatural. It is only this last kind which is morally blameworthy and can be (if extensively engaged in) socially harmful. The theory of Capitalism and modern economics do not know any such distinctions and, if anything, conceive trade and commerce in terms of the last kind. For money is thought to be the principal end of economic activity, and the desire for wealth in the sense of money (since they are treated as the same) the supreme motive of *homo oeconomicus*. Indeed, modern economics inevitably treats the unnatural form of exchange as the paradigm of all trade and commerce.

Moreover, the modern mind is locked into thinking of social

matters in materialist terms, and thus conceives money as the driving force or motor of all economic behaviour, which it is metaphorically only in the case of the second kind of exchange (MCM). On top of the perversion of language, therefore, in talking of private property where it has been almost totally misappropriated and of free competition in a situation of virtual monopoly, we have to contend with trade and commerce being practically identified with its unnatural mode.

This has had significant implications for the way people conduct their economic affairs. What in the past was looked upon as an unworthy way to engage in trade, namely, seeking to amass one's stock of money without limit by the simple process of buying and selling the same things and so making a profit, consumed as it were by the love of money (*philargyria*), came first to be regarded as a legitimate way to do business and then when fortunes were made by such businessmen or "entrepreneurs" even came to be looked upon as the very way business is done. The modern mind cannot understand why St. Thomas and the theologians and moralists of his time should have condemned this kind of business. For, in modern economics, this pursuit of profit (without any reason to be limited) is made the very thing that drives the economy. Such successful enterprise should be commended not condemned.

It is in this context that the notion of "profit" must be discussed. St. Thomas uses the notion (*lucrum*) specially in the discussion of the secondary kind of exchange (MCM), as he does also with the notion of business (*negotiatio*) (cf. *II-II, q. 77*).

Their modern use, however, for reasons that will be clear, has a more general sense, being extended to include the first kind of exchange (CMC). They are used in reference to any kind of commercial activity, naturally enough, since the modern mind, as noted above, makes no distinction between the kinds of exchange. The first kind of exchange according to St. Thomas, however, does not properly pertain to business people (*negotiatores*) but to ordinary households or public offices which have to provide for the necessities of life for the home or the city. "*talis commutatio non proprie pertinet ad negotiatores sed magis ad oeconomicos vel politicos, qui habent providere vel domui vel civitati de rebus necessariis vitae.*" (*II-II, 77, 4 c*)

This notion of *oeconomicos* in St. Thomas ought not to be taken in too restricted a sense. It is meant to bring out the fact that the first kind of exchange (CMC) is directly aimed at satisfying the ordinary needs of life. It would include therefore the multifarious trades (such as shoemaking) and activities productive of all kinds of goods and services, whereby people are able to obtain a reasonable living; it would include all activities ordered to exchange except those "business" activities directly aimed at increasing one's stock of money by buying and then re-selling the same things (MCM).

All economic activity, however, is seen in modern eyes as directed to the making of a profit in the sense of making money – indeed it is all seen to be motivated in the same way as the person who engages in what Aristotle and St. Thomas call unnatural exchange (MCM in its second sense), needing to start with money (capital – already possessed because one is a capitalist, or has borrowed from same), and engaging in business (whether productive or not) for the purpose of increasing their stock of money (or its equivalent), called economic "growth", without limit. All kinds of occupations are therefore conceived as if they were all modes of the same kind of "business".

All businesses, therefore, are the same from the modern economic standpoint, their *raison d'etre* being to make a profit. Does anyone suggest that they aim at making a loss? It is no wonder that there is great difficulty in applying Aristotle's and St. Thomas's economic analysis in this regard to modern conditions. One has to say that hardly anyone gets it quite right, even among Catholic theologians and moral philosophers. It is also not surprising when modern economists look with disdain on their efforts to criticise profit- making.

The discussion is inevitably at cross purposes. The economists cannot understand what the theologians are talking about; it all seems quite naïve and simplistic. The theologians cannot quite match their ideas with the workings of the modern economy; it all seems impossibly complicated and difficult to understand, as it must be if its object is something unnatural.

What the encyclical *Centesimus Annus* has to say on the matter is: "Profit is a regulator of the life of a business, but it is not the only one; other human and moral factors must also be considered which, in the long term, are at least equally important for the life of a business". This is all very true. But it does not make use of the important distinctions with regard to the notion of profit made by St. Thomas.

Just as some exchanges are naturally good (CMC), so their profits are naturally good. For their profits are not money as such but the things produced or provided from the activities engaged in. That does not mean that such profit cannot be badly used from another perspective; whiskey may be used to get drunk; nor that a business making a legitimate profit cannot be behaving badly in another respect, e.g. in relation to its treatment of employees and its customers. But these are all moral considerations or regulators outside the matter being discussed here.

The intent of the argument about the legitimacy of profit or the profit-motive concerns the nature of such themselves. St. Thomas does not use the word "profit" in the case of exchanges that are naturally good (ironically, there the concept of gain is used to indicate a proof of inequality or injustice in such exchanges). He reserves it for the money profit (*lucrum*) made from the secondary exchange activity (MCM). For it is only here that the question of its legitimacy or otherwise is raised. The goodness of "profit" in relation to the first kind of exchange is self-evident. It simply means the equivalent received of the product offered in exchange, expressed in terms of its monetary value.

In St. Thomas's analysis not all money profit obtained by buying and selling the same things is illegitimate. Like money itself it is good or bad depending on whether it is ordered to natural and rational purposes which in this context is the satisfaction of one's natural needs or reasonable wants, taking into account one's family and community needs and wants. If it is not so ordered but sought without any such limit, then it is not good.

There is then a sense in which the word "profit" is to be taken as bad or illegitimate. It does not immediately impinge upon anyone except the one who engages in it (for it is a form of the vice of avarice). But it can become socially significant if many engage in it or are encouraged to indulge their desire for money without limit. When the encyclical says that "profit is a regulator of the life of a business", it is necessarily taking profit in the good sense. So far as the "business" (e.g. shoemaking) is concerned it is the fundamental regulator – not much point in carrying it on at a loss.

It is true that there are other "regulators" (moral factors) involved even if one's motive for this kind of profit is a good thing. But that does not address the precise question of whether the motive for the other kind of profit (money increase - *lucrum*) is to be considered good or bad. As indicated, the encyclical is taking profit as something good in itself and it is true that other considerations or circumstances can make the profitable transactions not good.

But without taking into account the distinctions brought out by St. Thomas the argument about the legitimacy or otherwise of profit and the profit motive can still remain at cross purposes. Indeed, St. Thomas begins his analysis by adopting Aristotle's strictures against this kind of profit (*lucrum*). All such kind of "business" (*negotiatio*), i.e. buying in order to sell again at a profit, because their immediate object is the possession of (more) money, considered in itself (*secundum se consideratum*), has a certain turpitude (*quamdam turpitudinem*) (*II-II, q. 77, art. 4. c*). But that is because such a way of operating in the exchange system (the market), considered in itself lacks a due end; it is not natural, for a natural end bespeaks a limit. It can, however, be made good by the business person subordinating it voluntarily to natural needs or reasonable ends in relation to our need for material things.

Now it is clear that the modern economists, taking their lead from the practice of modern commerce, see no difference between the two kinds of trade (CMC and MCM), and correspondingly between the two kinds of "profit", the former of which is morally unquestionable, but the latter questionable. Indeed, as indicated above the modern economists have opted to defend a notion of profit and the profit motive that is morally illegitimate. It cannot possibly be a regulator of a business in any morally acceptable sense. For, it signifies the absence of any rational regulation or moderation in the business of "making money".

Catholics, then, have a problem here of joining issue on this matter with the modern mind. It is a perfect example of equivocation leading to sophistical reasoning. The two kinds of exchange or trade or commerce and, correspondingly, the two meanings of profit in the discussion are confused as one. Since the notion of profit has become associated with ordinary or natural exchange (CMC) it must be seen as good. When no distinction is made between this and the other more sophisticated exchange process (MCM) it becomes impossible to assert that profit in any sense, and the corresponding profit motive, is not good.

The strictures of the "mediaevals" against profit (lucrative profits) is then made to look ridiculous and out of touch with real economic life in the 21st century.

To a certain extent Catholic intellectuals writing in this area have been taken in by this sophism. There are some who are uncomfortable with the Church's critical attitude to Capitalism and read the last encyclical as softening its stance. Indeed, without the necessary distinctions being brought into play it can be seen how it is possible to so (mis)read the encyclical.

Chesterton, however, as mentioned above, had a kind of intuition into what was wrong (see his discussion on "trade", and its perverse nature as a modern phenomenon). But without the necessary distinctions outlined above it was not possible for even him to speak clearly and definitively about modern business and profits.

To summarise, some profits are naturally good obviously, as when applied to what the shoemaker makes over and above his expenses; in this material sense it means simply the shoes (expressed in terms of money value) he can offer for sale. But he is not interested in the shoes for his own use. That is where the social system of exchange or trade comes in. What he is interested in is not even the money he can obtain for them, but what useful things (for himself and his family) he can buy with the money. That is the real end of his "business" of shoemaking, and something eminently natural and rational. His engagement in exchange is the model for all natural exchange (CMC).

Other profits are not from these kinds of business. There is a way of doing business that operates in quite an opposite way. What is this kind of business? One does not produce any new material good or service, but first buys something, not to use it but to sell it on "at a profit" (MCM). As noted above, St. Thomas applies the word "business" (*negotiatio*) in this context only to this kind of business, not the other. It is a special kind of economic activity (like money itself *sui generis*), something "artificial" (in a moral sense), non-natural (but not for that necessarily unnatural). But it is unnatural if the profit is something sought for its own sake or without a (natural) limit; if it is reduced to the desire for money as such.

What is this kind of "profit"? Note here again, that in this context this is the only thing that St. Thomas calls "profit" (*lucrum*), intending something artificially (or accidentally) produced in the exchange process. It is not something like the equivalent of shoes that one had made and for which in exchange one obtains other things of equal value. The "profits" of the shoemaker's "business" is not what St. Thomas is referring to. There is no question of its being anything but good, <u>considered in itself</u>.

The kind of exchange with which St. Thomas is concerned is not based upon equivalence of value of two things in the process of selling one's own products (or services) and buying others, but on the differences in value in the process of buying and selling the same thing. The whole object of this second (and socially secondary) kind of activity is not quite "to buy cheap and sell dear", but certainly to buy cheaper than one sells, or sell dearer than one has bought. If one focuses exclusively on this kind of exchange (as modern minds, especially economists, tend to do), out the window goes the idea of equivalence of value or natural justice in exchanges (a just price). Some economic theorists then stupidly believe that all exchanges are based upon inequality of values.

The idea of profit here, then, is that of "making money" in the sense of the difference in monetary values resulting from the transactions, the "creation" of wealth (conceived as money). It is a pure money profit. Nothing more in terms of material utilities (such as shoes) has come into existence, but the trader is richer. How can that occur? It can only come about because of the potential for differences in the values, or fluctuations in the prices of things. Prices fluctuate (accidentally) for all sorts of reasons, objective and subjective. From the very nature of how prices are set there is scope for differences in value. For they are practical and based upon a common estimate of the uses of things that are not exactly determined (*non punctualiter* as St. Thomas says).

A just price rather expresses a range than an exact ratio, even though it must be set at an exact ratio where money is concerned. Hence, there is always scope for "negotiation" about the price. A shrewd negotiator can easily profit from this inherent quality of the pricing process. We might call this the subjective factor. There are all sorts of objective factors too that cause a variation in price over time and place without any suggestion of injustice

However, whatever the reason, the business of one who engages in this special kind of exchange (well known to Aristotle and St. Thomas) had a name and a nature which distinguished it from ordinary exchange or trade. Moreover, St. Thomas is primarily concerned with the uses of the terms *negotiatio* and *lucrum* in the moral context of this special form of business being used badly, and the profit therefrom, i.e. where one seeks profit without limit. The closest we have to it today is "dealing". but even this does not distinguish between the good and the bad. It is most confusing and misleading then when in modern translations of their works the word "trader", in its sense of an ordinary exchanger, is used.

St. Thomas is not saying that this second kind of exchange cannot be engaged in without blame. The profit therefrom can be legitimate if limited to one's natural needs for material things or by one's reasonable desires for things measurable in monetary terms.

This makes the moral judgment difficult in regard to any individual person. One would have to know a lot about his or her circumstances.

But St. Thomas and we are concerned with principles not with cases. The activity can be judged in general terms. When the leaders of society, led by the "intelligence" of their advisers, do not see the distinctions, or confuse all trading as of one kind only, all sorts of social and economic problems go unaddressed.

Chesterton was focused upon the more fundamental structural defects in the modern economy, as have been the social encyclicals. The modern economists, however, are concentrating more on the economy's functional aspects, taking their ideas mainly from commerce (and finance – which we do not deal with

here as it is material for the treatment of a separate question, that
of usury). By virtue of their perspective the economists do not see
any moral dimension in economics – it disappears altogether
with the disappearance of the notion of the just price. Everything
other than the activity of money-making is simply a given, no
questions asked, and money has no "colour".

That is what is meant by saying the modern economists and
the theologians and moral philosophers, with whom Chesterton
may be classified, are at cross purposes. They might as well be
studying two different worlds. The moderns tend to think of
Capitalism as a sophisticated money-driven system "creating"
wealth and even driving progress in technology and production.
The fact that the benefits of such wealth-creation and technical
progress seem to be disproportionately enjoyed by a relatively
small part of the population is something that does not enter into
their considerations. It is just the way things are.

Their world is the world of money, commerce and finance.
These are the realities that dominate the economic order. Might
it not be that the world that the modern economists believe they
are investigating is in fact the unnatural exchange economy
known to Aristotle and St. Thomas but "realised" in modern
times to an extent that they could not have imagined? Might it
not be that the real economy is the natural one that struggles to
function under the incubus of such a disordered scramble for
wealth (money)?

This would explain why there is such a disconnect between
the thought of Chesterton and that of serious students of the

modern economy. They are studying two different worlds. It happens that what Chesterton is examining is the fundamental part of the real economic world. The economists are basically studying an aspect of the real economy which has the reality only of a disorder or evil in the exchange system of the body economic; it is a subject matter or economic study only as the study of a disease is a necessary part of the study of health.

These two studies need to be corrected and then reconnected, the first by including once more Aristotle and St. Thomas's fine analysis of commerce in its twofold nature. We need to know about that part of the economy that the economists study; which today is "where the action is". But it cannot be studied simply as a socio-economic pathology which is not recognised as such.

Therefore the philosophy of Distributism needs to be supplemented by an explanation of the modern exchange system and a critique of its disordered state. We need to cure modern economic science of its virtue-blindness, and hence vice-blindness, the relevant virtue being the social one of justice. As indicated at the start, this abstraction in the name of science, or stance of neutrality, in social studies of itself engenders a distorted perspective – which allows many injustices to pass unacknowledged. There is not much prospect of a rapproachment between the Catholic social moralists and the "scientific" economists whilstever this warped vision persists.

On the other hand, the Catholic moral critique of modern economic life and thought will continue to be hampered without a clearer vision of St. Thomas's distinctions regarding trade and profit. Without such an addendum to his critique Chesterton's valuable insights in his social philosophy will continue to go unacknowledged and unappreciated, not just in the academic world, but also among most Catholic intellectuals many of whom are working earnestly in this field of socio-economic studies

ADVERTISEMENT

Just to show that Chesterton is not alone in his view of the perversity of the conditions of much of modern social and economic life, when most of us seem to have succumbed to the conditioning influence of advertising and the media, we set out below a few more quotes attributed to well known citizens of the New World, with a final quote from Chesterton.

Abraham Lincoln

"I see in the near future a crisis approaching that unnerves me and causes me to tremble for the safety of my country ... Corporations have been enthroned and an era of corruption in high places will follow, and the money power will endeavour to prolong its reign by working on the prejudices of the people until wealth is aggregated in a few hands and the Republic is destroyed."

Stephen Leacock

"Advertising may be described as the science of arresting human intelligence long enough to get money from it."

Ogden Nash

"I think that I shall never see a billboard lovely as a tree. Perhaps, unless the billboards fall I'll never see a tree at all."

G.K. Chesterton

"[In the pre-capitalist era] a fairly clear line separated advertisement from art... I should say the first effect of the triumph of the capitalist (if we allow him to triumph) will be that that line of demarcation will entirely disappear. There will be no art that might not just as well be advertisement. I do not necessarily mean that there will be no good art; much of it might be, much of it already is, very good art. You may put it, if you please, in the form that there has been a vast improvement in advertisements ... But the improvement of advertisements is the degradation of artists. It is their degradation for this clear and vital reason: that the artist will work, not only to please the rich, but only to increase their riches; which is a considerable step lower ... And no one who knows the small-minded cynicism of our plutocracy, its secrecy, its gambling spirit, its contempt of conscience, can doubt that the artist-advertiser will often be assisting enterprises over which he will have no moral control, and of which he could feel no moral approval. He will be working to spread quack medicines, queer investments ... And to this base ingenuity he will have to bend the proudest and purest of the virtues of the intellect, the power to attract his brethren, and the noble duty of praise." (*Utopia of Usurers c. I. Art and Avertisement*)

Appendix D

Marx's Small Mistake

Marx's criticism of Capitalism is a work of monumental proportions.[1] Convinced, as he was, and rightly so,[2] of its evil social

---

[1] I do not pretend in this short article to cover all aspects of his argument or thesis regarding Capitalism. Much that he had to say provided a genuine critique of the Political Economy of his time, which to a large extent was, as he saw it, a flawed defense of an economic system involving the exploitation of the many by the few. But the mistake we are concerned to highlight stands out from the first to the last part of his whole work and undercuts all the good work of such a critique.

[2] The word "Capitalism" does not signify a simple concept. Referring as it does to a concrete social and economic reality that inevitably has good and bad elements it can be taken for what is good in that economic system or for what is bad. Marx focused on what is bad and, as we shall see, mistook the true nature of Capitalism even in that regard. Others, however, can see only what is good or choose to ignore its defects. The notion of Capitalism derived from this corresponds to the first meaning referred to in the 1991 encyclical "Centesimus Annus" (para. 42), which as the encyclical notes would be better referred to simply as the naturally free economy. This meaning is the one fairly generally taken today when Marxism, with its criticism of Capitalism, is seen to be discredited. For, Communism, or some other form of Socialism, and Capitalism are presented as the only two alternative ways in which a modern economy can function. The more accurate usage

effects, he devoted the whole of his life to exposing how and why such an economic system produced, inevitably as he saw it, a degrading poverty to the point of virtual slavery in the greater part of the people subjected to it.

How is it, then, that the conclusions he came to were so far awry that those who tried to apply them to solving the social problem of the oppression of the poor by the rich in fact brought the people so impoverished to an even worse state?

Obviously, there was a mistake somewhere in his thinking, and therefore in his criticism. Now, one can come to wrong conclusions because of weak logic or false assumptions. We may pretty well rule out the former because there is no doubt that his was a great mind if one speaks only of reasoning capacity. As with other great minds that have also come to wrong conclusions it is hard to fault his logic, given his premises.

The fault then must lie in the premises from which he argued. Can we detect some falsity here? I believe we can and indeed at the very basis of his thinking on the matter. It may appear to be a small mistake, but, unfortunately, not just for Marx's economic

---

from a historical point of view, however, which is adopted here, is one that includes the whole phenomenon, both good and bad elements, and therefore describes Capitalism as the basically natural economy seriously affected by social injustice in regard to the distribution of property and work and consequently dominated, at times to an extreme degree, by those who control the capital and money within a society. This represents the second meaning referred to in "Centesimus Annus".

philosophy, but also for the whole of mankind which has suffered enormously as a consequence, the mistake is at the beginning of his thinking on the subject. As noted long ago by Aristotle: "a small mistake in the beginning is a big one in the end". (quoted in St. Thomas' *De Ente et Essentia*, "paruus error in principio magnus est in fine secundum Philosophum in *I Coeli et Mundi*").

The mistake, it seems, has not been noticed even by Marx's critics for they too, though drawing opposite conclusions to him, were and still are in a like confusion of mind regarding the exact nature of Capitalism.[3]

Most have been content to attack Marx in a more general way. But we are not talking here of his general philosophy in which he affected a theoretical materialism but which was more fundamentally a rationalism translated into a radical humanism. All this he had in common with the spirit of the age, being distinctive at this fundamental philosophical level only in his adaptation of the Hegelian dialectic to his purposes. The pragmatism and atheism of his thinking flowed naturally enough from such premises, as it did generally in modern culture. He was as much a child of the Enlightenment as any, but put together his own special mix of ancient Greek materialism, French social humanism, German dialectic and English Economics.

---

[3] That is to say they, like Marx, see part not the whole, except unlike Marx, they take Capitalism to be simply what is good in it, as explained above.

We can criticize him at this fundamental philosophical level, as many rightly do, but there the mistake is not peculiarly his, nor does it characterize precisely the way in which his thinking went distinctively awry. To identify this we have to fix our attention, as he did, at the socio-economic level on the phenomenon of Capitalism. For his was no merely theoretical interest in things. The general situation of the working poor was *in extremis* and he rightly declared in this context that the object of [a practical] philosophy was not to understand things but to change them.[4]

---

[4] Marx exaggerated the opposition between things to the point of contradiction. The more correct way to put what he evidently intended is that in practical matters the principal purpose of studying something is to do something about it. There is still a need for prior understanding, but understanding of itself is useless. St. Thomas explains this practical character of political (including economic) science at the very beginning of his commentary on Aristotle's Politics: "Secundo possumus accipere genus huius scientiae. Cum enim scientiae practicae a speculativis distinguantur in hoc quod speculativae ordinantur solum ad scientiam veritatis, practicae vero ad opus; necesse est hanc scientiam sub practica philosophia contineri, cum civitas sit quiddam totum, cujus humana ratio non solum est cognoscitiva, sed etiam operativa." *In Pol. proemium* (my trans: "Secondly, we can grasp the genus of this science. For since practical sciences are distinguished from theoretical in this that the theoretical are ordered solely to the knowledge of truth, the practical however to operation, it is necessary that this science be contained under practical philosophy, because the city is a cer-

What had come to be called Capitalism was the concrete state of social affairs in Europe (including England) that was later transported to the United States of America where it flourished. Marx correctly saw this as a new kind of regime[5], or system of power relations, that had come into being following the demise of the old regime, marking the change from the mediaeval world to the modern. Despite the breakup of a more or less united Christendom into independent nation states that that change brought about, the unity of Europe which was expressed formerly in a common religious faith found a new unity of thought in politico-economic terms.

In general this thinking presented itself as a philosophical liberalism, seen as overcoming the previous anti-liberalism of the regime it replaced, the Catholic Church becoming a convenient *bete noir* for the purposes of this argument. Things, however, were not as simple as they were so presented. For in reality what had occurred was rather a power play, a takeover, a social revolution in classical Aristotelian terms. What was the precise character of that revolution we will pass over for the present, for its po-

---

tain whole of which human reason is not only cognoscitive but also constitutive".

[5] The word "regime" is used here in a very general sense referring to a change that affected the whole of Europe. The change, though with effects at the political and especially economic levels, was of the most profound kind, both in regard to the personal worldview of individuals and the cultural and religious life in Europe.

litical dimension is complicated somewhat by the nationalism that accompanied it.

What is clear is that it became generally expressed in the politico-economic system that we know as Capitalism. This is not to say that such a system took over completely. No regime manages to subdue totally its subject population. Moreover, its success was varied, being more so in the newly formed nations that adopted Protestantism than in those that remained for the most part Catholic.[6] However, it became sufficiently predominant to justify us characterizing modern Europe as capitalist, with this kind of regime extending, thanks principally to England's and America's influence, to the whole modern world (penetrating now even into China).

How, then, are we to understand Capitalism, as concretely so realized? The best definition is that given by G. K. Chesterton who experienced it in its heyday. "When I say 'Capitalism' I commonly mean something that may be stated thus: 'That economic condition in which there is a class of capitalists, roughly recognizable and relatively small, in whose possession so much of

---

[6] Not that Capitalism was a consequence of Protestantism, as Weber argued. The "redistribution" of wealth that manifested itself in economic form as Capitalism was a political phenomenon, if it came into effect in different countries at more or less the same time as the beginning of Protestantism. The commercial revolution which saw the freeing of exchange to include MCM without restraint (regarding which see page 8 and following), and the consequent concentration on making money, was a phenomenon that appeared much earlier.

the capital is concentrated as to necessitate a very large majority of the citizens serving those capitalists for a wage."'[7] And this is essentially how things were in Marx's lifetime, though he tended to exaggerate the opposition between Capital and Labor.[8]

---

[7] Cf. G. K. Chesterton, "The Outline of Sanity", IHS Press, Norfolk, Virginia, 2001. This definition describes a social condition where the natural social economy is subject to a gross disproportion in the distribution of property or capital. How this might have come about is of course a matter for historians to determine.

[8] Marx had some insight into the phenomenon of Capitalism as defined by Chesterton. Thus in summarising the supposed dialectical process according to which property passes from primitive to capitalist to socialist he refers explicitly to the fact that private property which formerly belonged to many was misappropriated by a few. "The transformation of scattered private property, arising from individual labor, into capitalist private property is, naturally, a process, incomparably more protracted, violent, and difficult, than the transformation of capitalistic private property, already practically resting on socialized production, into socialized property. In the former case, we had the expropriation of the mass of the people by a few usurpers; in the latter, we have the expropriation of a few usurpers by the mass of the people". cf. CAPITAL, Part VIII: Ch. 32. His need to discover, however, a historically necessary dialectic shifted his attention to an aspect of the commercial process (MCM) which also characterises modern capitalism (fully discussed in the text). Thus he lost the moral significance of this expropriation in an imagined dialectic of violence (i.e., one expropriation being cancelled out by another). As we shall see, he missed the fundamental reason for the exploitation of workers in Capitalism and

It is a system where there is a marked division within society between those who own property and those who work, so much so that we can practically divide the populace into the relatively few whose living is from the ownership of property rather than work and the great majority with little or no property who have to work for a living. The name "proletariat" is given to this latter group from their lack of property, and the name "worker" is indeed applied to them almost exclusively. The name Capitalism is taken from the other group because of their position of dominance in the system.[9]

Effectively, of course, this signifies in political language a regime classified by Aristotle as an oligarchy, i.e., a rule by a powerful few designed primarily for the benefit of the rich.[10] However, because of the modern mind's adherence to political liberalism and the modern world's division into nation states Capitalism

---

sought to extract it from a misuse of exchange which, though significant and relevant, is secondary to the main cause, and misinterpreted by him.

[9] We are talking of Capitalism in its heyday during the nineteenth century. Much has occurred since then to modify the concrete expression of this divide and moderate its excesses. However, the system still survives and is quite capable of returning to its pristine form.

[10] That is how one must characterize a regime in which the extremity of the division between rich and poor points to its manifest injustice. That is not to say, however, that individual rich people might not see themselves in aristocratic terms, and that they may be genuinely motivated to act and use their great wealth for the common good.

does not operate directly as a political regime.[11] Its economic power structures and influence transcend national and political boundaries. Marx saw this and hence the slogan of the Communists "Workers of the world unite". For, in Marx's eyes, and indeed in truth, though the capitalists belonged to different nations, even at war with one another, their interests were common and combination at an international level was something natural to them.

In these circumstances liberalism is seen, on the one hand, as the natural ally of capitalism, simply representing in political or even general philosophical terms what capitalism is in economic terms. On the other hand, however, capitalism is seen as the natural enemy of true liberalism, a cruel despotic system of power through wealth hypocritically posing as the champion of freedom and democracy.

Marx, of course, espoused the second interpretation of liberal capitalism. In that we can say that he was nearer to the concrete truth of things in his time than those holding to the other interpretation but, unfortunately, in his critique of capitalism he made, right at the beginning, the "small" mistake referred to, which we must now explain.

---

[11] Indeed, the modern philosophy of Liberalism has coincided with the spread of democratic political ideas, so that nations have generally adopted democratic political forms. The underlying economic divide, however, is reflected in the fact that political power is exercised through the party system..

Even a cursory examination of his major work "Capital" discloses how the whole of his critique hinges upon the distinction, originally made by Aristotle, between the two ways in which goods and money circulate in exchange. To facilitate the discussion of these Marx adopts the symbols C for commodity[12] and M for money. The two processes of exchange can then be represented as CMC and MCM.[13] Money it will be seen functions in the first case as a pure medium for the exchange of two commodities; in the second, however, money becomes the principle and term of the whole transaction with a commodity acting as the medium.

If we separate each exchange process into two transactions, one of sale (CM) and the other of purchase (MC), we can see, as Marx did, that the second process of exchange is the reverse of the first; in the first a sale is followed by a purchase; in the second a prior purchase is for the sake of a subsequent sale. Marx's interest throughout the whole of his book focuses upon this second process of exchange, for he sees in it the clue to the nature of Capitalism.

----

[12] Marx gives a specialized meaning to "commodity" so that it names things as they are seen in the course of exchange. It is convenient here to adopt his symbolism. It is to be remembered, however, that C can stand for any kind of wealth or capital, such as buildings, which can be bought and sold.

[13] The whole basis of Marx's argument, elaborated in terms of this very symbolism, can be found in Capital, Book I, Part II: Ch. 4.

He brings into account more fundamental distinctions, also derived from Aristotle, and made use of by Adam Smith and his successors. These are the distinctions between the material things and their value, which latter concept divides into utility (use value) and value (exchange value).[14] But, as said above, the whole focus of Marx's attention is upon the significance of MCM in the modern economic system.

There is much to commend in Marx's insights in this regard. There is definitely a relationship between the change in social attitude in the late middle ages regarding this second process of exchange and the rise of Capitalism in modern times.[15] Marx also had valuable insights into how the mercantile mentality that characterizes Capitalism took over, as it were, the whole modern industrial process, so that labor itself (i.e. the laborers as an economic category or class) came to be treated like merchandise to be bought and sold like any other commodity.

---

[14] This distinction made famous by Adam Smith in his differentiation between value in use and value in exchange goes back to Aristotle's statement that "twofold is the use of the shoe" made in the very context of this discussion in chapters 8 & 9 of the *Politics*. Marx's argument uses to advantage the labor theory of value which he believed he found in the classical political economy. There was a great deal of plausibility in this explanation of exchange value by reason of the fact that employed labor played such a large part in the capitalist mode of production. We see below however how he was misled in this regard.

[15] Discussed by the author in other places, available on website of Centre for Thomistic Studies Inc., Sydney, Australia. www.cts.org.au.

However, he made a mistake in assessing the real significance of MCM. Let us say that, to put his mistake in preliminary terms, he gave MCM, and Capitalism as he understood it, a quasi-natural status in the socio-economic order that it does not have. He misunderstood the fact that Aristotle's analysis of the socio-economic order was an ethical one, not to be interpreted in a naturalistic way, as the classical political economy had done; furthermore, he read into the oppositions dealt with by Aristotle in this regard an absoluteness that came from Hegel.

If he had known his Aristotle a little better, he would not have made the mistake. If he had been a little less influenced by Hegel, he may not have magnified it so much.

In order to see how he went wrong we need to understand something more about the two opposed exchange processes and how Aristotle dealt with them. They are dealt with principally in chapters 8 and 9 of the first book of the Politics. They occur within a fuller discussion by Aristotle of the ways in which a household makes use of various arts whereby are acquired the things necessary for living. Being in the nature of an ethical study Aristotle brings into consideration to what extent a particular art of acquisition is in accordance with human nature or not. The basic test he applies is whether or not the art concerned is ordered to the satisfaction of the natural needs of the household, i.e. for the sake of such things as are useful within reason.

According to Aristotle exchange is simply one way in which a household acquires the things that are necessary and useful to it. The need for exchange comes about as communities grow in size.

Among small and primitive societies this exchange takes the form of barter (CC). In discussing this kind of exchange Aristotle has no difficulty in characterizing it as a natural development in the matter of satisfying our need for various material goods and services.

But sooner or later it becomes necessary to mediate the mutual exchange of goods by money. This process itself is simple to begin with, certain useful goods serving as a medium of exchange, but eventually those most suitable (e. g. gold and silver) are adopted universally, and so employed they are taken out of the sphere of their proper uses as metals etc.[16] With the introduction of this kind of exchange a complication arises, for it happens that some people become more interested in accumulating money than in acquiring the things that households have real need of. That is to say rather than using money as a medium only in the exchange process (CMC) it is made the end of the exchange (MCM).

Aristotle notes that this secondary use of exchange "has in fact suggested the notion that riches and property have no limit." For once money is introduced into the exchange process people

---

[16] Eventually, of course, money takes the form of documentary evidence of a credit/debt relationship between members of the community. Thus it is well described as "a bill of exchange endorsed by the whole community".

begin to confuse money with wealth.[17] "Indeed, riches are assumed by many to be only a quantity of money, because the arts of getting wealth [CMC] and retail trade [MCM] are concerned with money."

This leads Aristotle to discuss the question whether those who so think that the desire for wealth is unlimited are right or not. There are some highly regarded thinkers, such as Solon, who say that "no bound to riches has been fixed for man". But Aristotle refutes them. "But there is a limit fixed, just as there is in the other arts; for the instruments of any art are never unlimited, either in number or size, and riches may be defined as the number of instruments to be used in household or in a state."

With the adoption of money as a medium in exchange, then, there is developed an art of acquisition directed simply towards the acquisition of money. This, to Aristotle, is an unnatural development. For the possession of money as such does not serve the reasonable needs of the household. In fact money is only required to the extent that by means of it these needs can be satisfied. To accumulate money without limit is not rational. But that is what this particular art seems designed to do.

Aristotle describes the kind of person who engages in this particular art of acquisition. "Hence some persons are led to believe that getting wealth [i.e. money] is the object of household management and the whole idea of their lives is that they ought

---

[17] That is, between natural wealth and artificial wealth in St. Thomas's language.

either to increase their money without limit, or at any rate not to lose it. The origin of this disposition in men is that they are intent upon living only, and not upon living well; and, as their desires are unlimited, they also desire that the means of gratifying them should be without limit."

The meaning of "the good life" becomes for such people one of unlimited pleasure. "Those who do aim at a good life seek the means of obtaining bodily pleasures; and, since the enjoyment of these seem to depend on property, they are absorbed in getting wealth; and so there arises the second species of wealth-getting."

Indeed, this love of money necessarily tends to a desire for excess that affects the use of other noble arts and natural virtues. "For, as their enjoyment is in excess, they seek an art which produces the excess of enjoyment; and if they are not able to supply their pleasures by the art of getting wealth, they try other arts, using in turn every faculty in a manner contrary to nature. The quality of courage, for example, is not intended to make wealth, but to inspire confidence; neither is this the aim of the general's or of the physician's art; but the one aims at victory the other at health. Nevertheless some men turn every quality or art into a means of getting wealth; this they conceive to be the end, and to the promotion of the end they think all things must contribute."

A clear moral line is therefore drawn by Aristotle between those arts of acquiring wealth that are natural and those that are not. The basis of this division is in the nature of the end or aim of the arts. If the art is limited to human needs then it is one that is natural and good; if it is unlimited, it is unnatural and bad. If the object of the art is to acquire things that are necessary or useful for the good of the household it is a good art; if the object is simply to acquire money, it is a bad art. The moral problem with the latter arises from the fact that when the acquisition of money is the object there is no reason to stop – for one's desire for money as such can never be satisfied.

Now with regard to the arts that involve exchange, one, barter (CC), does not employ money; so obviously there is no problem with it. Where money is introduced, it is first used as a medium to the acquisition of what is needed for the household. This use of money (CMC) is not contrary to nature, for it is ordered to the satisfaction of the needs of the household. But when the acquisition of money is the sole object of the exchange we have an art that is contrary to nature. In this money is not used as the medium of exchange but is the principle and term of the exchange.

The most obvious form of this art of acquiring (more) money is dealing in monies, or money-changing (MM)[18]. But the same object is achieved by buying and selling the same thing for the sake of increasing one's stock of money (MCM). So far as the arts

---

[18] This exchange activity is not to be confused with usury, which involves different if related considerations. Indeed, MM is better symbolized as McM where c can be made to stand for money in a form or currency other than that in which the profit is made. For such "foreign currency" is seen as simply a commodity to be bought and sold at a profit. It is thus the most refined form of MCM.

of exchange are concerned, then, we have two extremes, the most natural is barter (CC), where no money is involved and the most "unnatural" is money-changing (MM)[19] where only money is involved. Between these two, however, we have the situations where in the first place money is used as a medium for the exchange of commodities (CMC) and in the second place commodities are used as a medium for the exchange of money (MCM). The former has the same end as barter, and therefore is not contrary to nature; the latter has the same end as money-changing and so is also "unnatural".

Aristotle was very strong in his condemnation of exchange where the object was simply to "make money". This commercial practice was apparently common enough in his day, as it is in ours. He was aware of the difficulty of distinguishing it from the other mode of exchange. Thus he says: "There is another variety of the art of acquisition and rightly called an art of wealth getting, and has in fact suggested the notion that riches and property have no limit. Being nearly connected with the preceding, it is often identified with it. But though they are not very different, neither are they the same. The kind already described is given by nature, the other is gained by experience and art."[20]

---

[19] Here again we are not talking about usury, which Aristotle will later say is the most unnatural of all uses of money.

[20] They are both arts but the first is from "nature" whilst the second is a pure invention of reason.

This distinction between the two modes of exchange or trade, however, is practically lost today. Indeed, Aristotle's description of the commercial mind of his time, "the art of getting wealth is generally thought to be chiefly concerned with it [the use of money], and to be the art which produces riches and wealth," might well be a description of the modern commercial mentality. When people, especially economists, think of trade, they have no notion of there being a secondary mode [MCM] different from the first [CMC]. If anything, all trade is thought of in terms of "making money", the accumulation of which has no necessary limit.

Economists and social scientists generally have not understood the distinction between the two modes of exchange. Part of the reason why modern economists fail to notice the difference is because they have ceased to think about matters economic in ethical terms. The true basis of Aristotle's distinction is ethical or moral. He speaks of the difference between the two in terms of what is natural and what is unnatural. But in this context "natural" equates with ethically good and "unnatural" with morally bad.[21]

---

[21] Adam Smith perhaps following David Hume's lead in adapting Newton's experimental method to the moral sciences, gives the new economic science a quasi-physical object. His followers came to view the universal law of self-interest in much the same terms as the universal law of gravitation.

Marx, however, was one who picked up the difference. But, unfortunately, he did not understand the basis of it and made too much of it. The classical political economy, reducing economic affairs, especially commerce, to a morally neutral natural order, could see no reason for the distinction.[22] Marx, saw Aristotle's distinction and its great significance for the functioning of the social economy. But, he accepted the moral neutrality of the modern approach, decrying any relevance of moral considerations in the "scientific" study of Economics. This led him to endow this secondary process with a quasi-natural status that had a historically necessary part to play in the dialectic which was expressed in the class conflict between Capital and Labor.

For Aristotle there is in the concrete such a dialectic, but it is a war between the good and the bad that has its roots in the hearts of men and women. The opposition within society even at the economic level is a moral one, between the virtuous and the vicious, between those able to control their desires for wealth and those not so able. The means to end or moderate such a conflict

---

[22] Indeed, the notion of economizing upon which the whole modern science of economics is based is that of the allocation of limited resources to unlimited wants, the very negation of Aristotle's position that the resources of nature, rationally managed, are sufficient for all our natural needs, and able to satisfy all our rational desires. "Nature does not default in necessaries". The first principle, therefore, of modern economic science is that of scarcity, as opposed to Aristotle's first principle of natural abundance. Such a fundamental difference can be directly related to the modern confusion of wealth with money.

are ultimately moral at the individual level,[23] though at the social level it is necessary also to have reforms that bring into effect good laws and institutions.

Marx, with disastrous consequences, converts this practical moral (and therefore reformable) dialectic into a historically necessary one. Nonetheless, he was able to draw much from the moral strictures Aristotle directed against those engaging in this form of commercial practice in an unrestrained way. It would be hard to find a more severe condemnation of this art of making money. The picture Aristotle paints is one of people subjecting all to the acquisition of money. Prompted by the profits to be made through the use of money in this way, they not only enslave themselves to a false god, but also they pervert their own good qualities and arts, and generally have a deleterious effect upon the society in which they live and do business.

Marx could then paint Capitalism, which he virtually identified with this commercial process, in the blackest terms, eschewing all the while any moral judgment in the matter. Marx had certainly plenty of material to work with in this regard. In his time the enormity of the contrast could not have been greater between the rich few seemingly bent of increasing their riches without limit and the great numbers of the rest of the population hardly able to subsist on their miserable wages.

---

[23] Hence it is that religion is indispensable to the possibility of the restoration of social justice.

Like the classical political economists he saw this as a natural phenomenon, a working out of scientific economic laws, but at least he did not accept it as a permanent state of nature. He was able to draw on the Hegelian dialectic to present what in moral terms was a great evil as at least a "contradiction" which, if historically necessary, was temporary. This gave his thinking on the matter much appeal, especially when compared with the hopelessness preached to the working poor by the prevailing "dismal science".

But the correctness of his analysis is another matter. As history attests, the application of his ideas led on to even greater evils. We can find fault with his understanding of the exchange process MCM. We will see that his definition of Capitalism in terms of this process is quite mistaken. Importantly, however, his notion of Capitalism, as necessarily exploitative of Labor, is a mistaken assumption flowing from his basic misunderstanding of MCM.

To appreciate these mistakes we need to examine a little further the exchange process MCM which Aristotle criticizes so severely and Marx relies on so much in his critique of Capitalism. We can do this with the help of St. Thomas whose interpretation of Aristotle is most highly regarded.

Aristotle's criticism is made on the supposition that the object, and the sole object, of buying and selling something is to make a profit, i.e. to increase one's stock of money. The exchange process itself, MCM, as it names a "second species of wealth-getting", does not have any other object. Aristotle is principally concerned with the kind of persons caught up in this art of acquisition whose "whole idea of their lives is that they ought either to increase their money without limit, or at any rate not to lose it."[24]

However, it is possible, as St. Thomas points out, to legitimize the art if one voluntarily imposes on its exercise the limit that it is required by natural morality. Hence, if the increase of money so gained is directed and limited to the supply of the reasonable requirements of oneself, family or nation, such a mode of ex-

---

[24] For a full exposition of the two species of exchange cf. St.Thomas's Summa Theologiae, II-II, 77, 4c: Ut autem philosophus dicit, in I Polit., duplex est rerum commutatio. Una quidem quasi naturalis et necessaria, per quam scilicet fit commutatio rei ad rem, vel rerum et denariorum, propter necessitatem vitae. Et talis commutatio non proprie pertinet ad negotiatores, sed magis ad oeconomicos vel politicos, qui habent providere vel domui vel civitati de rebus necessariis ad vitam. Alia vero commutationis species est vel denariorum ad denarios, vel quarumcumque rerum ad denarios, non propter res necessarias vitae, sed propter lucrum quaerendum. Et haec quidem negotiatio proprie videtur ad negotiatores pertinere. (my trans: "As the philosopher says in I Politics the exchange of things is twofold. One indeed is quasi natural and necessary, by which namely occurs exchange of thing for thing, or of things and money, on account of the necessities of life. And such exchange does not pertain to dealers but rather to householders or statesmen, who have to provide the necessities of life either for the home or the city. But the other species of exchange is either of money for money, or of whatsoever things for money, not on account of the necessities of life but for the sake of the profit sought. And indeed this business seems properly to belong to dealers."

change, or of making money, may be not only legitimate but also laudable.[25]

---

[25] This is fully elaborated by St. Thomas also in II-II, 77, 4 c: Secundum philosophum autem, prima commutatio laudabilis est, quia deservit naturali necessitati. Secunda autem iuste vituperatur, quia, quantum est de se, deservit cupiditati lucri, quae terminum nescit sed in infinitum tendit. Et ideo negotiatio, secundum se considerata, quandam turpitudinem habet, inquantum non importat de sui ratione finem honestum vel necessarium. Lucrum tamen, quod est negotiationis finis, etsi in sui ratione non importet aliquid honestum vel necessarium, nihil tamen importat in sui ratione vitiosum vel virtuti contrarium. Unde nihil prohibet lucrum ordinari ad aliquem finem necessarium, vel etiam honestum. Et sic negotiatio licita reddetur. Sicut cum aliquis lucrum moderatum, quod negotiando quaerit, ordinat ad domus suae sustentationem, vel etiam ad subveniendum indigentibus, vel etiam cum aliquis negotiationi intendit propter publicam utilitatem, ne scilicet res necessariae ad vitam patriae desint, et lucrum expetit non quasi finem, sed quasi stipendium laboris. (my trans: "According to the philosopher, however, the first [kind of] exchange is praiseworthy, because it serves natural necessity. The second, however, is justly condemned, because, as regards itself it serves the desire for profit, which knows no limit but tends to infinity. And so dealing, considered according to itself, has a certain turpitude, insofar as there is not within its notion any reference to a fitting or necessary end. However, although profit, which is the end of dealing, does not contain in its notion any reference to a fitting or necessary end, nevertheless neither does it contain in its notion anything immoral or contrary to virtue. Hence nothing prevents profit from being ordered to some necessary or even

This is something that is not brought out explicitly in Aristotle's treatment, though it is implicit in that the basis of his criticism lies in the lack of such a limit. It is something completely overlooked by Marx.[26] For his thesis depends on giving to the

---

fitting end; and thereby the dealing may be rendered licit; as when someone directs a moderate profit, which he pursues by dealing, to the sustenance of his home, or even to the succour of the poor or even when someone in dealing looks to the public welfare, so that the things necessary for one's country be not lacking, and he seeks the profit not as an end but as a kind of payment for labour."

[26] For Marx the exchange process MCM cannot be thought of except as without limits. The capitalist is then defined in terms of this unlimited appetite for more money. This personification of the process, as evil, gives a substantial status to the process which is then made a necessary part of the social dialectic. One quotation suffices to verify this. "The simple circulation of commodities - selling in order to buy - is a means of carrying out a purpose unconnected with circulation, namely, the appropriation of use-values, the satisfaction of wants. The circulation of money as capital is, on the contrary, an end in itself, for the expansion of value takes place only within this constantly renewed movement. The circulation of capital has therefore no limits. As the conscious representative of this movement, the possessor of money becomes a capitalist. His person, or rather his pocket, is the point from which the money starts and to which it returns. The expansion of value, which is the objective basis or main-spring of the circulation M-C-M, becomes his subjective aim, and it is only in so far as the appropriation of ever more and more wealth in the abstract becomes the sole motive of his operations, that he functions as a capitalist, that is, as cap-

exchange process itself an intrinsic exploitative character, with which he can identify the system of Capitalism.

But St. Thomas shows that there is nothing necessary about its misuse. It is, indeed, an activity that people will find difficult to engage in with the necessary moderation, as was clearly the case in Aristotle's time, and is more obviously the situation in our own. It is important to remember, however, that its management is a moral matter and if its abuse works to the detriment of a society it points to a loss of moral and religious values in regard to the acquisition of wealth. A society that ceases to worship God will soon begin to worship money.

This is the first and most fundamental respect in which Marx misunderstands the nature of the exchange process MCM. It cannot be given any quasi-natural necessity. It remains one that depends upon human free will and accordingly carries with it moral responsibility.

Marx compounds his mistake in this regard by defining Capitalism in terms of this misuse of MCM. Though it makes some sense to highlight the opposition between the good and bad elements in the exchange economy, this must only be done in moral terms and always with the proviso that the good has a priority and superiority over the bad, despite appearances at any particular time. For the good has reality and power from its very nature

---

ital personified and endowed with consciousness and a will." Capital, Book 1, Part 8, ch. 32.

whereas the substance and strength of the bad comes only from the partial goodness that it has.

It was inevitable, however, given Marx's deterministic interpretation of the economy and his adoption of the Hegelian methodology, that he should reify and exaggerate the evil element in this bad commercial practice so as to make it an effective contradictory force in a dialectical clash of social forces. Capitalism, so understood in such a socio-economic system, is meant for destruction in the historical working out of this conflict.

But there is one further aspect of the matter that needs to be considered in order to appreciate the full extent of Marx's error in this regard. There is a puzzle in understanding why anyone would want to engage in the second exchange process (MCM) at all. For a normal exchange process (CMC) takes place upon the basis of an equivalence of exchange value in the goods exchanged. The original seller expects to be able to buy with the money he has obtained goods of the same value of those he has sold. Equality is of the very essence of a just and fair exchange and MCM involves the same process of exchange except in reverse.

Neither Aristotle nor St. Thomas directly discuss how it is that the merchant makes his money, though they are well aware that his object is to buy cheap and sell dear. But how can he do this if everyone is aware of the true value of things in the market? If the merchant is to make a profit, must he not buy the commodity for less than it is generally worth and/or sell it for more? To some extent this differential can be explained by the fact of distance: the merchant brings the commodity from places where it is less appreciated and sells it where it is more. This means that he is not selling in the same market but rather in two different ones. Aristotle was aware of this. Neither does St. Thomas see any moral problem with this.

However, assuming that people are operating in the same market, it does not seem possible to justify the same commodity being bought and sold at different prices. The function of money is to express the common price of things. How could it vary in regard to the same commodity? Yet, the process itself makes no sense if there is not something to be gained from it. Marx was persuaded that there had to be some sinister reason for this lack of equality in the MCM exchange process. He came up with a quite original and ingenious solution.

There had to be, he argued, something intrinsically involved in the exchange process that enabled a commodity to be purchased at a certain price or exchange value and then later sold at a higher price, or at a value that included a "surplus value" over the original value of the commodity. The exchange process itself demanded an essential equality between the two prices or exchange values but in the capitalist industrial system there was something (labor-power) that, though not strictly a commodity, was first bought at a certain price (in the form of wages paid) and later sold (as incorporated in the product) at a profit.

The capitalist mode of production mirrored this very exchange process (MCM). It begins with capital (in the form of money) and is ordered to the making of money (the increase or growth of capital). The "commodity" used in this process is labor-power (i.e., the productive power of workers) or this plus technical capital which is but the product of previous labor. How is it possible to buy this commodity and sell it for more than what was paid for it?

Well, Marx explains, it is in the way the free market operates in a capitalist economy. Taking advantage of his money power the capitalist can acquire the labor–power of workers generally at a low price; indeed, the system of free competition tends to force wages down to subsistence level as explained in the classical political economy. When they come to sell the product of the labor-power they have purchased the capitalists are in the same market which is governed by the same laws of supply and demand, but which generally will enable them to obtain more for the product than they were obliged to pay for its production. Their profit is simply the surplus value arising from the difference between the value of labor in the form of wages and in the form of labor incorporated into its product.

The laborers are exploited insofar as they receive less in terms of value of their share of the product on sale than what they put into it. But legally they cannot complain because it was all done in a free market system. The capitalists have bought their labor power at its competitive value in a free market. And the product which now belonged to them has been sold at its market price in a free market. Nor does Marx assert that there is anything immoral in the process. It is the way the system has to work.

There is an element of truth in Marx's analysis; but only if it is understood in moral terms. We can see from the definition of Capitalism given by Chesterton that it must involve some degree of injustice. For the extreme division of society in terms of wealth is a sure indication of an unjust disproportion in the distribution of wealth within such a community. This inevitably enables the few rich to take advantage of the many poor when it comes to the exchange of goods and services.

The taking advantage by the capitalists of the laborers' impoverished circumstances so that they are constrained to accept a wage below what is fair and proportionate to their contribution to the value of the product is in fact a sin against commutative justice, an immoral exploitation, one of those crimes that cry out to God for vengeance. The fact that it is done by an apparently free contract in a free market is a cruel deception. For insofar as the workers are constrained by necessity to accept the terms of the wage contract (not having any other resources to fall back on) they are not truly free, as explained forcefully by Pope Leo XIII in *Rerum Novarum*.[27]

---

[27] "Let it be granted then that worker and employer may enter freely into agreements and, in particular, concerning the amount of the wage; yet there is always underlying such agreements an element of natural justice, and one greater and more ancient than the free consent of contracting parties, namely, that the wage shall not be less than enough to support a worker who is thrifty and upright. If, compelled by necessity or moved by fear of a worse evil, a worker accepts a harder condition, which although against his will he must accept because an

But Marx missed the opportunity to make a true critique of Capitalism in moral terms. He tried to force the opposed interests of capitalist and workers, of the excessively rich few and the excessively poor majority, into a pre-conceived system of logical (dialectical) and historical necessity, thought to be expressed in a process of exchange that was inherently exploitative.

We have seen that he was wrong in his general assessment of the significance of MCM. He was wrong too in assuming that the profit derived from this species of exchange was necessarily exploitative. If it were intrinsically exploitative it could not be justified by even a good end, which St. Thomas allows.

Marx was mistaken in assuming that the essential equality required in regard to every exchange admitted of no inequality at all. He forgot that he was dealing not with mathematical equations but with practical equivalences, which allowed not only for some elasticity in the measurements but also for variability in values caused by accidental factors such as time and place.

The merchant/dealer can and does buy things cheaper and sell the same things dearer even in the same place in a very short time span without the essential equality required of the transactions being violated. For, the justice of the prices of things is not always fixed with mathematical exactitude[28] (though their ex-

---

employer or contractor imposes it, he certainly submits to force, against which justice cries out in protest." (*R.N*, 63.)

[28] Cf. S.T. II-II, 77, 1, ad 1: Quod ideo dico quia iustum pretium rerum quandoque non est punctualiter determinatum, sed magis in

pression in money makes it seem so). It is at times a matter of estimation so that the fair price names a range rather than a fixed ratio. Hence, provided there is not too great a discrepancy, a greater or lesser price may be regarded as fair and just.

Moreover, the values of things are not fixed but changeable and depend on all sorts of accidental or extrinsic factors. The right price is not determined according to some abstract calculation but concretely depending on time of purchase and sale and other circumstances. By a close study of such details and movements the merchant/dealer can profit from these accidental variables without the essential equality of their exchanges being disturbed.

There may be of course a great temptation to influence if one can the extent of these variations by political or fraudulent means, but this is beside the point, which is that the possibility of profit from MCM can be readily explained by factors that do not touch the essential equality demanded for justice in exchange. Marx was mistaken then in thinking that he needed to look for an exploitative explanation in the very process MCM.

This refutes as well his contention regarding the essentially exploitative character of Capitalism, as he conceived it. Even if

---

quadam aestimatone consistit, ita quod modica addition vel minution non videtur tollere aequalitatem iustitiae. (my trans: "I say this because sometimes the just price is not determined exactly but rather consists in a certain estimation, so that a small addition or subtraction does not seem to take away the equality of justice.")

we identify it in some way with the commercial practice of MCM, the exploitation of labor is not needed to explain the possibility of profit from such a use of money.

Nor is this commercial process needed to explain the poverty of laborers in Capitalism. Such a fact is rather to be found in the mal-distribution of property which, of itself, without any necessary under-payment of workers, puts them in a proletarian position, as is clear from Chesterton's definition. The principal cure, therefore, to the problem of social injustice does not, as he clearly saw, consist in the abolition of property and money, but in the better sharing of control over them.

Capitalism, as it names a disordered economic system, involves the misappropriation of capital (natural wealth) by a few to the detriment of the rest of the community.[29] The misuse of money (artificial wealth) is indeed a significant part of the overall disorder, but only insofar as it is fueled by greed, for which MCM gives particular opportunity.[30] This disordered appetite for even more riches, *ad infinitum* as Aristotle shows, is built upon an already excessively disproportionate control of capital by a relatively few in the community.

The more fundamental disorder regarding capital, as ordinarily understood, is in its being commandeered, as it were, by "a class of capitalists, roughly recognizable and relatively small"

---

[29] This can only take place though the abuse of power or at least the failure of government to control the powerful.

[30] Usury also plays a significant role but it is a separate issue.

which necessitates, as Chesterton observed, "a very large majority of the citizens serving those capitalists for a wage." How this deep division in modern societies in terms of property and work, or Capital and Labor, came about belongs to the study of history.[31]

Things are not as bad as they were in Marx's or in Chesterton's time. For the extremity of the division has been greatly moderated by social legislation and a renewed spirit of social justice inspired to a large extent by the social encyclicals. Nonetheless, the roots of the division remain, and there is an ever-present danger of things being pushed again to extremes.[32] One can see evidence of this in most recent times.

To sum up Marx's mistake we can say that though he rightly identified the distinction made by Aristotle between the two modes of exchange, which most others have failed to notice, he

---

[31] The author has attempted to provide a historical survey of the misappropriation in other places. Available at https://www.cts.org.au.

[32] Alluded to by late pope John Paul II in 1994 in his encyclical The Gospel of Life , 10: "And how can we fail to consider the violence against life done to millions of human beings, especially children, who are forced into poverty, malnutrition and hunger because of an unjust distribution of resources between peoples and between social classes?" cf. also C.A. 42 " ... there is a risk that a radical capitalistic ideology could spread which refuses even to consider these problems [inter alia, the fact that "vast multitudes are still living in conditions of great material and moral poverty"], in the a priori belief that any attempt to solve them is doomed to failure, and which blindly entrusts their solution to the free development of market forces".

badly misread the nature and significance of this distinction. He gave to the second mode (MCM) a necessarily exploitative character that it does not have and thought he had discovered in this the clue to the exploitative nature of Capitalism. He then attempted to explain this capitalist mode of exploitation as an exploitation of labor.[33]

If he had limited himself to saying that laborers were systematically treated like commodities by capitalists, their labor bought in a sham labor market at a "price" below what was just, so that excessive profits could be made from the products of such labor, there may have been some truth in what he was saying.

But this was no result of any historically determined system. It was the fault of heartless employers[34] driving an unconsciona-

---

[33] His explanation derives much plausibility from the fact that laborers, including small children, were being exploited in a most inhuman manner. This called out for an explanation which was not being provided except in terms that such injustice was a necessary law of Economics. But fact and explanation are two quite different things. Marx made the mistake of trying to fight the enemy with its own weapons, i.e., of expropriation.

[34] Cf. R.N. 3: "Hence, by degrees it has come to pass that working men have been surrendered, isolated and helpless, to the hardheartedness of employers and the greed of unchecked competition ... to this must be added the fact that the hiring of labor and the conduct of trade are concentrated in the hands of comparatively few; so that a small number of very rich men have been able to lay upon the teeming masses of the laboring poor a yoke little better than that of slavery itself."

ble "bargain" with workers in no position to do otherwise than agree to what the employers offered. Furthermore, it could not be imputed to all capitalists or employers, for the fault, even if general, was a moral one.

A serious moral responsibility rested too on those in government to ensure that those unable to protect themselves were protected by the community. The prevailing philosophy of liberalism blinded governments to their responsibilities in this regard. The fact that some few in the community were in such a dominant position that they could so impose their will upon so many should make us ponder on the reason for this. But the exercise of such power remains a matter of personal will, not of some impersonal historical dialectic.

If Marx had limited himself to saying that the exchange process MCM encouraged capitalists to use their money to go into business or production where they could make great profits by exploiting labor in the fashion referred to (i. e. by reducing labor costs, wages, to a minimum) there may have been something in what he was saying. But such profits would depend upon concerted acts of injustice to the workers, if masked by the appearance of freedom of contract. They would not belong to the nature of the exchange process MCM as such.

This function of capitalists as employers is exercised either directly as owners of the factory, business etc or indirectly through limited liability companies.

If Marx had said that under Capitalism this second mode of exchange MCM, as the pursuit of money without limit, thrives and the notion that riches and property have no limit is so common that it is hard to dissociate it from Capitalism itself, then there would have been something in what he said.

But the root causes of the disorder in Capitalism are not in the use of money so much as in the underlying "take-over" by a powerful few of the wealth or riches within a community which Aristotle defines as the number of instruments to be used in household or in a state.[35] For, "capital" fundamentally stands for such wealth generally, but it is particularly applied to wealth that is not immediately used up in consumption. Its original sense, therefore, lies outside the processes of exchange, in what Adam Smith called fixed capital, and Marx called technical capital.

The very notion of instrument makes it clear that man or Labor is prior to nature or Capital. How it has come about that, in the modern notion of Capitalism, capital is seen as having priori-

---

[35] Aristotle saw such capital as naturally belonging to individuals. That is to say he defended strenuously the institution of private property. Marx, of course, thought that his criticism of Capitalism entailed the rejection of private property. But this only confused the issue. For in this regard, he was not arguing against Capitalism as an exploitative system, but, in the other sense adverted to above, as a natural economy free of any injustice. We may see here how his concentration on what was bad in Capitalism blinded him to what was good, aside from the fact, with which we are mainly concerned here, that it distorted his thinking even regarding the defects in the economic system.

ty or superiority over labor becomes clear when we take into account the superiority gained by the virtually exclusive possession of property by "the capitalists", over those who need such "instruments", i. e. property or capital, to gain a living by their labor ("the workers"). This is reinforced by the fact that the notion of worker becomes virtually equated with hired worker or employee, and the notion of employer becomes associated with those who have the capital or money necessary to engage in production or trade.

There do remain, to a more or less degree depending on the particular community, workers in the original sense who are self employed, who have sufficient property or money (their own or borrowed) to avoid the necessity of working for others. But, the more a particular society is affected by the disproportion in the distribution of property or capital, the fewer the numbers of these independent operators and the smaller the scale of their operations. Many, indeed, sacrifice income for love of the land or their art or just for the sake of independence. But the tendency is for them to "go under" and become absorbed into the general wage-earning "workforce".

The general situation of disproportionate social distribution in regard to property and work, then, according to which Capitalism has been defined, is the basic reason why Capital seems to make use of Labor, rather than the reverse.

A further cause of the impression that capital is the prime mover in the economy comes from the notion that money is capital, in that money is naturally productive, as it appears to be in

MCM. But this productivity is an illusion created by looking at the matter from an individualistic point of view.[36] There is a monetary gain made by the individual who practices this art and, certainly, one can legitimately obtain a profit from this exchange process, as we have seen. But such a profit is not a positive addition to the stock of wealth or utility socially considered. It is purely relative, one person's gain being another's loss, though, by reason of the accidents of the measuring process, the loss is not counted, even if perceived. The whole focus is on the gain to astute individuals, which is allowed because it has not interfered essentially with the social exchange process.

This "second species" of the exchange process (MCM) can be applied, in a way, to the area of production. Marx believed he saw this happening and called it the capitalist mode of production. One who has money, can buy or hire the necessary fixed capital, and can "buy" the labor needed, and then sell it again as "incorporated" in the product. But, in truth, the labor is hired, not bought and sold. For if the capitalist has paid the (hired) laborer a just wage the product is his alone to sell.

However, if the capitalist has underpaid the laborer, the product is not all his to sell. Part of the profit on sale, then, can be seen as belonging to the laborer.[37] In that case, there is an analogy

---

[36] The illusion is also used by many to argue against the immorality of usury.

[37] Where the workers are intimately associated with the whole production, as is often the case in modern industrial and commercial op-

to be drawn in terms of buying and selling the labor of another, and profiting thereby. This is effectively how Marx saw it, providing for him the explanation for the possibility of profit from the exchange process MCM. Such an engagement of labor is, of course, exploitative only on a supposition (that the wage contract is unjust). This supposition may have verification on an extensive scale in actual fact, but Marx saw it as necessarily verified in all capitalist production.

Thus, his confusion of capital with money, and his misreading of that peculiar, if common, misuse of money in the second mode of exchange (MCM) led Marx to mistake the cause of the impoverishment and virtual slavery of the working class of his time. He identified the cause in an exchange process that in his mind was essentially exploitative. This meant that he presented Capitalism in absolutely negative terms, which in practical language signifies something purely evil, needing to be totally destroyed.

Yet nothing concrete is totally evil, for evil can only exist in a subject that is fundamentally good. Capitalism, then, even if it signifies a disordered society in terms of the distribution of prop-

---

erations, their role approaches that of partners rather than hired hands. For the capitalists have little more role than that of providers of the "instruments" wherewith the production takes place, in which case there is something to be said for regarding the workers (which term here includes anyone actively engaged in the productive process) as the true principals in the production.

erty and work, and an irrational use of money, will be fundamentally good. This is not to say that Capitalism, so understood, has not in the past worked huge injustices, and is capable even now of causing extreme misery to the great majority of the population. But this does not call for the abolition of property and money, or even the outlawing altogether of exchange according to the derived and secondary mode MCM. It does however call for the elimination of injustices and abuses in the distribution of property and in the use of money, particularly in regard to the exchange process MCM.

Marx's mistake was to make of these undoubtedly great evils, which have so adversely affected the modern social economy, "a necessary part of the world's dialectical process".[38] He identified Capitalism with its defects[39] and thus saw it as one part of such a dialectic destined for destruction in the path of history. But Capitalism, rightly viewed, is but the natural economic order into which there have been introduced these disorders, admittedly of a most serious kind.

---

[38] Cf. Cardinal J. Ratzinger, "Truth and Tolerance', Ignatius Press p. 48.

[39] The opposite mistake, which we have noted the defenders of Capitalism generally make, is to ignore the existence of these defects and identify Capitalism, as it refers to the existing extreme disproportion in the distribution of property and money, with the natural economy. Or they may see Capitalism in terms of commerce and identify it, as Marx did, with the second mode of exchange, but deny that there is anything wrong with the pursuit of profit or money without limit.

Marx's philosophy, which included this misconception of market processes and Capitalism, misled whole peoples, many of whom believed they were championing the cause of the oppressed workers of the world, and almost resulted in the destruction of the natural socio-economic order itself, after involving tragically and senselessly "the sacrifice of countless thousands of victims".[40]

The recognition of his mistake, however, should not induce us into making the opposite mistake of simply identifying Capitalism with the natural socio-economic order, choosing to ignore the great social injustices that flow from the having by a few of far too much property compounded by a use of money that promotes further avarice.

It is incumbent upon us to identify the evil aspects of the social and economic order and the injustice that condemns so many to unremitting work just in order to obtain a living, while a few are put in a position to enjoy "the good life" without the need to work.[41]

However, it is one thing to diagnose a disease and quite another to cure it. In Marx's case, unfortunately, the diagnosis was

---

[40] Cf. Ratzinger Ibid.

[41] It goes without saying that not all are aware of the injustice of their over-privileged position and many of great wealth work hard for the good of the "underprivileged". Being fundamentally a matter of morals, one cannot judge the individual without knowing all the circumstances and the particular person's state of mind.

mistaken, and the cure turned out to be worse than the disease.[42] Our principal concern here has been to show up the mistakes in the Marxian diagnosis which led to the attempted cure being nearly fatal. It is not our purpose here to propose any cure to present social evils. That is matter for another discussion, one that necessarily involves religious considerations, a moral attitude that includes patience, and the recognition that politics is the art of the possible.[43]

---

[42] This point is made in the encyclical Centesimus Annus (1991): "Two things must be emphasized here: first, the great clarity [of Leo XIII] in perceiving, in all its harshness, the actual condition of the working class — men, women and children; secondly, equal clarity in recognizing the evil of a solution which, by appearing to reverse the positions of the poor and the rich, was in reality detrimental to the very people whom it was meant to help. The remedy would prove worse than the sickness." CA 12

[43] The quotations from Aristotle, St. Thomas and Marx used in this article were taken from the following: *Politics*, trans. B. Jowett in The Basic Works of Aristotle, ed R. McKeon, Random House Inc., 1941; *Summa Theologiae*, Martietti, Rome, 1952. *In Politica*, Corpus Thomisticum, ed. E. Alarcon (www.corpusthomisticum.org); *Capital* Vol. I. ed. F. Engels, trans. Moore & Aveling, Marx/Engels Internet Archive (Marxists.org) 1991.

www.ingramcontent.com/pod-product-compliance
Lightning Source LLC
Chambersburg PA
CBHW071729270326
41928CB00013B/2610